On Education—Sociological Perspectives

On Education—

Sociological Perspectives

Edited by Donald A. Hansen and Joel E. Gerstl

NEW YORK   LONDON   SYDNEY   JOHN WILEY & SONS, INC.

With Essays and Commentaries by

Raymond S. Adams

    University of Queensland

Ronald G. Corwin

    The Ohio State University

John Forster

    Victoria University of Wellington

Joel E. Gerstl

    Temple University

Donald A. Hansen

    University of California, Santa Barbara

Reece McGee

    Macalester College

Robert Perrucci

    Purdue University

John Sirjamaki

    State University of New York at Buffalo

Asher Tropp

    University of London

Preface

From the time of the Great Depression to the Sputnik fright, all but a few sociologists in the United States remained comparatively indifferent both to the problems of education and to education as a social institution. In the last decade interest has increased, but even today most sociologists evidence scant enthusiasm for the sociological study of education. The indifference is strange, for few subjects are more appropriate to sociological research and theory. Indeed, formal education in complex societies today is of such importance in meeting basic problems of socialization, of technology and economy, and of social control that neither contemporary men nor contemporary societies can be understood without continuing reference to it. However harsh, it is not unjust to suggest that a sociology that neglects such a major area is not yet an adequate sociology.

The indifference of the sociologist is all the more arresting when statements and in some cases continued efforts of early sociologists are considered. Many of these men who so strongly influenced the course of the development of sociology, emphasized that formal education is central among the social realities of complex societies and urged continuing investigation of educational institutions, processes, and practices.

In some countries, their advice has been followed less laggardly than in the United States. In England and other Commonwealth countries—perhaps partly because of the belated acceptance of sociology as a distinct discipline, which forced it into alliances with subjects earlier established—the two areas have been closely connected. A symbol of the relationship was the appointment of German sociologist Karl Mannheim to the Chair of Sociology and Education in the University of London by the educator Sir Fred Clarke. The intimacy of English sociology and education is not merely symbolic, however. Today a listing of the most eminent sociologists in England would be heavily weighted with those who have devoted a considerable part of their energies and time to the sociological study of education.

The relationship of sociology and education has been less close in France, despite the early efforts of Emile Durkheim. When accepting his chair at the Sorbonne—a chair, it should be recalled, in Pedagogy—he lectured on education and sociology, with words in many respects pertinent today:

". . . if there was ever a time and a country in which the sociological point of view was indicated, in a particularly urgent fashion, for pedagogues, it is certainly our country and our time. When a society finds itself in a state of relative stability, of temporary equilibrium, as for example, French society in the seventeenth century; when, consequently, a system of education is established which, while it lasts, is not contested by anyone, the only pressing questions which are put are questions of application. . . . I do not have to tell you that this intellectual and moral security is not of our century; this is at the same time its trouble and its greatness. The profound transformations which contemporary societies have undergone or which they are in process of undergoing, necessitate corresponding transformations in the national education. But although we may be well aware that changes are necessary, we do not know what they should be. Whatever may be the private convictions of individuals or factions, public opinion remains undecided and anxious. The pedagogical problem is, then, posed for us with greater urgency than it was for the men of the seventeenth century. It is no longer a matter of putting verified ideas into practice, but of finding ideas to guide us. How to discover them if we do not go back to the very source of educational life, that is to say, to society? It is society that must be examined; it is society's needs that must be satisfied. To be content with looking inside ourselves would be to turn our attention away from the very reality that we must attain; this would make it impossible for us to understand anything about the forces which influence the world around us and ourselves with it. I do not believe that I am following a mere prejudice or yielding to an immoderate love for a science which I have cultivated all my life, in saying that never was a sociological approach more necessary for the educator. It is not because sociology can give us ready-made procedures which we need only use. Are there, in any case, any of this sort? But it can do more and it can do better. It can give us what we need most urgently; I mean to say a body of guiding ideas that may be the core of our practice and that sustain it, that give a meaning to our action, and that attach us to it; which is the necessary condition for this action to be fruitful." (Emile Durkheim, *Education and Sociology*, New York: The Free Press, 1956, pp. 133–134. Trans. by Sherwood D. Fox.)

To this it need only be added that if a sociology of education were needed in Durkheim's France, it is vital, even crucial, to contemporary societies. Unfortunately, the crucial is often the neglected, and the growth of sociology in the twentieth century has been characterized by a studied indifference to many socially important subjects. There are increasing indications, however, that the field is now sufficiently mature to accept some social responsibilities which are compatible with empirical pursuits—a move that could well bring to its theories and research the richness and incisiveness they today so frequently lack. The sociology of education is one of the many promising areas in which such development might be sought. Some few steps in the search are suggested in the essays following.

      ❉   ❉   ❉   ❉   ❉   ❉

In these essays, six sociologists examine some of the areas of education and sociology which today seem to hold high potential for one another. We have attempted to develop the collection in a more integrated form than is usual in symposia. Our method has been simple: to bring into collaboration colleagues who are similar in basic perspectives and to encourage among them a free exchange of suggestions and criticisms starting early in the planning stages of the work. The result, we hope, is an assembly of essays each bearing the character, writing style, and arguments of its author yet integrated in substance, structure, and perspectives with the rest.

With the exception of the first chapter—which, discussing the curious relationship of education and sociology, is necessarily of different structure—each essay is presented in three major sections. In the first section is identified a major area of sociological theory and research: the study of social institutions, of social change, of stratification and mobility, of organizations, of occupations. In the second section of each essay, the authors synthesize the major data and arguments available in existing literature which relate education and their sociological area. The final section of each essay offers suggestions and speculations for future inquiry and theory.

The final section of the book offers brief critiques of the analyses, from cross-cultural perspectives. To the overseas reader, these critiques might offer perspectives emphasizing the relevancies and irrelevancies of the analyses to their societies. To the reader in the United States they should sensitize to promising modifications of propositions which—in the character of contemporary American sociology—rest largely on research and observation carried on within a single culture.

✿ ✿ ✿ ✿ ✿ ✿

Like most authors and editors, we are indebted to a great many people for their assistance, advice, and skepticism. Penny Edgert was especially helpful in various stages of editing, and more than anyone else she is responsible for the index. Chris Lauderdale, Laurie Newberg, and Karl Alexander were exceptionally skillful and tolerant in the preparation of the final manuscript.

We are also indebted to the many authors and copyright holders who have granted permission to reprint from their works. Most of those who granted permission are clearly identified in the bibliographic references; to these men and organizations, our thanks. Thanks, too, to Harrison-Blaine of New Jersey, Inc., for permission to reprint from Christopher Jencks' article, "Education: What Next?", *The New Republic*, 1965; to the Regents of the University of Wisconsin for permission to reprint from Bernard Bailyn's chapter in *The Discipline of Education*, edited by Walton and Kueth; to Holt, Rinehart and Winston, Inc., for permission to reprint from Joseph A. Kahl, *The American Class Structure*.

D.A.H.

J.G.

December, 1966
Santa Barbara
and Philadelphia

Contents

On Education—Sociological Perspectives

PART ONE   ESSAYS

1 The Uncomfortable Relation of Sociology and Education

Donald A. Hansen

University of California

Santa Barbara

Short years ago few sociologists might have resented the charge that their indifference to education was but a minor thing, compared to their ignorance of it. Few might have objected even if it were suggested that their ignorance was so perfect it matched the sociological acumen enjoyed in most departments of education. Today, on hearing such comments many sociologists would note a certain tightening of the viscera, a tightening not dissimilar to that the eavesdropping educator might experience. For things have changed, and such charges have grown as outdated as they are unjust. Sociologists and educators have begun to heed one another, actively to cooperate, responsibly to criticize and question.

It is difficult to exaggerate the potentials of these renewed interchanges. Yet, seen in the context of differences and mutual dislikes which have become traditional in the relation of sociology and education, and from the perspective of the essential (as well as the unessential) character of each, the current interest is not entirely encouraging. The problem is not only that sociologists and educators might fail to cooperate more fully, it is also that they might cooperate too fully. As there is real danger that professional norms, ideologies, and organizations of the separate disciplines will continue to thwart efforts to develop a productive relationship, there is also danger that energetic efforts to move together will threaten the essential nature of one or both of the disciplines, by ignoring differences that cannot be ignored.

In the following section it is suggested that the common explanations for the uncomfortable relation of sociology and education appear both

3

valid and rather superficial. In response to somewhat different problems
the two disciplines have developed irritatingly different attitudes and
operations, some of which are petty and unnecessary. But, it is argued
in the second section, other differences are essential to the goals of the
disciplines. Indeed, it appears that at the base of the uncomfortable
relation of sociology and education is an essential hiatus that has long
plagued human inquiry, and has resisted repeated efforts to resolve it.
The hiatus, separating empirical and normative enterprises, must be
recognized and specified if a maximally effective relation of sociology
and education is to develop. Toward specification, a redefinition of the
terms "educational sociology" and "sociology of education" is offered. It
is argued in the third section that the hiatus may be essential, but in
some social contexts it need not frustrate all efforts to interrelate empirical and normative inquiry. Thus, in the essential discomfort between education and sociology today can be seen not only critical problems, but also arguments for their interdependence.

DIVERGENCE

As the twentieth century neared, both sociology and the formal study
of education emerged as disciplines in American universities. Though
they differed markedly, their distinctive cultures were parallel in their
growing commitment to positivism, and in the popularity of the doctrines of social progressivism and social reform. It is not surprising that
fields similar in such basic ways moved together in the development of
an educational sociology which was both social-progressive and reform-
oriented. Even before the century had begun, the pioneering sociologist,
Lester F. Ward (1924), wrote of education as "the proximate means of
progress" and of the powers of education to stimulate "social telesis."
Such ideas in later decades became part of the foundation on which
Finney, Good, Elwood and other students built their educational
sociology; ideas, unfortunately, no more firm than shifting sand, ill-
suited to support the weight of structures of knowledge. The infirmity
of the structure was revealed in passing decades, as the two disciplines
altered in distinctly different ways. Rather than correct the basic deficiencies in educational sociology, however, both sociologist and educator turned to other problems and other areas. With notable exceptions, the brassy flourishes that had announced the early educational
sociology scarcely lasted out the twenties; the erratic brilliance turned
to a drone and then but a whimper through the thirties and forties.

These changing fortunes of educational sociology are more than simply interesting—they are pertinent to an understanding of the current reemergence of sociology of education and of its potentials. Most importantly, it appears that educational sociology was allowed to eclipse not because the subject had been exhausted, nor simply because it had proved too difficult for research or unreceptive to theoretical formulations. It was not abandoned in frustration—certainly efforts to develop systematic methods were frustrating, but no more so than in many other fields that continued to emerge. But educational sociology was different from most other fields, and the difference that made the difference appears to have been that no one, or too few, cared to be associated with a field of suspect parentage and undesirable character— for to all but a few, the educational sociology that had developed in the late twenties was a most unappealing waif, whose legitimacy was doubted by almost all who did not deny it. The eclipse of educational sociology, that is, may well have been essentially a result of the uncomfortable relation of the two parent disciplines—a relation which appears in great part unaltered today.

Superficial analysis of this relation might lead to optimism about the future of current developments, for it is apparent that the discomfort is related to conditions that are today improving. Unfortunately, whether developments continue depends on far more than increased status security or even seductive research monies—for the discomfort is grounded in problems deeply and firmly entrenched in the traditions and character of the two disciplines. Before these are considered, however, it will be useful to consider some of the superficials, for, appropriately, they help in understanding the current re-emergence of interest between education and sociology.

1. Some Conditions and Stimulants of Interest

However unpleasant, it must be recognized that the difficulty between sociologists and educators is apparent in the common presumption of sociologists that education and some other human arts are "Mickey Mouse" and not to be associated with. Nor can it be ignored that many educators are scathing about the "ivory-tower nonsense" of sociologists, who say little that is worthwhile, but take a long time saying it.

That each of these perspectives may have some basis in fact[1] does not fully explain their existence. The sociologist's stance is especially interesting, for few other academic types have been so fearful of contact with education as have sociologists. This suggests that it is not only the perceived status of education that determines the attitude, but in part it may be the very similarity of the two fields. Turning to engineering, medicine, psychiatry, or law, the sociologist is secure in his identity, certain that he is contributing uniquely, working in his own special ways on problems peripheral but important to the field with which he is cooperating. He can expect that his work will be evaluated more or less on its own merits. In collaborating with education, the story is quite different: not only is little prestige available to be borrowed from the discipline, there is also strong possibility that his research will be confused with that of the educator (risking offhand rejection of his publications by many in his own field, and even by some in education), and that he himself may be mistaken for "an educationist" by his fellow sociologists.

To put it another way: the sociologist's snobbery may rest not only on the alleged mediocrity in education, but also on his own status insecurity. For, at least until recent years, sociologists in this country might have been described as "marginal" academicians—and sociologists themselves point out (usually in other contexts) that the marginal man is the most fearful of integration with the peripheral, for integration may cost him his few shreds of acceptance.

In the last fifteen years or so, however, the status of sociology appears to have improved.[2] Today on many campuses the field is accepted as roughly equal to most other social and behavioral sciences, and the social sciences, in general, "in comparison with the rest of academia, are like a Cinderella who has come into splendor" (Riesman, 1958, p. 66).[3] A causal relation between this change in status and the re-emergence of attention of sociologists to education would be questionable, however: at most it might be argued that the sociologist's status security allowed developments which were otherwise unlikely. Even if status security is accepted as a more-or-less necessary condition for the development of a vital sociology of education, it is no more a sufficient condition than the renewed willingness of some educators to allow and urge others to study education, or than the experience of the sociologist who finds highly capable collaborators among the education faculties.

Other factors also contribute to the renewed interest, notably the rapid upsurge in the numbers of sociologists and educators, and in the sizes of major university departments. These developments allow departments to support ever more specialists; they allow some professors freedom to seek new fields as they find others overpopulated with teachers or nearing "saturation" of seminal ideas. In sociology especially this latter condition may be influential. For it is likely that some, if not many, sociologists have been attracted to the field by its pioneering quality; they are interested in exploring new and unknown areas rather than systematizing older ones. Thus, the increasing size of academic departments and partial settling of traditional subjects may encourage academic explorers to a sociology of education, or sociology of almost any area previously ignored.

At the same time of departmental growth and increasing status security another influence, perhaps even more potent, has been felt. It may be suggested, not without some cynicism, that the sociology of education has been stimulated by the emphasis on "education and excellence" in the United States since the Korean War and especially since Sputnik. The important point is not that many sociologists and educators share the general concern about the effects of education on our society and future—many do, but such concerns by themselves would likely generate only polemics or interpretive essays, for the cries of alarm over national success are of only passing importance to researchers in pursuit of acceptable publications. Far more stimulating to the generation of systematic inquiry is the fact that federal and foundation's money has been directed to the study of educational problems. Even in academics, distant sticks are not nearly so persuasive as snatchable carrots.

To summarize: some insights into the recent reemergence of interest in a sociology of education may be gained by considering (1) the unprecedented financial support being channeled into educational research; (2) the growth and specialization of sociology departments; (3) the increasing status security of the sociologist, which eases the sanctions in his profession against fraternization with any but the prestigious; (4) the effective cooperation of some educators with some sociological analysts.

It has been suggested that these stimulants to early interest are not adequate to assure continued strengthening of the relationship of education and sociology. Indeed, even if they were adequate, they could not be taken as unconditionally encouraging. For the sociologist is still far from secure in his status. Sanctions, though eased, discourage the dabbler in educational problems from serious work, and often dissuade the impressionable sociology student from seriously considering education as a legitimate focus. Further, to mention but one other continuing irritant, much of the basic research sociologists would prefer to do in educational settings has little appeal to those who control public and private research funds.

It is apparent that the problem goes far beyond these surface difficulties, however, for even among educators and sociologists who have cooperated for long periods of time frustration and misunderstanding are common; however highly they may regard certain individuals, both sociologist and educator often feel quiet discomfort with the other's field. For in a real sense the sociologist and educator live in different worlds; they do not share important concepts and attitudes, and their perspectives differ.[4] However similar at the turn of the century, each discipline changed, and as the years went on, similarities faded and the psychological space between them expanded.

How did this happen? Most simply stated, it appears that both were caught in a press toward positivism and "scientific method"; a press that was in a great part a condition of their similar positions in the American university system, but that helped move them apart, because of their differing positions in the American community. For it appears that sociologists in increasing numbers were able to cloister themselves from the demands of their society for advice and action, while educators were continually exposed. As most simple statements, however, this one obscures many essential facts.

2. From Social Inquiry to Sociological Methods

Sociology originally was conceived as the "Queen of Sciences," in which all knowledge relating to man's behavior would one day be integrated. This conception is apparent in the works of the sociological pioneers, works which suggest that, whatever the cost, sociologists indeed intended to strive relentlessly for all-inclusiveness. Such men espoused positivism, yet allowed that position to interfer little with their continuing inquiry into the ways and relationships of man and society; that is, they were preeminently concerned with substantive problems, with "reality." In their sociology they developed competing theories, two of which especially captured the attention of early sociologists in the United States; of these one figured importantly in educational sociology.

Early educational sociologists gave scant attention to the popular "Social Conflict" theories, which emphasized conflict as a natural consequence of human interaction, and as essential to social processes and organization. By contrast, the Social Progressive ideas of Spencer and Comte, reflected in the American, Ward, offered theoretical support for the missionary emphasis so important in early educational sociology. As other social reformers, the educational sociologist perhaps felt more at home with social progressivism because it represented a "positive" attitude toward human and social capacities, and was less destructive of reform efforts than conflict theory, which, seeming to emphasize that "might makes right," threw unflattering light on the reformer and made his every move politically suspect.[5]

In sociology in general, however, both types of theories were influential, and helped to maintain a distinctive orientation toward subject matter. For both types of theory were essentially substantive: however much they differed, each focused attention on the stuff of on-going social life; neither was especially burdened with methodological questions or with "conceptual frameworks" or "systems of analysis." Though dedicated to positivism, in basic assumptions, propositions, and tenets the theories were little involved with questions of *how to study* man and society. Each addressed questions *about* the essential nature of man, the qualities of his relationships, the patterns of his behavior.

But American universities were not receptive to such concerns: an emerging discipline had to be demonstrated as unique, and such questions were already being pursued in established disciplines. Sociologists in America were in quite different situations than those in England and France, where the substantive social theories originated. In those countries, early sociologists were not closely affiliated with the universities but were free lance, usually practicing sociology only part time. However heroic their achievements in this perspective, these sociologists enjoyed one striking advantage: they did not suffer the jealous scrutiny of those in established disciplines engaged in the study of social facts; they were free of the criticisms and attendant self-doubts which would beset the sociologist who attempted to win a place in a university. In France and England no place was to be competed for— the sociologist was an academic outcast, and hence free to work as he pleased.

Things were different in America, where higher education took a form similar to that in Germany. There, as Nisbet (1964) argued, the strict differentiation of subject matter and scholarly specialization which have characterized the late nineteenth and twentieth centuries came to fruition. In Germany, sociology faced academic situations closely parallel to those soon to develop in America. To enjoy popular prestige, it was necessary to become a university discipline. Further, to be accepted by disciplines already established, it was necessary to develop a scope and method that did not transgress on those previously developed, in law, history, political science, and economics.

"Hence, German sociology, almost from the very beginning, was preoccupied with questions of self-definition and self-image; with problems of methodology, of scope, and of objective. Sociology manifested, after its first grudging acceptance in the university, a good many of the qualities we generally sum up in the term 'marginality.' Regarded by others in the academic hierarchy as a kind of interloper, as a threatening poacher, as, at best, a dubious rival, it was necessary for sociology to justify itself to the older disciplines. It could do this, obviously, only by proving that in sociology there lay an insight and method, a subject matter and objective, that no other existing discipline contained. It is thus not strange, given this environmental context, that so much of the work done by Tonnies, Weber, Simmel, Troeltsch, and others proves to have, on close examination, a self-consciousness that is not to be seen at all in England and hardly before Emile Durkheim in France. The German sociologist, perhaps like modern man in general in the twentieth century, was preoccupied by the questions, what am I, what is my true role, what is my end in life.

"Given the historical fact that the American university (which does not much precede 1890) looked to Germany for its curricular model, it is not strange that similar status strivings should have characterized the history of sociology in this country. Here too the fields of philosophy, economics, government, and history achieved positions of influence earliest, looking with a dark eye upon disciplines such as psychology and sociology that seemed to threaten their empires. Sociology, in this country, unlike the case of Germany or any other part of Europe, had in addition the special difficulty of distinguishing itself from the old social work courses that had been part of almost every theological seminary. There was, finally, the complication of the vast intellectual influence of Spencer in this country, which made some of the earliest academic manifestations of sociology undistinguishable from ethnological schemes of social development and progress. . . .

". . . There was the general exodus of American university scholars almost single-mindedly to the universities and institutes in Germany. Here, in addition to obtaining a highly superior conception of the mission of the university, it was possible for American sociologists to get a vivid picture of sociology as a special science, one that could be charged with neither imperialism, at one extreme, or social uplift, at the other. I am not unmindful of the influence of France on the thinking of such key figures as Charles H. Cooley and George Herbert Mead, but no one will challenge, I think, the assertion that it was the German example that did the most to remake the American college into a university and the example of German sociology that did the most to rescue American sociology from the Scylla of social work and the Charybdis of social developmentalism." (Nisbet, 1964, 71-73.)

Most striking of the changes in American sociology stimulated by the contact with German sociology—changes increasingly apparent in the twenties, and consummating in the dominance of an empiricism heavily weighted with methods of research and "systems of analysis" by the end of the thirties—were concern with methodology and a conception of objectivity which, many held, required insulation from practical affairs. The sociologist was thereby kept from public controversy and public responsibility, and hence from restraints.

This increased orientation toward methodology was the dominant move of sociology away from the earlier character which was more compatible with education. Concepts of social progressivism, "telesis," and "passive mentation" were recognized as value-laden and reform-oriented, and by the thirties were clearly out of line with the dominant trends of sociology, which emphasized that the sociologist must work only for the establishment of objective knowledge—an emphasis that has remained influential in sociology until the present day. Stimulated by increasing research grants for specialized investigations, the age of "statistical sociology" has developed, an age, Talcott Parsons (1964) has warned, in which sociology may coalesce into a rigid discipline of quantification. Agreeing from a different perspective, C. Wright Mills (1959) derisively tagged statistics-dominated inquiry with the label "Abstracted Empiricism." Mills also saw another kind of fixation on methodology in what he called "Grand Theory"—that is, the elaborated system of concepts supposedly adequate to societal analysis at any or all levels of complexity. Mills did not argue that the methodological efforts to establish conceptual systems of analysis, or the use of statistical techniques, is undesirable. Nor did he deny that they might be useful tools. Rather, he insisted that no tool should be exalted to a central position in sociology, thereby displacing social inquiry and social theory. As practices, he suggested, Grand Theory and Abstrated Empiricism "may be understood as insuring that we do not learn too much about man and society—the first by formal and cloudy obscurantism, the second by formal and empty ingenuity" (Mills, 1959, 75).

Not all sociologists agree with Mills' description or evaluation of the tendencies in the use of concepts and statistics, but few would disagree that the movement toward methodological sophistication in both statistical techniques and conceptual systems has increasingly dominated American sociology in recent decades. From a position of world and reform consciousness at the turn of the century, sociology developed into a predominantly self-conscious discipline, emphasizing methods and systems of analysis, and guarding against value bias by insulating itself from the demands of practical problems and social action.[6]

3. From Science and Pragmatism to Practicality and Scientism

The discipline of education developed quite differently. Though suffering problems within the university similar to those of sociologists, educators have also had to face continuing demands for practical research and theory useful in the preparation and work of teachers and administrators. The diverse challenges have been met at times brilliantly as in the influential theories of the pragmatists, and especially of John Dewey. The same theories, however, have often been interpreted in the practical setting as if there were no breach between theory and action, and distorted to imply that only effective action is important, that application is the supreme concern of not only the teacher, but also the theorist and researcher. Whatever other influences were present, it seems that these theories or their distortions have contributed to the increased involvement with techniques and methods, in which "effectiveness" is redefined as "efficiency." Closer examination might reveal this orientation as akin to the statistics and research-methods developments in sociology; it might be argued that they are both in great part reactions to organizational pressures, but that the exposure to practical problems has led education to concern with methods of actions, while the cloistered sociologist has developed a concern with methods of research. The risk involved in either type of pursuit may also be seen as similar: that the pursuit of effectiveness is distorted into a pursuit of efficiency.

That a "cult of efficiency" has emerged in education has been suggested widely, argued actively by Callahan (1962) in a discussion of educational administration, and succinctly described by Bailyn (1963). Bailyn traced the present character of education to the first two decades of this century, when the "evangelists of professionalism" such as Cubberly, Monroe, Suzzallo, and Kilpatrick pursued with humorless method a vision of education as something more than a discipline, something grander, more esoteric and important. It was nothing less than a science—but exactly what "science" was, early educators appeared unable to agree. Yet their quest for science rode on the powerful tides of empiricism, and their efforts to build academic enterprises were dramatically successful in the exploding educational institutions of the early twentieth century. New and academically respectable things were happening in the world of education, and it appeared that the study was entering new and elevated stages of developments.

The response of these early educators was to attempt to develop an entirely autonomous academic discipline of education. National and regional professional organizations developed, journals were established, new educational institutions sprang up almost overnight.

"The result was remarkable. The study of education leapt ahead on all fronts, stimulated and supported by the intellectual and institutional force built up by this first generation of professional educators. Great good resulted: a broadening and deepening of the knowledge of educational processes and rapid improvement in the practice of teaching as new information and expert analyses of experience were disseminated through an increasingly well-trained, unified, and self-conscious profession.

"But then, in the passage of time, limits were found and a reaction set in. By the end of the 1920's and in the 1930's the primary assumption of the founders of professionalism in education that the study of education rests, or should rest, upon the solid intellectual basis of a science or at least a discipline of its own, came into question. The various strands of traditional scholarship that had been brought into combination in the centers of educational research either remained stubbornly separate, tied individually to their original bases, or, when removed from these roots and woven into a distinct scholarly entity called education, lost their resiliency and strength. Indeed, it seemed to many that when education took the scholarship of its origins with it into seclusion and nurtured it in isolation, a retrogression, relative to the advances in the contributing disciplines—some kind of intellectual calcification— took place. . . .

"The result, by the end of World War II, was an extreme disillusion on the part of scholars with the aims and practices of professional educators and a feeling, widely shared by the public at large, that what was needed was a total reversal, a return to the very assumption the founders of educational professionalism had so vehemently rejected, the assumption that—as it was put derisively in a classic nineteenth century statement—'there is (no) science about (teaching) except that of the branch of learning to be taught.' Efforts to reverse the direction of the founder's impetus took place rapidly within the colleges and universities and in the various professional organizations of the academic community. . . .

"But the full implications of this great pendulum swing, this motion first towards and then away from the study of education as separate scholarly enterprise resting on the sense of a special body of knowledge and special methods of investigation—the full implications cannot be grasped in these general terms. One must reach into the substance of the fields involved in order to see the implications with any degree of completeness. Unfortunately, I am competent to discuss the development in detail only in one field, history; but what has happened there —and what is happening now—is suggestive, I believe, of more general conclusions.

"In history, one cannot avoid concluding that a process of desiccation set in as the result of the emphasis upon the peculiar concerns of education, reinforced by institutional barriers that served for two generations to limit contacts between the general practitioners of history and the specialists in education. So far has this process gone that the consequences are now perversely attractive. The general historian finds the ruling formulations of the history of education so parochial, so restricted by the presumption of special purpose, and consequently so far behind the frontiers of contemporary scholarship in the field at large that the entire subject appears to be one great and intriguing question mark. It is not merely a matter of factual accumulation and narrative coherence. It is a matter of understanding as well, so that wherever one touches the subject—even where the monographic masonry appears to be most solid—it proves to be weak and insubstantial. Everything, it seems, is out of focus, askew." (Bailyn, 1963, 128-131.)

The educator's attention to techniques is not directed only at effectiveness; this tends to be replaced with a drive for efficiency, so that, for instance, less concern is spent on whether the children are learning than on whether the teacher is conforming to accepted patterns. In short, education—from kindergarten to university education department—evidences the negative effects of rapid bureaucratization and of harsh demands of an expanding society, as well as the legacy of efforts to be "self-sufficient" and scientific.

The compromise of "scientism" with "the wisdom of experience" is rather surprising, for the "wisdom of experience" is often faulty, especially in a fluid world, and the critical objectivity of "science" should reveal at least some of the faults. Though sometimes evidenced brilliantly, the critical stance necessary to productive objectivity (a stance by no means courageous among other university faculty) appears noticeably tentative in many departments of education. Ideas are readily reduced to practicalities, they are judged for their utility rather than their validity, and in the process, utility becomes the validation, thereby limiting discussion to immediate possibilities or even probabilities and proportionately hobbling creative imagination.

As any caricatures, the preceding sketches of sociology and education are gross and critically unfair—the more appealing features of the fields have been ignored, the unappealing emphasized. Yet it is in these unappealing features that the problems and the relationships of the disciplines are critical. In education, American pragmatism has become art, but it is an art often employed for the evasion of all but the immediately useful. At the same time, sociology has developed a marked concern for methodologies—which, not dissimilarly, are judged by the criterion of utility. There is still willingness among some sociologists to relate to social action and practical problems, and interest in a return to emphasis on substantive theories appears to be spreading. But the willingness and the interest are today scattered and tentative—the general mood favors concern for concepts and methods rather than for man and his community.[7]

THE ESSENTIAL HIATUS

However petty some of the differences between sociology and education, others are not easily disparaged. One source of frustration is the fact that sociology is by nature an abstracting and generalizing discipline, while education is oriented toward predictive statements required in diagnosis and planning. Though both employ summary statements which adequately describe an assembly of data, from such statements the educator typically presses for the concrete, the diagnostic, the specific, the predictive, and the applicable, while the sociologist seeks abstract generalization, which may have little immediate utility. This means, for one thing, that the educator may be frustrated in his efforts to interpret the sociologist's findings in ways useful in application. And it means that the sociologist, unused to the pressures of practicalities, may be frustrated as he realizes that educators fail to properly evaluate his work: that which seems to the sociologist his least worthy effort may win the greatest applause, while his most serious work is greeted with shaking heads. Similarly, an interdisciplinary project that begins with apparent agreement may suddenly be rent by strife, as the collaborators attempt to move in separate directions, each confused and upset by the other's lack of proper interest.

Such differences—differences in the techniques for gaining the ends of the discipline—can only be recognized and accepted. They are important, yet they are far from the most difficult to be met. A more profound hiatus frustrates the relations of sociology and education, and it cannot be breached without crippling one or both. Paradoxically, the hiatus is not only essential, it also argues for the interdependence of the disciplines.

1. The Normative and the Empirical

The essential hiatus in the relation of education and sociology is, in fact, not between the two disciplines, but rather between two basic modes in the study of man and society. The modes differ in criteria, each imposing restrictions and demands on problem selection and specification, each contributing to the establishment of differing types of theory. The distinction is between normative and empirical inquiry.

Empirical inquiry is dedicated to the establishment of verified knowledge, internally consistent, cogent, and adequate to its subject. In such inquiry and from such theory emerge statements of what is, what has been, what is possible, and what is likely. In contrast, normative inquiry is dedicated to the establishment of imperatives for the development of policies, programs, and actions, and to the establishment of normative theory; that is, to an internally consistent and cogent body of prescription, adequate to the realization of desired goals and consistent with a valid ethic.

The problem of the relationship of empirical and normative theory has plagued modern man especially since Kant, and still awaits resolution. Many efforts have been made to bridge the gap without violating the essential nature of either the empirical or the normative, but each has fallen short of success, and none has emerged free from scathing criticism.

One of the more notable and intriguing efforts in recent times—also the subject of strong criticism—was that of F. S. C. Northrop (1959). The essence of his argument was that normative theories should be based on and verified by the philosophy of nature developed from the exact sciences. Northrop suggested that there are three different kinds of deductively formulated scientific theories. For two of these the methods of natural science are appropriate: the theories of natural science itself (as have developed in, say, physics and biology), which are verified by applying the methods of natural science to the facts of nature, and the theories of empirical social science, which are verified by applying the methods of natural science to the facts of de facto society. But for the third type of theory—deductively formulated normative social theory—such methods are not appropriate: "Otherwise factual social theory and normative social theory would be identical;

also, the distinction between what is actually the case in society and what ought to be the case in society would not exist."

Instead, normative social theory is defined by a set of philosophical premises (akin to what Edel describes as Ethical Theory—see below). These philosophical premises are verified in the same way as the theory of natural science—that is, by appealing through the methods of natural science to the facts of nature. More simply, this means that the "correct" normative social theory is that in which the basic philosophical primitive ideas and postulates are identical with the primitive ideas and postulates of the philosophy of *natural* science. This philosophy of natural science is arrived at by analysis of the verified theories of natural science, forcing into the open its basic methodological, epistemological, and ontological assumptions.

In short, whereas it is commonly suggested that normative social theory build from empirical social theory, Northrop suggested quite a different approach. For empirical social theory is based on the methods of natural science, and the methods of natural science are capable of giving only factual theory—not normative. But this does not mean that the methods of science and empirical social science cannot be used in establishing normative theory, or in determining the ends for which their discoveries are or should be used:

"There are other ways of scientifically verifying normative social theory than that of applying the methods of natural science to the facts of *de facto* society. This other way is to note the role of the deductive method in deductively formulated scientific theory, which exhibits itself both in the verified theory of natural science and in the normative theory of social science. Any deductive theory analyzes into its primitive concepts and basic postulates or assumptions. By making these primitive concepts and postulates identical in both the normative theory of social science and the factual theory of natural science, one thereby obtains normative social theory which is different from factual theory and at the same time obtains normative social theory which can be verified, since the deductively formulated theory of natural science is scientifically verifiable.

"One also solves the basic paradox of moral authority. This paradox is that a normative theory, if we are to claim cognitive value for it, that is, claim that it is true or false, must be at one and the same time both normative and verifiable. To be normative it must, in part at least, prescribe a form for society different from that which is in fact the case, but to be cognitive and verifiable it must, with respect to some subject matter, be completely in accord with what is the case. These two attributes are impossible to achieve if both the normative and the cognitive or verifiable properties of normative social theory are referred to the facts of society. For to be verifiable with respect to these facts the normative social theory must accord completely with them. Then the distinction between factual social theory and normative social theory evaporates. And to be normative with respect to social facts a normative social theory must in part at least differ from the facts of society and attempt to remove or change them. If this condition is satisfied, then the normative social theory cannot be verified by an appeal to the facts of *de facto* society.

"This paradox of moral authority can be resolved only if one refers the normative property of normative social theory to the facts of one subject matter and the cognitive or verifiable property of normative social theory to the facts of another subject matter. This is precisely what is done by the method at which we have arrived. Normative theory projects its normative prescriptions upon society; it receives its empirical verification from nature." (Northrop, 1959, 343-344.)

To repeat: Northrop suggested that normative social theory be based on the philosophy of natural science, rather than on verified empirical social theory. He would resist the suggestion that this empirical social theory might be equally germane to the philosophy of natural science as are the theories of natural science. In essence, seeking to resolve the gulf between ethical theory and scientific theory, and seeking to skirt the fallacy of identifying the "ought" for culture with the historical "is," Northrop proposed the construction of some sort of ethical base established on theories of natural fact.

Others, however, would argue that such a base is inadequate; that developing theories of social sciences—including exact psychology—might one day, and do to some degree even today, offer factual indications and clues to essential nature and especially to the essential nature of man. There is, indeed, danger that historical specificity and the particular value involvement of any individual and peoples will invalidate the efforts in the social sciences to identify the "essential nature" of man. Perhaps, however, this is a difficulty the ethical philosopher (and the educational sociologist) must accept: the question is not whether the data of the natural sciences are pertinent in an ethical theory—all knowledge and validated theory might be taken as pertinent. Rather, the question is whether they are adequate.

Northrop appears to have ignored the implications of the interpenetration of community and individual. He suggested the essential nature of man be the base on which values be formed and against which they be evaluated, but he skirted the question of what is the essential nature of man. For, whether an essentialist or existentialist concept of man is embraced, it seems that this must be accepted as a fact of the human condition: that the essential being is impossible to identify, apart from existential contexts. If this is so, then the efforts of the "value-laden" behavioral and social studies must be considered as potential resources in the formation and verification of normative theories. Northrop's message, given this modification, is hauntingly similar to that of the contemporary psychologists, anthropologists, and sociologists—Linton, Lee, Allport, Fromm, and Maslow, for example—who speak of man's essential being or his existant reality as a fundamental and ultimate base of ethics and as a final measure of the value of any social action or structure.

Edel (1962) approached the hiatus differently, recognizing that the empirical and normative enterprises are distinct, but seeking for methodological compatibilities. Arguments such as Northrop's which pose a deductive model and ask how to deduce value conclusions from scientific premises, Edel suggested, oversimplify the relation to the point of irrelevance. He offers the alternative of distinguishing four "methodologies or enterprises": analytic, descriptive, causal-explanatory, evaluative. Each is distinct, each has its own aims and forms of results. Yet each deals with the same materials, and has "unlimited" scope. "Analysis may go after the concepts of science as well as those of value. Description may focus on the activity of men having a purpose, or making moral choice, or reflective in ethical authorizing, just as it may focus on men moving or behaving" (1962, pp. 234-235). Similarly, causal-explanatory and evaluative methods are appropriate to any substance. The distinctions between empirical and normative, then, may be but artifacts, historically grounded, and having no "ultimate rationality." Careful study may reveal that each is closely compatible with the others—it is already commonplace, for example, that developments in one area of investigation force developments in the others.

It is possible that efforts such as Edel's and Northrop's may lead eventually not only to a respecification of the present empirical-normative dichotomy, but even to a methodological realignment of the present relation of empirical theory (and "pure" science), normative theory (and "applied science"), and social action.

Thus, it may be that our conception of an empirical-normative relation is crude and simplistic. Yet for the present it remains, as do the problems it is used to identify. In a world of perfect understanding and ethical certainty, the problems would not exist and the distinction between the empirical and normative modes would be unnecessary. For if we knew and agreed on what should be, the empirical effort could be accepted as a component of, or even identical to, the normative. In an uncertain society, however, the problems do exist, and the distinctions are widely drawn, though not always explicitly. Unfortunately, the distinctions are also widely worshipped.

Sociology contains its share of worshippers. Most sociologists agree that establishment of objective knowledge and theory is their primary goal, and are far from unsympathetic to the repeated efforts made to commit sociology solely to the pursuit of empirical inquiry. Traditionally, however, a sizable and vocal minority insists that sociologists must also use their sociological knowledge and theory to approach demanding practical problems, and perhaps even to aid in developing normative theory. Although the distinction is not always honored, and in controversy is not always perfectly clear, sociologists have developed a tradition of close attention to the relation of empirical and normative inquiry, and an awareness of the confusions and distortions that can result from an indiscriminate combination of the two.

In education the distinction is less well defined. However sensitively aware educational theorists and philosophers have been of the problem, in general the field has not encouraged attention to the differences between the empirical and the normative. In part, this may be due to a confusion of research techniques with the entire empirical effort; often the educational researcher attempts empirical research, but because of a normative position succeeds only in adopting bits of technical jargon and manipulation. This is unfortunate, for normative commitment rarely allows substantial contribution to empirical theory, and emulation of empirical methods often renders normative efforts ineffectual.

The researcher or theorist, that is, who attempts to resolve normative problems of education armed only with the techniques of empirical sociology runs a high risk of failure. However careful his research, however impressive his analyses, however well-received his reports, there is but low probability that he will make an effective contribution to empirical or normative inquiry or theory.

In the currently developing relations of sociology and education, the distinction—or the failure to recognize and honor it—is critical. Close attention needs to be given to the role of both the empirical and the normative, and the distinctive character of each enterprise identified, both to allow each to increase in effectiveness and to allow their compatabilities to develop.

A start toward this may be made by clearing the current confusion in usage of the apparently similar terms, "sociology of education" and "educational sociology." In these terms is, often, an implicit but muddy distinction between the empirical and the normative.

2. "Educational Sociology" and "Sociology of Education"

How does the term "sociology of education" differ from the more traditional term "educational sociology"? Often the two are used interchangeably, the implication being that the user may employ the one which best suits his mood or taste. In this perspective, it is interesting that the sociologist active in the study of education will often insist that his specialty be called a sociology of education (and that when the American Sociological Association adopted the *Journal of Educational Sociology*, it changed the name to *The Sociology of Education*). It appears that often (though certainly not always) the intent is to set up a contrast with counterparts in education departments, that the terms are used in a sort of academic one-upmanship, in which the sociologist may not be attempting to one-up the educator so much as to protect himself from onedownery at the hands of his colleagues.

At times, the terms are better rationalized to imply a difference in research operation or in research sophistication, or to designate a difference in focus of interest, indicating that the sociology of education is more global. At other times, the terms are used to distinguish between the perspective employed by the investigator, for example:

"From one perspective, sociology can focus *within* education, examining educational theory, practices, and processes. With such a focus, sociology performs much as does educational psychology and this approach is labelled "educational sociology." From another perspective, sociology can focus *on* education and attempt to understand educators, schools, and other educational institutions in their social and cultural contexts. This "sociology of education" is concerned with the relationship between education and society. In brutally simple terms, sociology from the one perspective might ask education, 'What can I do to serve you?' From the other perspective it might ask, 'What, in the name of society *are* you and what in the world are you doing?' " (Hansen, 1962, 313.)

Whatever the merits of such arguments, they add up to confusion. Methods are but supplements to investigation. Though at any time the methods employed by one field may differ from those employed in another, in following years these tools may be exchanged. Is the sociology of education of today to be the educational sociology of tomorrow—or vice versa? The argument that the terms should designate differences in subject matter is similarly faulty: though the distinction may serve at any one time, it is inadequate to cope with exchange of foci, for example, if those who call themselves "sociologists of education" are sensitized by and adopt a current focus of "educational sociologists," say, on the social contexts and consequences of curricular innovation.

Such confusion is avoided and more critical gains promised if the term "educational sociology" is used to refer to the pursuit of a normative theory of education and to research that is primarily directed to furthering that normative theory or to direct application. "Sociology of education" would then refer to the pursuit of empirical theory and to research that is essentially directed toward furthering it.

The distinction between the efforts has little to do with methods employed (both certainly require objective research), or the subject matter, or even the "scope" of the perspective. Either empirical or normative inquiry can focus on the individual or on the entire society; indeed, any pretense to adequacy in theory of either type requires individual-societal breadth. (Worthy investigations and attempts to establish components of each type of theory on both individual and societal scales are already developed.) Similarly, either type of theory can be served by historical or comparative analysis, or by any useful research methodology extant; obviously, it is possible that any given project will contribute to both.

The distinction does not necessarily separate the research of sociology from that of education. Although sociology may be, grossly, characterized as empirical, and education as normative, it is clear that neither sociology nor education can claim sole proprietorship of either mode of inquiry; it may even be that neither field can effectively develop without both.

The essential distinction is between the effort to develop knowledge and the effort to develop a base for effective action. A sociology of education, that is, would be an essential component of the effort toward general empirical theory, an educational sociology an essential part of the effort to establish action prescriptions and normative theory.

In educational sociology, then, inquiry is necessarily relative to some conception of present conditions to be improved. It follows that an adequate normative theory is served by an adequate conception of the current state and potentials of education and society; thus that an adequate normative theory requires an adequate sociology of education. But this is not to say that the normative educational sociology will be *based* on the empirical sociology of education. For empirical theory, no matter how adequate, can only tell the reformer what can be changed *from*, to help to make him aware of the special problems that might be faced in change, and assess the probabilities of consequences. The conception of what should be established, of what education should become, must be erected from a conception of the ideal. From where is this conception to come? Faced with pressing demands and plagued with egocentrism, reformers and educators have traditionally attempted to articulate a conception of the good society or the good education, resorting, where articulation was either impossible or obviously vulnerable to objective analysis, to "intuition" or "conscience." Although such makeshift criteria will likely continue to guide educational decisions and actions, ideally an adequate educational sociology would require a valid base in a cogent ethical theory from which constructive prescriptions might develop.

Educational sociology, then, is revealed as far more than an assemblage of investigations, responses to immediate, practical problems, or attempts to remove inadequacies in existing practice. Although today much, perhaps most, existing research that might be categorized as educational sociology is of this muddling-through, problem-oriented research type, educational sociology can be seen to be part of a larger enterprise to establish more adequate education in the society of today and tomorrow. But this statement may hide its own essential implication: the pursuit of an adequate normative theory of education, to which educational sociology might be an essential contributor, could be one of the most urgent efforts of our time. It can be argued readily and convincingly that in contemporary society as never before, exhaustive effort must be turned to establishing valid educational goals and programs.

It is apparent that the preceding discussion deals with ideals; that such adequacy in normative theory is at least equally beyond current capabilities as is adequate empirical theory. The discussion is of practical importance, however, in two critical points. *First, the task of an educational sociology is far broader than current research and discussion even vaguely imply. Second, an educational sociology is not but a simple extension of a sociology of education; normative inquiry cannot be validated simply through the application of empirical methods or empirical theory and knowledge.*

In summary, both empirical and normative enterprises—both sociology of education and educational sociology—are important today, and if they are to effectively develop, they must be carefully and explicitly distinguished as independent enterprises. But this is not to say that they cannot and should not contribute to one another. For in fact (as will be suggested), the two may be in many ways closely compatible.

To state that a mutually productive relation is possible, however, is not to prove it practicable. Among the most tenacious barriers to realization of potentials, and even to their explicit identification, are the perennial questions:

1. What is the nature of "objectivity"—does it allow any conception of the empirical enterprise as anything but "value-free"?
2. Does "involvement in human life" by the researcher and theorist add to, or detract from, the empirical enterprise?

The potential relation of educational sociology and a sociology of education may be in large part determined by the answers to these questions. One set of answers is suggested in the following section.

COMPATIBILITY

Many sociologists are human—or so it seems, at least to a sociologist. This is in a sense unfortunate, for it means the sociologist suffers the weaknesses and vulnerabilities that have so long plagued man in his efforts to be objective. A popular response in sociology, as was suggested earlier, has been to seek objectivity by insulating sociology from practical concerns. This, it was argued, would allow it to become "value-free."

Values, however, are not that easily avoided. Dewey (1938) was hardly the first to point out the presence of values even in the most carefully designed of scientific enterprise. Nor was he the last; indeed, the point has been made over and over again in recent decades, for example, in Myrdal's suggestion that the ideal of a purely factual analysis independent of any valuations is empiricism grown naive, resting on the assumption that if we observe without preconceptions, facts will organize themselves into some pre-existing system.

". . . But without questions there are no answers. And the answers are preconceived in the formulation of the questions. The questions express our interest in the matter. The interests can never be purely scientific.

They are choices, the products of our valuations. 'Without valuations we have no interest, no sense of relevance or of significance and, consequently, no object,' my late friend Louis Wirth once wrote to me when we corresponded about this problem. This is, indeed, the principal paradox of science: the value premise, as I pointed out, cannot even be formulated except in relation to all elements in all the alternatively possible development processes laid bare by factual analysis: the factual analysis cannot be carried out except when guided by the value premise. . . . Chaos does not organize itself into any cosmos. We need viewpoints and they presume valuations. A 'disinterested social science' is, from this viewpoint, pure nonsense. It never existed, and it will never exist. We can strive to make our thinking rational in spite of this, but only by facing the valuations, not by evading them." (1950, 240, 242.)

Today, few would seriously contest such an argument. But even given agreement that viewpoints cannot be avoided and that they presume valuations, there is still room for debate over the two questions that introduced this section: What are the costs and profits of the pursuit of a value-free sociology? Can "objectivity" actually ever be approached?

The Price of Enduring Virginity

Quite apart from questions of validity, a major desideratum for empirical pursuits is that probability be maximized for cogent, incisive, and socially pertinent research and theory. This desideratum suggests that sociologist's isolation from society can be detrimental to his work. Not only does the isolated or insulated individual have a difficult time selecting research topics most promising for empirical theory, he also risks confusing mere knowledge with understanding. Whatever its merits, if it is too consistently assumed, the dispassionate stance places a sociologist in danger of ignoring the essential nature of his subject. Interestingly, Weber is often referred to by those who would support the image of a value-free sociology. Considering his awareness and concern with the influence of values and the importance of political and social action, it is ironic that he became the symbol for the "frightened virginity" of later sociology. Gouldner (1962) suggested that Weber's arguments on this point—which were agonizing expressions of highly personal faith—have today become hallow catechisms and an excuse for no longer thinking seriously. The value-free image today is a face-saving device; yesterday, it appeared to be a tacit agreement with society allowing the sociologist to develop his methodologies in cloistered isolation. The value-free image may have been popular not because of its truth or logical elegance but because it was somehow useful to those who believe in it. "Applauding the dancer for her grace is often the audience's way of concealing its lust" (1962, 199).

That the belief in the value-free sociology is a "group myth" rather than a valid and cogent belief is apparent when the belief is examined:

". . . Does the belief in a value-free sociology mean that, in point of fact, sociology is a discipline actually free of values and that it successfully excludes all non-scientific assumptions in selecting, studying, and reporting on a problem? Or does it mean that sociology *should* do so? Clearly, the first is untrue and I know of no one who even holds it possible for sociologists to exclude completely their non-scientific beliefs from their scientific work; and if this is so, on what grounds can this impossible task be held to be morally incumbent on sociologists?

"Does the belief in a value-free sociology mean that sociologists cannot, do not, or should not make value judgments concerning things outside their sphere of technical competence? . . . If technical competence does provide a warrant for making value judgments then there is nothing to prohibit sociologists from making them within the area of their expertise. If, on the contrary, technical competence provides no warrant for making value judgments then, at least sociologists are as *free* to do so as anyone else; then their value judgments are at least as good as anyone else's, say, a twelve-year-old child's. And, by the way, if technical competence provides no warrant for making value judgments, then what does? . . .

"I fear that there are many sociologists today who, in conceiving social science to be value-free, mean widely different things, that many hold these beliefs dogmatically without having examined seriously the grounds upon which they are credible, and that some few affirm a value-free sociology ritualistically without having any clear idea of what it might mean. Weber's own views on the relation between values and social science, and some current today are scarcely identical. While Weber saw grave hazards in the sociologist's expression of value judgments, he also held that these might be voiced if caution was exercised to distinguish them from statements of fact. If Weber insisted on the need to maintain scientific objectivity, he also warned that this was altogether different from moral indifference.

"Not only was the cautious expression of value judgments deemed permissible by Weber but, he emphasized, these were positively mandatory under certain circumstances." (Gouldner, 1962, 199-200.)

As Gouldner's discussion implies, isolation of the sociologist from social action both profits and costs social research. The question is, do the profits outweigh the costs? The answer is necessarily socially relative—profits and losses are closely dependent on the social situation of the researcher and the condition of his society. In Weber's time, it appears, the profits were heavy, but times have changed.

What does isolation afford the sociologist today? For one thing, some protection against manipulation by economic and political interests: as long as the sociologist is removed from the ongoing activity of his society, his cooperation and efforts may be little wooed. But this generalization requires a critical modifier, as Shils (1962) has suggested. For isolation offers protection—indeed, the individual is allowed such isolation—only so long as his discipline holds little potential for economic and political forces. Security of a discipline, that is, may have been gained through isolation yesterday, but perhaps not today, and most probably not tomorrow.

Of all the profits isolation might afford an emerging discipline, one of the most important is the opportunity to develop a solid core of methods or of theory. This function of the sociologists' isolation in the earlier part of this century cannot be denied, but is such isolation today the most profitable condition for continued development? To consider this question is to consider the costs of sociological isolation. As suggested in Gouldner's argument, one of the greatest deficits is the sense of alienation that pervades the work of the socially aware sociologist. Such alienation is not a simple black or white proposition: it does offer the individual a critical stance and perspective excitingly productive of insights; the role of the "stranger" is critical to sociology. But when the socially aware "branch" of sociology is entirely of this alienated sort, other critical developments in both empirical and normative theory are not made, or are made much too slowly. For the stranger's analyses, however suggestive and exciting, are often distorted and grotesque caricatures, weak in objectivity and of questionable validity. On the other hand, when the dominant character of the field favors isolation and dispassionate objectivity, the majority of the work emerging from that field will—regardless of its validity—suffer from a lack of significance, and an inadequacy to the richness of the subject matter addressed.

In brief, then, the dominant character of sociology which would carefully insulate the sociologist *qua* sociologist from the social arena risks irrelevance and a poverty of understanding; the humanistic (or in the perspective of some, the lunatic) fringe, on the other hand, risks wild invalidity. As the field is split on the critical question of involvement, the stances appear to polarize, and the middle ground is a wasteland trod by but a lonely few.

In contemporary society, the dispassionate, isolated stance may be far more costly than profitable. Interestingly, it is most often defended with the argument that it allows an otherwise unavailable objectivity— an argument which moves with surprising grace from a near-truism (that objectivity is essential to empirical theory) to an awkward error (that objectivity requires isolation of the individual researcher).

For even objectivity is a social matter.

Objectivity and Methodological Compatibility

That is, the rage for isolated dispassion is based on a faulty conception of the processes of establishing objectivity. However successfully the individual sociologist insulates himself from worldly contacts, yet he is a human being, born into a human world and socialized into a specific value system. However successful his rigorous methodology in reducing the effect of values—values which he has internalized, or which are perhaps even integral to his individual and cultural identity —it can never be totally successful.

What is needed, Popper (1952) argued, is not an objectivity based on the frail and inadequate resources of the individual human, but rather one based on a *community* of theorists. Scientific objectivity, Popper pointed out, is not a consequence of the individual's effort to prune his approach of value commitments or presuppositions, but rather is "a product of the social or public character of scientific method; and the individual scientist's impartiality is, as far as it exists, not the cause but rather the result of the socially or institutionalized objectivity of science" (1952, p. 220). Objectivity, that is, can be gained only by the collective and critical efforts of many. Even so, objectivity is not an automatic result of collective effort; bias can be, and often is, shared and encouraged by an entire generation of thinkers, as was harshly evidenced by social scientists in Hitler's Germany. How, then, can an "institutionally organized objectivity" be gained?

"The only course open to the social scientist," Popper suggested, is ". . . to tackle the practical problems of our times with the help of the theoretical methods . . . of trial and error, of inventing hypotheses which can be practically tested, and of submitting them to practical tests." In short, Popper argued that to develop objective theory and research, empirical researchers must engage in social action, must test their ideas with "piece-meal social engineering" (1952, 222). Similar themes are familiar in the work of Dewey (1938), who suggested that *normative* theory presents a judgment of existing social structure, and predicts that another structure would not only be preferable, but also possible. Hence, verification of normative theory also requires social action.

The potentials of interrelated empirical and normative efforts is suggested in these themes. Though each effort might exist without the other, *if each is effectively independent, they can be productively symbiotic.* For to ask the empirical question of what is, is to ask what might be; to fully establish knowledge of existing human and social reality, it is necessary to objectively verify theories of potentialities. Whether the emphasis is placed on the objectivity or on the potentiality it is clear that the empirical enterprise can be profoundly advanced through intelligent cooperation with programs of social action. Normative theory, too, finds its verification as well as its justification in social action. The question of what should be involves both the questions of what is and what might be. In at least certain instances, then, both empirical and normative pursuits can be served by efforts to systematically control change.

The promises of methodological compatibility are not the only potentials in the interrelations of empirical and normative efforts, however. Others can be seen. The above argument—that a sociology of education and an educational sociology, though separated by an essential hiatus, are in some ways methodologically compatible—is important, but it can easily be distorted, limiting the effectiveness of research. For the adequate advance of empirical theory requires moves far beyond those actions and programs which might be prescribed by normative theory. Yet (as anyone who has watched the mad scientist on the late-late show knows) the empirical scientist cannot be indiscriminate in his "piece-meal social engineering," no matter how important he may consider the theory which might thereby be tested. Certain programs of action, and even pursuit of certain theory and techniques, might be dangerous whatever their contribution to empirical pursuits. Verification might be socially disastrous, as in the case of demonstrating techniques of political manipulation just as an unenlightened dictator emerges to power. As normative and ethical theory develop in adequacy, their potential contribution to political pursuits also develops, and increasingly they offer empirical sociology the conscience and control that can help save it from the political traps of becoming a manipulated or a manipulative discipline. As sociology cannot not hope to develop a value-free methodology, neither can it ignore the value bearings and potential powers of its developed theories. Paradoxically, the nature of empirical theory is in great part a normative question—and the nature of normative theory is in large part an empirical question.

However sensical this apparent nonsense, neither it nor the identified compatibility should lead to the conclusion that the hiatus between the empirical and normative theory is artificial. As divorce courts evidence daily, even complete mutuality in certain operations does not necessarily bring identity, or even a general compatibility.

Yet, at least in contemporary society, neither the empirical nor the normative enterprises can afford to divorce itself from the other. For the normative has much to gain from the less value-laden structure of empirical theory. And the empirical will benefit in enhanced relevance and significance, as well as in potentials for verification, as normative efforts offer opportunities for testing and safeguards against manipulation. For each to develop effectively, and for the two to productively interrelate, it is vital that the value bases of a sociology of education, and the empirical bases of educational sociology be recognized, in the context of their distinctive natures.

It cannot be overstressed that the development of both types of theory is important in contemporary society. But it must not be ignored that the development of each type can go awry: it must be recognized that in the current state of development of sociology and education and in their relationship with one another are to be found threats to both pursuits.

THE DANGER

A note of caution remains. It may be that neither an effective sociology of education nor an effective educational sociology will develop from the current rush of interest. If so, the fault could not be fixed on the individual sociologists and educators who have made the effort. For it may well be that the disciplines of sociology and education are today so organized and so related to one another and to other disciplines that productive cooperation is rather improbable.

It has been argued that an essential hiatus separates the sociology of education and educational sociology and, more roughly, separates sociology and education. Each type of effort—the one empirical, pursuing the establishment of objective knowledge and theories, the other pursuing the establishment of normative prescriptions of theories—is essential to contemporary education and society. It has also been argued that the two can interrelate, and are compatible in many ways, even offering increased relevance and opportunities for validation.

But potentials are not automatically realized, and disciplines are made up of individuals who may cling to traditional ideologies, prejudices and practices. In his actions the sociologist (even though his words suggest otherwise) often continues the virtuous defense of a purity never really possessed. As the existing structures of rewards may discourage many serious efforts of sociologists, the myopic practicality of the educator may often frustrate those sociologists who do make an effort, and the unforgiving snobbery in both fields may lead to wounds that run deep.

In such conditions, what could well develop is a pathetic and petty educational sociology, pretending to be empirical, but devoted to normative pursuits—and in the pretense destroying the devotion. The situation could even grow worse, leading to circular destruction: as such an educational sociology developed, the empirical sociologist might withdraw even further from contact with educational fields, ever more fearing guilt by association. Conditions existing in the fields today, that is, could lead to development of a tradition such as that which has so long hindered the development of some research areas in both fields— a tradition characterized by doubtful validity and significance. Once established, such traditions die but slowly.

In the current conditions of sociology and education and in their relations there are, indeed, grounds for pessimism. Joyous reports that the professional virgin has stepped from the crumbling clay of her pedestal, or that the practical myopic has gained effective vision are greatly exaggerated. Yet there have been marked improvements on both sides of the campus, and one need not be totally naive to grow excited over the possibilities of intimacies to come. For, just as there are dangers in current relations, there are also potentials.

It is rare that two disciplines—the one essentially normative, the other essentially empirical—which overlap so widely in foci have had the opportunity to converge just at a time at which each appears to be emerging from rather narrow methodological and technical states. It is possible that an effective relationship between sociology and education could not only result in effective empirical and normative theories of education, but could also point the way to valuable developments in sociological theory and inquiry.

For it is today clear that an effective sociology requires more than sterile objectivity and the laying of layer upon layer of statistical fact and generalization. It is also clear that it is not enough to add to this the dramatic contrast of suggestive imagination. Between these extremes lies the real potential of sociology, in a type of inquiry not yet supported by tradition—an inquiry characterized by systematic, insightful analyses and understanding synthesis, an inquiry supported but not dominated by the technological pursuits of the rigorous empiricists, and the swinging imagination of the not always loyal opposition. Movements toward this potential can be seen today, as in the field of political sociology. Whatever else such developments might require, one essential appears to be an intimate contact with materials which are the subjects of investigation and theory. Empirical sociology divorced from its substance can become a distorted imitation of what it might be; exactness and precision (even if entirely possible) alone do not establish validity any more than does loosely-anchored imagination.

If sanctions and snobbery continue to relax, and if enough men of academic excellence are available, it is possible that exciting developments in both sociological and educational theory could result.

To the reader who has followed the preceding discussion, the prescriptions for development of effective research and theory should be clear. Though in application they will undoubtedly be exceedingly complex, they can be stated simply:

That the distinction between empirical and normative enterprises —between a sociology of education and an educational sociology—be exactly identified and supported;

That those who would pursue an empirical sociology of education be encouraged and supported in developing an intimate awareness of educational realities—an intimacy in which they are free from practical responsibilities and pressures to develop immediately useful statements;

That the essential character and requirements of normative educational sociology be identified and that the enterprise be recognized both as critically important to contemporary society, and as a legitimate academic activity;

That the existing and potential compatibilities of the two enterprises be identified and serious effort begun to maximize productive cooperation.

There is little doubt that undulating frustrations will be the lot of those who attempt to satisfy such prescriptions—for they will be caught between two disciplines whose relationship remains one of the most uncomfortable and tantalizingly unproductive in university academics.

Donald A. Hansen is Assistant Professor of Sociology at the University of California, Santa Barbara. He received a Ph.D. in Sociology from the University of Minnesota and a Ph.D. in Education from Northwestern University, and has taught at Purdue University and at the University of Otago (New Zealand). His inquiries have focused on sociology of the family, counseling and therapy, and on the mass media.

NOTES

1. It matters little that many sociological constructs have crept or leapt into the stock of common language and are reflected in the perspectives of contemporary legislators, after-dinner speakers and newspaper pundits. Nor is the lucid economy in the writings of a few score writers adequate to disturb the general belief that sociologists write badly, their messages (and perhaps their ideas) imprisoned in conceptual cages. The evidence is, undeniably, on record. Too, brilliant minds, worthy theory and useful research do appear in departments of education, but—as educators themselves are quick to point out—a major problem facing the field is in recruitment, reflected by the fact that disproportionately many of the least capable graduate students and few of the most capable, are majoring in education. See Wolfle and Oxtoby (1952).

2. See the Sibley report (1963) on training in sociology.

3. Riesman's simile might be extended. This essay argues in essence that one job of social inquiry is social criticism—but public suspicion of the parvenu suggests that the criticism should proceed with restraint. Perhaps the Cinderella sciences must ask a very practical question: How hard is it wise to kick with a glass slipper?

4. For a suggestive discussion of the differing "conventional wisdom" of educators and sociologists, see Bressler (1964).

5. Martindale (1957) has more fully discussed this possibility in an examination of the development of theories of social disorganization.

6. The "world-conscious" facet of sociology never completely disappeared, but rather went into partial disfavor, especially among the more prestigious sociologists; indeed, after hitting its nadir somewhere after World War II, it has gained strength as articulate and brilliant writers have begun to insist that it is time for even the most rigorous sociology to return to a concern with

man and with society. This development may hold seeds for rich produce to feed an emaciated sociology of education as it recovers from the near-starvation suffered for nearly three decades.

7. Things are changing in both fields, but even if they were not, a caution would be necessary: The preceding descriptions attempt to characterize general moods and developments, and can easily be faulted by lists of notable exceptions in each field who have worked effectively and wisely. These exceptions do not necessarily prove the generalization—but they do offer dramatic contrast to the general trends in their fields. Why is it, for exámple, that the works of Hughes, Lipset, or Mills so vividly contrast with the main streams of productivity in their field—even the productivity of men of similar standing and competence?

WORKS CITED

Bailyn, Bernard (1963), "Education as a Discipline: Some Historical Notes," in John Walton and James L. Kuethe (eds.), The Discipline of Education, University of Wisconsin Press, Madison.

Bressler, Marvin (1964), "The Conventional Wisdom of Education and Sociology," in Sociology and Contemporary Education, Charles Page (ed.), Random House, New York.

Callahan, Raymond E. (1962), Education and the Cult of Efficiency, University of Chicago Press, Chicago.

Dewey, John (1938), Logic, the Theory of Inquiry, Holt, Rinehart & Winston, New York.

Edel, Abraham (1965), "Social Science and Value: A Study in Interrelations," The New Sociology, Irving L. Horowitz (ed.), Oxford University Press, New York.

Gouldner, Alvin W. (1962), "Anti-Minotaur: The Myth of a Value-Free Sociology," Social Problems, 9: 199–213.

Hansen, Donald A. (1963), "The Responsibility of the Sociologist to Education," Harvard Educational Review, 33 (Summer), 312–325.

Martindale, Don (1957), "Social Disorganization: The Conflict of Normative and Empirical Approaches," in Howard Becker and Alvin Boskoff (eds.), Modern Sociological Theory, Dryden Press, New York.

Mills, C. Wright (1959), The Sociological Imagination, Oxford University Press, New York.

Myrdal, Gunnar (1953), "The Relation Between Social Theory and Social Policy," British Journal of Sociology, 4: 210–242.

Nisbet, Robert A. (1964), "Sociology in the Academy" in Sociology and Contemporary Education, Charles H. Page (ed.), Random House, New York.

Northrop, F. S. C. (1959), The Logic of the Sciences and the Humanities, Meridian Books, Cleveland.

Parsons, Talcott (1964), "The Sibley Report on Training in Sociology," American Sociological Review, 29 (October), 747–748.

Popper, Karl (1952), *The Open Society and Its Enemies,* Vol II, Princeton University Press, Princeton, N.J.

Riesman, David (1958), *Constraint and Variety in American Education,* Doubleday, Garden City, N.Y.

Shils, Edward (1962), "The Calling of Sociology," in *Theories of Society,* Talcott Parsons et al., (eds.), The Free Press, New York.

Sibley, Elbridge (1963), *The Education of Sociologists in the United States,* Russell Sage Foundation, New York.

Ward, Lester F. (1924) (orig. 1883), *Dynamic Sociology,* Appleton-Century-Crofts, New York.

Wolfle, Dael, and Toby Oxtoby (1952), "Distributions of Ability of Students Specializing in Different Fields," *Science,* 116: 311–314.

2 Education as a Social Institution

John Sirjamaki
State University of New York
at Buffalo

The concept, institution, refers to social arrangements of life in human societies. These are the procedures by which societies organize and regulate their social and cultural activities to meet the necessities of individual and collective existence, and to persist through time.

Sociologists have struggled to specify the cultural principles which the term institution denotes, and have produced a large number of definitions (Hertzler, 1946, 3-4). But they have not always succeeded in making its meaning clear, or even in differentiating it from other terms, notably from culture, group, organization, and norms. As a result, the concept has been an ambiguous one, and its use in sociological analysis of limited value (Schneider, 1964, 339).

Most sociologists concur nonetheless, somewhat paradoxically, that institution is one of the concepts indispensable to their science. All societies have institutions—familial, economic, political, religious, and others—and could not survive without them. Their social organization rests on institutions, and adapts through new institutions to changing conditions of existence. Were sociologists not to study the institutional configurations of human life and endeavor, they could not comprehend societies as wholes or understand their social and cultural events.

The difficulties that sociologists have with the concept of institution are in its operational, not generic, definition. Institution, as a collective term, refers to complex social behavior with diffuse meaning and variable content in societies, whose signification is therefore hard to specify. To make use of the term, sociologists must clarify its denotation, as well as fit it into their system of concepts and bodies of theory.

One may appreciate these difficulties of definition by considering the

36

title of this chapter: the institution of education. An institution of education signifies a society's system of education. But does it denote, more specifically, all its schools and colleges, their students and faculties, administration, public financing, educational policies, methods of instruction, adult education, vocational training, and parochial schools? If the institution of education concerns all educational matters, the term is too comprehensive for service in sociological analysis.

Sociologists however have succeeded relatively recently in delimiting the meaning of institution, and employ the term now with increasing assurance and profit. These remarks will become clearer if the efforts to define institutions and to develop methods of institutional analysis are reviewed briefly.

THE MEANING OF INSTITUTIONS

The word, institution, has existed in the English language since 1450, and has acquired a number of meanings over the centuries, of which sociologists use two principally now. One is the definition of institutions as established practices in the social and political life of a people (1551); the other is the orderly arrangement and regulation of human activities (1821) (*Oxford Universal Dictionary*). Sociologists have retained these meanings of institutions while elaborating them to fit their systems of concepts and to indicate their use of them.

Early sociologists, especially Spencer (1958), employed institutions in their first sense as established practices, but gave the term an organic connotation. Spencer conceived of societies as social organisms, and institutions as "organs" performing sustaining, distributing, and regulating functions in societies. He identified six types of institutions— domestic, ceremonial, political, ecclesiastical, professional, and industrial—and compared their structures and functions in primitive and modern societies. His assumptions about societies and institutions rested on postulates of social evolution, and led him to believe that, as societies progressed toward higher levels of cultural development, their institutions became increasingly specialized in form and activities, but continued nevertheless integrated and interdependent.

Sumner (1906, 53–54) introduced a comparable organismic definition of institutions into American sociology. He defined institutions as consisting of a concept (idea, notion, doctrine, interest) and a structure (framework, apparatus, functionary). Institutions arose, for the most part, from the mores (Sumner called them crescive institutions) as the mores "were made more definite and specific as regards the rules, the prescribed acts, and the apparatus to be employed." Sumner identified property, marriage, and religion as institutions "still almost entirely in the mores." But he recognized also the existence of enacted institutions which "were the product of rational invention" in modern societies.

Chapin (1935, 14–15) added to Sumner's concept of institutions by discussing their nature more fully. Like Sumner, he believed that institutions arose as groups strove to satisfy basic needs of individual survival and group maintenance (sex, hunger, fear) and established stable patterns of activities in doing so. He further asserted that these institutional activities were characterized by such attitudes and behavior patterns as affection, love, loyalty, and respect; symbolic and utilitarian culture symbols; and norms and codes of behavior. On their basis, he identified two types of institutions, nucleated and diffuse. He defined nucleated institutions as groups or organizations that carry on institutional activities, such as schools, churches, and government, and diffuse institutions as such cultural activities as language and the arts.

To base institution on needs, however, aroused objections that the relations of institutions and needs are, at best, indirect and unpredictable. The sex drive, for example, does not dictate the institutions of marriage and family, although it is closely associated with them. Therefore other sociologists have treated institutions as man's adjustments to his conditions of life rather than as derived from his needs. In this perspective, Hobhouse (1924, 49) defined institutions as the usages and principles governing the relations of men. Martindale (1962, 39–43) defined them as "standardized solutions to the problems of collective life," such as mastery of nature, socialization of human personality, and social control. This definition has the merit of removing institutions from an organismic mould, and permits empirical investigation of how societies develop institutions and integrate them into their social orders.

In a comparable manner, sociologists have recast the second meaning of institutions as the arrangements and regulation of human behavior. To regulate behavior implies that groups set standards of behavior and enforce compliance to them. Early theorists recognized that groups developed institutions through collective action, but were never entirely clear about the two terms, group and institutions, and often, indeed, used them interchangeably. MacIver (1949, 15) explicitly differentiated them: he defined groups and organizations as the associations through which men act, and institutions as "the established forms or conditions of procedure" they follow in doing so. Following MacIver's lead, other sociologists have defined institutions as systems of norms, patterns of relationship, or structures of roles (Parsons, 1951, 39) which regulate human behavior and bring it under the control of rules. They also use institution in its infinitive form, to institutionalize, to indicate the process of which behavior is organized into stable patterns of activities and regulated by norms (Parsons and Shils, 1959, 40).

With concurrence on the definition of institutions, sociologists employ the concept at several levels of meaning. Thus they use institutions in practice to indicate the following:

1. CULTURAL SYSTEM. When they treat institutions as cultural solutions to societal problems, they intend institutions to signify the system of structures, practices, and norms by which societies have organized behavior in the sectors of life. Institutions thus denote the stable, enduring constellations of cultural activities which societies have developed historically to ensure their continuity and welfare. The educational system of a society—or its organized education—is an example of an institution in this sense.

2. CULTURAL COMPLEX. Sociologists also treat institutions as solutions to problems within cultural systems; hence as normative principles which sanction procedures and structures of roles to regulate behavior. In the American educational system, for example, academic freedom, public education, objective examinations, and the scientific method are institutions according to this meaning.

3. INSTITUTIONALIZATION. Sociologists deal with the efforts of groups and organizations to find solutions to problems, hence to institutionalize practices which bring order and stability to hitherto unregulated or partially controlled behavior. In the American educational system, public transportation of students, free lunch programs, systems of accreditation of schools, and counseling programs are in process of institutionalization to the extent that they are not fully accepted and sanctioned.

4. INSTITUTIONS IN THE SOCIAL ORDER. In large-scale perspective, sociologists are concerned also with the roles of institutions in the social organization of societies. Within the social order, institutions are held in a hierarchical arrangement, with some institution or set of institutions dominant in it, and the others of lesser status. Groups and organizations associated with paramount institutions have larger access to wealth, prestige, and social power, which enables them to maintain stability and integration in societies. In the American social order,

economic and political institutions dominate, and educational institutions, despite their manifest importance, have smaller importance.

This discussion of institutions has conveyed some sense perhaps of how sociologists proceed with institutional analysis. For the most part, they fix attention on societies, and investigate the historical and cultural development of their institutions. Their method of investigation is a comparative one: they make historical and cross-cultural comparisons of institutions in one or several societies at the same or different times and places. Through comparative analysis they discover the universal or general as opposed to local or temporal traits of institutions.

EDUCATION: AN INSTITUTIONAL ANALYSIS

All societies organize—or institutionalize—education in order to socialize their human generations, and to secure their social and cultural survival. The term, socialization, means the enculturation of persons and their assimilation into groups so that they become active members of society. Such socialization of persons is necessary because they are born biological organisms and are made into human beings by their experiences in society.

Modern societies employ many institutions—notably educational, familial, and religious institutions—to socialize their populations. In the specialization among these institutions, they make use of education to accumulate and communicate knowledge by which to train and instruct their people, particularly children and youth. The functions of education thus include academic education, technical instruction, vocational training, inculcation of values, discovery of new knowledge, and application of knowledge to solve problems of society and to advance its standards of living.

A society's institution of education denotes its system of education. This consists of its schools and colleges, their academic practices, policies, and facilities, and the structure of faculties and students who teach and learn in them. It comprises the organization, principles, and procedures by which a society educates its people, and preserves and enriches its civilization.

Many persons and groups—school administrators, faculties, public officials, and citizens—take part in building a society's system of education. They establish and operate schools, and organize them into a national system of schools which provide education for children and young adults from the elementary through secondary and higher grades of school. In these schools they teach students, professionalize instruction, develop curricula, add library, laboratory, and other facilities, and promote extracurricular activities. At the same time, they develop the rules and regulations which control these academic activities.

These schoolmen and public groups are guided in their endeavors by the needs of their society for particular kinds and amounts of education of children and youth. They establish educational programs and formulate objectives in awareness of the society's level of culture, industrial development, extent of urbanization, political order, stratification, and other characteristics. Similarly they relate the schools to other institutions, and integrate them into the social order of the society.

In actual conduct of the schools they thus create a system of education, and establish the academic patterns and policies that faculties and students follow in them. They embellish these procedures as they adopt new practices which solve fresh problems. To the extent that such practices work and are accepted as legitimate and equitable, they are institutionalized and incorporated into the activities of the schools.

To generalize, organizations (schools) are necessary to develop institutions (education); and organizations tend to follow institutionalized practices in their operations (Bierstedt, 1963, 344). Through institutionalization the schools achieve permanence, stability, and public support, and, by acquisition of new institutions, they continue capable of adapting to changing conditions in society.

An understanding of educational institutions will be enhanced if these observations are applied to analysis of the American school system. The American schools may be regarded, in the sense of these remarks, as the cultural solution of Americans to their needs to accumulate and communicate knowledge in order to socialize the generations and to maintain the society and its civilization. Much historical and cultural data concerning the schools are available for institutional appraisal of them, and for comparison between them and the schools of other countries.

This analysis of American schools may be organized by employing the four usages of institutions. Each usage presents the schools in a distinctive perspective and permits investigation of them from that aspect; taken together, these usages comprehend the schools as wholes as they function in American society. Thus, when the schools are considered as a system of education, they may be seen in large-scale, or holistic, perspective within the society, which permits analysis of their major cultural and structural characteristics and facilitates cross-cultural comparisons between them and other systems of schools. Second, a consideration of the schools in terms of institutionalized practices directs analysis to their normative procedures and policies, which represent solutions to problems of accumulation and dissemination of knowledge. Third, when analysis of new practices in the process of institutionalization is made, the schools are examined in their efforts to innovate and therefore to adapt to social changes in the society. Finally, the role of the schools in American society and the importance of educational institutions in its social order may be evaluated when the schools are considered in this fourth perspective.

The American School System

The United States has a mixed public-private educational system composed of autonomous schools and colleges which provide elementary, secondary, and higher education. Its earliest schools were private schools founded in the colonial period, which were largely controlled by church groups and offered a religiously oriented curriculum for children of the upper classes. These schools flourished in the nineteenth century and are especially prominent at the college and university levels today. Except for parochial schools, they have largely abandoned their denominational affiliations. Although some public education was available in the colonies, the public schools arose in the nineteenth century, and predominate in numbers and total student enrollment in this century. As a corollary of the doctrine of state-church separation, they represent school-church separation in educational institutions.

Public schools were established to educate the middle and working classes, including the children of immigrants who came in vast numbers to this country. Their institutions reflect their educational mission: these include universal, or mass, education with children compelled to attend school to a stipulated age; tax-supported education given free of charge to children from elementary grades through high school; and secular, or nondenominational, education. Another institution of the schools is the comprehensive curriculum, designed to provide children with a common general education and diversified specialized education in addition.

Still another institution of the schools is their public control, which rests with state rather than the federal government, and is exercised by local communities in the states. Political control of the schools is, therefore, highly decentralized. Elected boards of officials of school districts, most of them autonomous and with taxing powers, govern the public schools in their communities, but hire superintendents of schools to whom they entrust the actual administration of the schools. State educational boards maintain general supervision and fiscal regulation of schools, but do not commonly intervene in their actual conduct. Until recently, the Federal government provided only general services to educational institutions; but now it expends large sums for school construction and various curricular, welfare, and research programs in the schools.

Private schools are of secular and parochial types, the former consisting of preparatory schools and colleges, many of them in existence for one or more centuries, and the latter mainly Roman Catholic schools and colleges. The former are independent schools controlled by private boards of trustees, and financed by endowments, grants, and tuition. They provide an education of quality to children of wealthy families, and cater to their class interests. As a result, they are socially prestigious schools, and hold their students and alumni as partisan status groups.

The Catholic schools are the largest school system under religious control in the United States. They are private in the sense that they are not supported by public funds, but Catholics consider their parish, or parochial, schools—most elementary schools and many high schools— as quasi-public. Other high schools are maintained by dioceses, and colleges are associated with religious orders. Catholic schools are financed by parents' contributions, tuition fees, charitable or endowment funds, and parish and diocesan funds. They provide a Catholic education in that they espouse the moral and spiritual teachings of the Catholic church, and have predominantly clerical faculties composed of Catholic priests and nuns. However they offer curricula of study similar to those of non-Catholic public and private schools. They educate students by comparable methods and standards to enable them to transfer to secular colleges if desired and to prepare them for their lives and work.

Public and private schools, taken together, have attained a considerable number and size as indicated by their student enrollments and faculties. They enrolled a total of 50 million students, 5 to 34 years of age, in 1963, who were 58.5 percent of the entire population in their age distribution. Students attended some 105,000 elementary schools, 30,000 secondary schools, and 2,000 schools of higher education in 1960. Public elementary and secondary teachers were more than 1,500,000 in 1963; the faculties in schools of higher education numbered 38,000 in 1960. The cost of the schools was correspondingly high; expenditures for elementary and secondary schools, public and nonpublic, exceeded 18 billion dollars in 1960; those for colleges and universities, public and nonpublic, were more than 6.5 billions of dollars. The American school system is one of the great industries of the United States.

Public Schools

An institutional analysis of the American schools involves examination of their historical development. The schools were established originally in emulation of European schools, but took on an American character as they became adapted through new structures and institutions to American society. A historical knowledge of the schools reveals the course of their growth, the values and purposes they embodied, the embellishment of their programs and procedures, their relations to other institutions, and their present status in the society.

Institutional and historical analysis however are not synonymous: the former does not undertake to produce a history of an institution. Rather it utilizes historical data to analyze an institution at different times and places in one or more societies. In the case of the schools, its concern is with their organization, policies, institutionalized practices, systems of value, and cultural content, which it strives to understand in historical perspective. It does not neglect the persons and groups who have built the schools, but its interest in them is much less than is the historian's.

To demonstrate institutional analysis of the schools, the common school as it emerged in the nineteenth century (which has been admirably analyzed by Cremin, 1951) may be used as an example. This school—from which emerged the public elementary and high schools of today—was an indigenous American development intended to establish universal literacy among the people. It arose as a school common to all of them, and fostered a curriculum that provided a general education, which has developed into the comprehensive curriculum of modern high schools. Children of middle and working classes received an instruction common in kind and quality, which served to equalize opportunity for them and abetted their assimilation and mobility in the society.

Four developments in the early national life, according to Cremin, favored the rise of the common school and imposed demands on it which eventually determined its mission and character. These events were the democratizing of politics, the struggle for social equality, the change in the conception of man and society, and the rise of nationalism (1951, 28). The demands they gave rise to were several:

"The first, and perhaps the most widespread, demand on education grew out of the new pattern of republicanism. It was increasingly argued that if there was to be universal exercise of the rights of suffrage and citizenship, all of society would have to be educated to this task. Although the liberal intellectual envisioned such education as a means of equipping the citizenry to make intelligent political choices, his conservative counterpart saw it largely as a propaganda agency to save society from the 'tyranny of democratic anarchy.' In education, the latter saw the only way of counteracting the incipient radicalism of the newly enfranchised lower classes. The end result of both, however, emerged as a vigorous demand for the universal education of the people —a demand conceived by its proponents to be at the very heart of republican society and government." (1951, 29.)

"A second crucial demand on education came from the increasingly vocal labor groups in the larger cities. Fearful of the political and social consequences of the new industry and commerce, and mindful of the gaps between principle and reality in the democratic ethic of the nation, they waged a vigorous campaign for 'equality of citizenship.' The newly enfranchised workingmen saw in the equal education of all children the only means by which the sense of community among the American people might be perpetuated, and rigid class stratification avoided. Revealing as it did the contemporary faith that a given reform could rectify a multitude of social evils, the cry of 'Free, Equal, and Republican' education became both a focus and a rallying point of early labor agitation. One after another, the various workingmen's associations and political parties went on record vigorously urging such a system on their respective state legislatures. Their pressures rose to the extent where some historians have held them to be the deciding factor in the institution of the American free school systems.

"In general, two distinct patterns may be delineated in the approach of this early agitation. One represented the efforts of workingmen, through their associations and parties, to secure the improvement and extension of existing public facilities. The other represented the efforts of intellectuals in the movement to develop a drastically new system which they saw befitting an age of industrialism. In view of the importance with which labor looked on educational reform during this period, it is not surprising that the conflicting claims of these courses of action became so highly controversial that in New York, for example, they actually destroyed the very unity of the movement itself." (1951, 33–34.)

"A third fundamental demand on education grew out of the newly emergent American nationality; and, as with the latter, it was sharply accentuated by the steady immigrations of the 1830's and 40's. Tending as they did to live in homogeneous communities apart from the rest of the population, the immigrants contributed to a rising illiteracy rate. Their gregariousness, when combined with their poor economic status, made it practically impossible for them to allow their children any schooling. The adults, nurtured in a foreign culture, tended to follow the older patterns with but a few adjustments to the new way of life.

"With the rise of nationalism among the American people, leaders began to fear the presence of a large body of persons whose patterns of thought and living were incompatible with the American way of life. They felt that such persons could well become a debilitating influence on the virility of the republic. Gradually they began to call for some means of educating them in the basic concepts and practices of democracy, in order that they might be more readily integrated into the community. In the proposals which came forth the school figured prominently as an Americanizing institution." (1951, 43–44.)

"What then, was the total effect of these forces upon the character of educational institutions? What new qualities in the American schools would they require in adjustment to the new cultural developments? Any synthesis seems to revolve largely around a demand for a new, functional, and positive conception of the school's role in society.

"In recognizing the demands of a republican system on its all-important electorate, certain groups demanded that the school provide universal preparation for the exercise of citizenship. They acknowledged, then, that the school had to do something which could no longer be haphazardly left to the family, the church, or even simple participation in the life of the community. The school was now entrusted with a responsibility on which depended the perpetuation and progress of the society.

"Similarly, demands from the growing laboring classes cast another functional role for the school. It now took on the role of a democratizing institution—an agency for preventing that rigid class stratification which these groups saw inherent in the new industrial system. While some saw the fulfillment of this role merely in the provision for universal education, others carried it further. Feeling that it was only out of an experience common to all groups that intergroup hostilities might be rendered ineffectual and class lines kept fluid, they urged the establishment of institutions cutting across traditional family, class, and religious lines. Essentially, they maintained, valid republican education could be carried on only within the social context of a miniature of the broader community. Such experience would tend to neutralize the undemocratic qualities inherent in the life of the wider society—thereby serving constantly to bolster equality of citizenship.

"In the demands for the school as an Americanizing institution, an agency for integrating newly arrived immigrants into the American community, lay a third positive role for the school. For in this area, leaders saw the school actually changing the habits of thought and action of people—molding them in such a way that they could adequately participate in the unique way of life required by republican society. The school, then, had not only to accomplish for newcomers all that it did for the native young (as implied above), but also to combat vigorously the undemocratic patterns which it encountered in the acculturation process. Admittedly, the newcomer could no longer integrate through mere social intercourse with American society. His tendency to live among his own fellows, when coupled with the increasing complexity of American social and political institutions, made the task almost insurmountable. Only through a vigorous, positive effort, utilizing a special institution such as the school, could American society hope to make the newcomer an effective participant in the democratic community.

"Thus, the effects of these new pressures on the American school all converge at one significant point: namely, the demand for an education which would exercise a positive and necessary influence on the life of every member of American society—uniquely providing each with those basic skills, techniques, attitudes, and loyalties necessary for a proper exercise of the prerogatives of republican citizenship." (1951, 47–49.)

Diverse groups, called "educational reformers" by Cremin, struggled to build a common school system which would satisfy these demands, "elevating the whole condition of society and thereby bringing about human progress." (1951, 49.) They worked through groups and organizations, published in educational and popular journals, and assumed posts in educational administration in state government or in school systems to carry on their mission. Thus they enunciated the educational principles which they hoped would express the ideal of the common school.

"At the base of the conception, and perhaps the most important element involved in it, was the idea that the means of education must be made available to all members of the community. This evolved as the result of two separate commitments. First, it was the responsibility of the republican community, in the preservation and furtherance of its own ends, to provide for the education of its constituents." (1951, 52.)

"It was apparent, though, that if such facilities were to be truly 'available,' two conditions would have to be fulfilled. First, they would have to be free; for it was evident that even the slightest cost for education automatically excluded large segments of the population." (1951, 52–53.)

"A second condition of true 'availability' was that such schools as furnished this free education would have to be of high quality—equivalent to any institution which could be established through private means." (1951, 53.)

A second principle was

"A conception of the common school as a leveling institution—one which would, during early childhood, remove the barriers which inevitably arose from different standards of living among different socio-economic groups. Only a common school which was attended by the whole community contained the seeds of a fully republican society. Only in a school where children of all classes, faiths, temperaments, etc., mingled freely together could the odious distinctions of a rigidly hierarchical society be neutralized. Thus the reformers sought to effect a conception of education which would embrace the young of the whole community in one great democratic effort." (1951, 56.)

Still another principle involved the curriculum of the common school which should be concerned with three areas of instruction: (1) education for everyday living, (2) education for moral adequacy, and (3) education for the intelligent and responsible exercise of citizenship. "The common school must be genuinely universal in scope" (1951, 76).

Finally, a fourth principle expressed a concept of public support and control of the common school.

"The basis of thought concerning means of support centered in the argument that if the state was to be dependent on common education for its very life, then it was the responsibility of the state to provide this education for its young." (1951, 76–77.)

"The means by which the whole community could support education was through the appropriation of public funds. Although there were several different kinds of public sources, the reform group early perceived the necessity of resorting to taxation—the traditional agency through which society supported all matters of common responsibility. Education would have to stand along with the functions of law and justice as one more crucial protection to the normal functioning and perpetuation of society." (1951, 77–78.)

"If the role of the state as "common mother" involved community responsibility for the support of education, it similarly made it incumbent upon the community to control and supervise the facilities established. The state was the only authority all-embracing enough to maintain the kind of community school which the reform group envisioned. Any lesser authority would carry the implicit danger of a curriculum that would violate the interest of one or more groups in the community, and tend to break down the all-inclusive character of the community school. The intellectual sectarianism which was potential in control by any less-inclusive body would most certainly act on segments of the school population so as to exclude.

"The implications of this argument struck most powerfully, perhaps, at the conception of education supported by tax funds, but controlled by the several religious groups—each maintaining tax-supported schools for the children of its own faith." (1951, 79–80.)

"If one condition for the success of the common school was the maintenance of high quality instruction, another question which presented itself to the reform group was: What level of the community could best accomplish this through its control of education? In the optimum, the reformers say this is the state. Although they urged responsibility at all levels—local through state—both their writings and actions indicate a vehement maintenance of the final authority of the state in educational matters. Though this probably arose from a variety of reasons, the one which seems most consistent with the total conception of common education revolved around the ability of the state, as the highest level, to compel minimum standards and to equalize opportunity. Through the exercise of its regulatory powers, the state could contribute much toward raising standards to the point where local populations would freely avail themselves of local facilities. Thus, the only control pattern compatible with common education was control by the community. Final authority would rest with the states; delegated and assumed responsibilities would accrue from the local levels on up. Similarly, the only compatible pattern of support capable of maintaining these desired qualities was public community support, including taxation." (1951, 80–81.)

Catholic Schools

Institutional analysis also involves cross-cultural analysis of the American schools. Such analysis entails systematic historical and cultural comparisons of schools in American society, or of American schools and the schools of other societies. Its purpose is to reveal the common characteristics of schools in all societies, which may be accepted as their universal traits, and their characteristics peculiar to specific societies, which may be accepted as cultural traits. Such comparisons further clarify the historical development of the schools and provide cultural content and meaning to their practices.

A logical use of cross-cultural analysis is to compare the public and private schools in the United States. The Catholic schools, discussed by Brickman (1964), are examples of private schools, whose comparison with public schools shows both similarities and differences between them. As American schools, Catholic schools share many academic patterns with public schools; but as schools under religious rather than civil control, with the duty to provide religious as well as secular education, they have a separate character also.

One-half of Catholic children attend Catholic schools in the United States. Their number in 1960 was 4,373,422 pupils enrolled in 10,501 elementary schools, and 880,369 students in 2,392 secondary schools. They were taught by a total of 108,169 teachers in the elementary grades, and 43,733 instructors in secondary schools, of whom the majority were nuns, priests, and brothers. Despite these impressive figures, not all Catholic children enroll in Catholic schools because of "the lack of sufficient schools, the costs to the parent, the complications of intermarriage, the critical attitude by some parents toward the results achieved, the large size of classes, inadequate teaching materials, and the narrow curriculum" (1964, 60).

The administrative control of the Catholic schools is as follows:

"Catholic education in the U.S. is organized by archdioceses (under an archbishop) and dioceses (under a bishop). The highest ecclesiastical officer is actually the archbishop or bishop, but because of manifold duties he entrusts the direction of education to an archdiocesan or diocesan superintendent of schools, who corresponds to a state or county superintendent of public instruction. The diocesan superintendent, or secretary for education as he is sometimes called, is a priest (often with the rank of monsignor) who has had special training in professional education in a Catholic or secular college or in both. The superintendent administers and supervises the entire school system of the diocese, and he helps in the coordination of the courses of study and in raising the standards of education in every respect. In a highly populous diocese, such as Brooklyn, the superintendent will have a staff of priest-educators to assist him. As the educational right-hand man of the bishop, the superintendent is in charge of all parochial and diocesan schools, as well as all schools operated by the religious orders of priests, brothers, and nuns.

"The vast majority of Catholic elementary schools and a number of the high schools are parochial; that is, they are financed by the Catholics of a particular parish and are under the direct supervision of the parish priest, who is responsible to his bishop and to the parents. As a general rule, the instruction in the parochial elementary schools is carried on by nuns who are members of religious orders. The parish priest, if qualified, is the principal; otherwise, the school is directed by a nun.

"The diocesan department of education, like the state department, has school boards, which are required under the orders of the Third Plenary Council. Although these boards at one time were actively engaged in raising the standards of education, in recent times they have functioned as advisory groups to the bishop and superintendent. The diocesan school board of Pittsburgh consists of twelve priests (including the superintendent, who acts as secretary) under the chairmanship of the bishop. Since all the board members reside in the diocese, they are subordinate to the bishop; but the bishop is interested in the views of the board members, who have had rich and varied educational experience.

"Again, as in the state school systems, the superintendent of a large diocese will be aided by supervisors of special fields of instruction, such as music and art. Superintendents, supervisors, and teachers are prepared in Catholic and non-Catholic colleges, teachers' colleges, and universities. They are organized into special associations such as the Jesuit Education Association, and these groups are usually constituents of the National Catholic Education Association (founded in 1904) which holds annual conferences, issues publications, and is otherwise active in arising the standards of the Catholic educational profession." (1964, 62–64.)

Under this system of religious control, Catholic schools follow the directives of the Catholic church; but they have also to educate children at standards corresponding to those in secular public and private schools. They confront a dilemma in pursuing these objectives; on the one hand, they separate and parochialize Catholic children in parish schools to ensure their religious training; and, on the other hand, they strive to prepare children for lives and activities in American society as well as in the Catholic subcommunity. In solving this dilemma the Catholic schools take on a distinctive character.

"The Catholic school is neither a carbon copy of the public school in the neighborhood nor an 'all-week Sunday school,' where the children are drilled for six hours daily in the catechism by nuns, pray in the church next door, and bear the parish priest's exhortations (McClusky, 1959, 73). On the basis of such an image, anyone might believe that the real objective of Catholic educational work is indoctrination pure and simple. While Catholic education does have a supernatural foundation and seeks to infuse the entire curriculum with Christian values, it is still concerned with the development of young people 'as scholars and citizens.' This means that the content of the subject matter taught in the Catholic schools must be substantially the same as the public schools. The difference is that the Catholic courses will modify the content in order to highlight Catholic values. These differences do not alter the fact that the Catholic student is expected to know what all others do when he takes a uniform state examination, as in New York State or the College Entrance Examination." (1964, 61.)

"The Catholic elementary schools offer the same basic curriculum taught in the public schools, with the addition of Catholic values. Their leaders, too, are reorganizing and modifying the content and the methodology in science, mathematics, and other subjects. Experiments are being initiated with team teaching, television, tapes, electronics, and other modern procedures and facilities. Cooperation is taking place between parents and teachers in conferences and in home-school associations." (1964, 65.)

"Any discussion of the curriculum in the parochial school must take the religious factor into consideration. Since at the bottom of the Catholic aim and effort in education lies the inculcation of religious ideals and attitudes, it has been felt necessary by the church authorities to produce Catholic textbooks in science, social studies, literature, and certainly religion. At the present time, there are Catholic series of textbooks for practically every school subject to make certain that no undercurrent of materialistic and naturalistic philosophy runs through the instruction in the parochial schools.

"According to one Catholic educational expert, the average elementary parochial school teaches formal religion five daily periods of half an hour each. The content of the religion course comprises catechism, doctrine, Bible, and church history. The classes are taught by nuns, priests, and lay teachers. While some schools may stress the teaching of religion more than others, most appear to preserve some sort of balance between the religious and the secular subjects. The schedule of time in the eighth grade of one parochial school indicates that the pupils spent 25 hours a week according to the following breakdown: English, 37.3 percent; social studies, 16 percent; arithmetic, 15 percent; religion, 10 percent; music, 6.7 percent; science and health, 5.3 percent; art, 4 percent; and recess and miscellaneous, 5.7 percent. In other words, two and a half hours out of 25 are taken up with the study of religion. The priest-sociologist (Fichter, 1958, 106) who made an investigation of this school admitted that the incidental religious activities, such as talks on religious vocations, choir singing, and altar serving, may cut down the time allotted in public schools to shop, sewing, and physical training, but he insisted that these were of an educative nature and were an integral and necessary part of the education of the parochial school pupil." (1964, 66.)

"The curriculum of the Catholic high school (Janet, 1949, 65–92) resembles that of the public high school: mathematics, the sciences, ancient and modern foreign languages, English, social studies, fine arts, practical arts, and physical education. Religion, of course, is present in every Catholic curriculum as a required subject for four years. The teaching of religion in some schools may be quite minimal—as little as thirty minutes per week—although many institutions devote from three to five clock hours each week to this subject. As in the elementary parochial school, additional time is spent on various religious activities which contribute to the realization of the basic objectives of Catholic education. The formal course content covers the study of Catholic doctrine, Bible and church history, apologetics, the liturgy, the Papal Encyclicals, and other sources of Catholic moral and social teachings.

"The courses of study in social studies in Catholic secondary schools comprise American, world, ancient, medieval, and modern history, civics, sociology, problems of American education, and other subjects. The foreign languages offered are mainly Latin, Spanish, and French, although a number of schools teach German, Greek, Polish, and Italian. The stress on Latin is understandable because of the close connection between this classical language and the liturgy and literature of the Catholic Church. In fact, in recent decades there has been a trend to-

ward courses in Church Latin, in which pupils read portions of the
Church Fathers, the Epistles, and the liturgy in the original. In general,
however, the role of Latin in Catholic secondary education may not be
as strong today as a quarter of a century ago. The current changes in
subject matter, equipment, and methodology are also affecting the
curriculum of the Catholic secondary school." (1964, 67.)

American Public Education

An understanding of American schools is advanced further by cross-
cultural comparisons between them and European schools. American
colleges and universities especially have been enormously influenced
by their European counterparts, from whom they have copied liberally.
In turn, colleges and universities have had a considerable influence on
the high schools, which as comprehensive institutions are a native
product. Conant (1959) delineated the salient characteristics of American and European education by contrasting their colleges and universities.

Like Cremin, Conant believed that historical knowledge is necessary
to comprehend public education. In historical perspective, he selected
two American values which helped to shape the schools: the belief in
equality of opportunity—"an equal start in a competitive struggle"—
and equality of status—"equality of status of all honest labor" (1959,
5,6). One outcome of these values was the establishment of a new type
of college, the "land-grant colleges," with federal support under the
Morrill Act, which helped to give higher education its modern
character.

"As these institutions developed, collegiate instruction in such practical fields as animal husbandry came to have the same academic standing as that of education for the professions. A proliferation of professional and semiprofessional areas of instruction, running from architec-
ture to wild life conservation, started in the closing decades of the last
century and has continued in this century until today a catalogue of
many an institution (privately controlled or publicly supported) bears
little resemblance to a corresponding pamphlet issued by a European
university.

"The widening of the fields of instruction in the nineteenth century
was part of a drastic educational reform that was taking place on both
sides of the Atlantic. The main objective of this reform was the recognition of the physical and biological sciences as reputable subjects to be

studied in a university. On this continent, because of the special history of the American people, the movement took on many special characteristics. The definition of what was a "university subject" widened and widened as the decades passed.

"As the fields of study of applied science and practical subjects broadened at the university level, instruction at the secondary level also changed. A hundred years ago one assumed a lawyer would have studied Greek and Latin; it was argued that a classical education was essential for him as a professional man. Fifty years later, it was hard to make a convincing case that the preprofessional education of an electrical engineer or an agriculturist should include instruction in reading Latin. And at no time in the educational history of this country has mastery of a modern foreign language come to be recognized as the hallmark of a well-educated man or woman." (1959, 3–4.)

To realize these twin ideals of equality of opportunity and of status, Americans have used the means of more and more education. Hence the numbers and percentages of young people enrolled in high school and in colleges has increased enormously. But two other factors have also influenced the burgeoning enrollments of the schools.

"First, there was the urge for institutional expansion—the drive for larger faculties and student bodies in the colleges and universities; fifty years ago expansion was more than welcomed. Second, there was a radical change in the picture regarding the employment of youth. When this century began, approximately half of the boys and girls fifteen years of age were not attending school; many were at work. Thirty years later the percentage of this group attending school had reached 85. This alteration was not a consequence of state laws raising the school-leaving age; the laws were rather a consequence of profound economic and social changes. To explore adequately the background of this shift in the American scene would require many pages; suffice it to remind the reader that in the second decade of this century the campaign against child labor was being pushed vigorously at the state and national levels. Today, as a result of laws affecting employment as well as the attitude of management and labor, it is difficult for boys even at the age of seventeen to obtain many types of jobs. In European countries three quarters or more of the youth go to work at fourteen or fifteen years of age." (1959, 7.)

"As a consequence of all these changes, the American public high school has become an institution which has no counterpart in any other country. With few exceptions, for the most part in large eastern cities, the public high school is expected to provide education for all the youth living in a town, city or district. Such a high school has become known as a 'comprehensive' high school in contrast to the 'specialized' high schools which provide vocational education or which admit on a selective basis and offer only an academic curriculum." (1959, 7–8.)

American colleges and universities have diverged in character through these developments from European universities.

"In European universities there is no equivalent of our undergraduate liberal arts college, no provision for general education. European universities are essentially a collection of faculties concerned with the education of future members of the learned professions. The general or liberal education of the doctor, lawyer, theologian, engineer, scientist, or professional scholar is provided by special secondary schools, admission to which is determined by a highly selective procedure at age ten or eleven. Not more than 20 percent of an age group are selected from the elementary school and enrolled in the preuniversity schools. Therefore there is a waste of talent under the European system. No one has estimated how much potential talent goes undeveloped in Germany, France, Italy, and Switzerland because of the early selection of the preuniversity students—a selection often influenced by the class system of European lands. The other 80 to 85 percent stop their formal education at age fourteen and go to work. Of course, the selection of those who are to be enrolled in the preuniversity school is on the basis of academic ability, but family tradition plays a big role and many boys and girls from the farm and working class never even think of trying to enter a preuniversity school.

"In the European preuniversity schools an eight- or nine-year rigorous course in languages, mathematics, science, history, and literature prepares the student to pass a state examination for a certificate which admits him to a university. The failures during the long course are many, and a considerable number fall by the wayside, but those who succeed finish with a mastery of two foreign languages, a knowledge of mathematics through calculus and of physics and chemistry at the level of our sophomore college courses. Those who are not enrolled in the preuniversity schools, except for a small fraction who enter an intermediate school, complete their full-time education at age fourteen." (1959, 2–3.)

EDUCATIONAL PRACTICES. To European visitors, the American educational system, with tens of thousands of local school boards having vast powers over public elementary and secondary schools, and with lay and ecclesiastical boards controlling private schools and colleges, sometimes seems hardly a system at all, but rather a chaos (Conant, 1959, 8). They cannot conceive how the schools, with such extensive localized autonomy, can function effectively as a system of schools and fulfill their tasks of education.

But, as Conant goes on to say, the system of schools works, and most Americans like it (1959, 8). The schools function successfully, however many, scattered, and free they are, for two main reasons. One is that they are organized much alike and have a structural unity. The other reason is that they follow similar institutionalized practices and have a normative unity.

The organization of the schools is discussed in Chapter five and need not be anticipated here. But several observations about their organization will indicate its relation to their institutionalized practices and emphasize the importance of the latter, which is the burden of this chapter.

School organization—more apparent in colleges and universities than in grade and high schools—rests on bureaucratic, professional, and collegial principles of organization, whose combinations and utilization vary with functional activities of the schools. The schools are administered by academic officials exercising bureaucratic authority, who are appointed and controlled by public and private boards. But these officials share power with academic departments and faculties, who have collegial and professional authority; and with government offices and officials, citizens groups, interest groups, and even students. Not only centralization but decentralization of power thus occurs in the schools, and many groups participate in decision-making processes in their operation. To control conflict with or among these groups, often by avoiding a confrontation of authority over them, school officials resort to rules and regulations to govern interactions and relations with them. This predilection for rules to mask exercise of authority is not unique to the schools, but occurs in all American organizations, and reflects American values of equalitarianism and due process of law (Crozier, 1964, 231–236). Officials and faculties also devise rules of course to regulate academic activities in the schools.

This promulgation of regulations has a further significance for the schools. Rules necessarily have a substantive content: they embody norms, they express value configurations, they have sanctions. As rules multiply, they develop into systems of norms or institutions, according to the second usage of this concept. Through common institutions schools achieve a normative unity, and are integrated into a system of schools.

Some institutions of the public schools have already been mentioned; other institutions are readily added to them. A paramount institution surely is the autonomy of the schools: their freedom to carry on activities according to their own norms, and their freedom from pressures by outside groups and organizations which interfere with these activities. Their independence requires the institution of academic freedom: the freedom of faculties to discover and communicate knowledge objectively and without constraint, and the freedom of students to learn without consideration of their race, religion, or class.

The autonomy of the schools however is relative. The schools strive also to fulfill the educational needs of the society, and to develop institutions which serve these purposes. These institutions include scientific research, vocational instruction, professional training, academic publication, technological research and application, public service, and public entertainment. These institutions currently expand and multiply, and increasingly involve the schools in the society.

But the schools have developed institutions principally to regulate their own instructional activities, and to solve academic problems. These institutions—to name only a few of them—include objective examinations, laboratory research, academic libraries, extracurricular activities, organized athletics, vocational guidance, medical care, counseling services, and student government. As these institutions suggest, the schools define students as persons as well as scholars, and provide for both their intellectual and social needs.

NEW INSTITUTIONS. The schools strive constantly to improve or expand their educational practices to function more effectively, and to meet the challenges which social changes bring them. They must be capable of developing new institutions to solve fresh problems, and thereby to adapt to altered conditions in society.

An analysis of social change and its bearing on the schools is discussed in Chapter three. But some comment on how social changes affect institutions and the processes of institutionalization is desirable here. The society experiences social changes continuously, brought about by population growth or movement, urbanization, technological advances, industrialization, scientific progress, war, or other causes. These devel-

opments engulf the schools in problems such as swelling student enrollments, mounting costs, student disaffection, and excessive faculty mobility. Or academic and public groups demand new or better services
from them: perhaps technical education, mass instruction by television,
more graduate instruction, desegregation of schools, or preschool training for children of the poor. The schools are compelled to find remedies
for the problems which assail them, and sometimes develop new institutions in the course of doing so.

To expatiate, the growth of institutions occurs through three stages
of development. In the first stage, the schools confront difficult situations which present problems for them, and which they come to define
as problems; next, they attempt to solve problems by devising procedures to deal with them; finally, they possibly come upon remedies
that appear to work and become accepted as legitimate solutions by the
society, when they may become institutions. These stages are by no
means inevitable: the schools may find no solutions or only inadequate
ones, or groups may oppose new procedures and prevent their legitimation as solutions.

School administrators and faculties initially encounter difficult conditions in the schools resulting from social changes which disrupt their
activities. They become aware also of an increasing discrepancy between what they ought to do and what they actually do in performance
of their duties and in adjusting to new circumstances. In experiencing
the burden of these conditions they come to recognize the problems
involved in them, and to define their nature and severity. They pursue
thereafter a discussion of these problems in their oral discourses and
scholarly publications.

These same groups also likely initiate efforts to solve the problems
they encounter in line of duty. But action in finding solutions involves
higher school and public officials who have authority and control funds.
The latter establish the committees and procedures to embark on the
tasks of finding remedies for problems, but ordinarily depend on the
former groups to propose tentative solutions which they have the power
to accept or not. Still other groups—professional, public, political, and
ethnic, representing diverse interests—may also participate in these
efforts.

Still later, schools and organizations across the land also become
involved, as well as public officials of state and federal governments. At
this stage, the entire society is concerned, and national offices of power
and authority have been reached. When national groups and organizations finally concur on solutions, their decisions appear to uphold the

interest and welfare of all the people. Their solutions, when tried out and found to work, become standard procedures and are thereafter followed in the society. They have evolved into institutions.

How these processes occur may be illustrated by a problem which harrasses the schools, and for which no solution is at hand at present. This is the problem of racial integration of the schools. Negroes are embarked in mass movements to redress racial imbalances and injustices in the society, and have attacked, among other things, segregation in the schools and the "neighborhood school" concept which sustains it. Local school boards draw school boundaries on basis of residence, and children attend schools in the districts in which their homes are located. But Negro children, who dwell in Negro neighborhoods or ghettos, are thus assigned to schools in which they compose the large majority of students. Negro groups allege that racially segregated schools are academically inferior schools, and penalize Negro children. Recent efforts to solve these problems include redrawing of school district lines more equitably, "bussing" of students to schools in other districts, specialized schools to replace neighborhood schools, and improved Negro schools. From these efforts and others still to come, some solution will eventually be discovered which mitigates segregation and establishes equity in schools. When it comes, it will provide procedures supported by emergent norms, and will constitute new institutions.

Schools in the Social Order

The society's institutions compose its social organization. Its institutions stabilize and control activities in the various sectors of societal life; together they provide a complete regulation of the activities of the society. This involves an integration of institutions in the social order, with core institutions—political and economic institutions in American society—dominant in a hierarchical arrangement and accommodation of institutions. The groups and organizations associated with core institutions exercise the power necessary to support this structure of institutions, and to maintain order and stability in the society.

The schools, although not core institutions, are nevertheless of large and increasing importance. Their position and influence in the social order, as well as their relations with other institutions, are actually hard to state reliably. But the schools may be evaluated by the access they provide to power, prestige, and wealth in the society, and the time, costs, and energies which persons devote to becoming educated. Such analysis of the schools may be made in two perspectives.

First, the schools perform functions of socialization and enculturation which are of incalculable significance to the society, and win a
high place for them in it. Without trained, educated citizens the society
could not survive nor its civilization long endure. The people show
their appreciation of the schools by their support and largesse: mounting enrollments, huge expenditures, vast school plants, diversified facilities, and professional faculties.

However, the position of the schools in the social order is not so high
as their scale and wealth might indicate. The society cannot be organized readily by educational institutions: its order scarcely resembles a
classroom, and intellectual oligarchies are not important in its system of
stratification. Also, education has an instrumental character, that is, it
serves to attain other goals rather than constituting a goal in itself.
For the society the goal is social control of the people—control of
access to higher education perpetuates the upper classes in positions
of dominance, and the working classes in lower strata. For individuals
the goal is the use of the schools as vehicles of mobility, which tends to
stress vocationalism in education. Like other institutions, the schools
fail to attain the high standards that one might wish for them. Therefore they are vulnerable to criticism of their quality of education which,
when it becomes excessive, nurtures derogation of the schools and
anti-intellectualism in the people.

Second, the schools, in another perspective, are increasing in status
in the social order because they function to discover and communicate
new knowledge, which has assumed transcendent value in modern
societies. The universities especially serve this purpose through scientific research and technological development, producing seminal ideas
and applications of them which instigate social changes in the society
and enhance the influence of the schools over other institutions. Among
their discoveries of new knowledge are, for example, atomic energy and
electronic technology, whose impact on government, industry, war,
indeed on all institutions, is revolutionary. Modern societies consider
scientific knowledge and advanced technology as enormous cultural
assets, whose possession, indeed, serves to differentiate the advanced
from the developing nations. "The highly educated man," as Drucker
asserted, "has become the central resource of today's society, the supply
of such men the true measure of its economic, military and even its
political potential" (1959, 87). The appearance of "multiversities" to
pursue and accumulate knowledge by rational inquiry and organized
research attests to the importance of the schools and the respect which
learning has.

An analysis of the role of universities in promoting social changes in modern societies by Halsey (1960)—he called them technological societies—"towards which Western industrial countries are more or less rapidly moving," will augment these observations. Halsey dealt with universities mainly in their relations to economic systems:

"This is basically because development of knowledge is always likely to issue from its conservation and, in fact, has done so intermittently throughout the history of higher learning. More particularly it is so because, in response to the demands set up by modern industrialism and scientific warfare, research has become institutionalized in universities. The universities have therefore become an established source of instability to the technology and hence to the economy. And at the same time they are the training institutions for the skilled manpower required by a complex technology." (1960, 20.)

The role of universities in the growth of technological society began with the application in the nineteenth century of science to industrial processes, the

"'invention of invention,' and the slow subsequent development of technological professions in agriculture, chemistry, metallurgy, mechanical and electrical engineering, etc. However it begins to become clear as a direct relationship of economic organization to the higher learning only with escape from the economic depressions of the 1930's and the search for high productivity of the war and post war years. Both as research organizations and as training establishments, the institutions of higher education in this period have been drawn more closely into the economy either directly or through the state. The exchange of ideas, people, and contracts between university departments and research institutes and their counterparts in private industry and government agencies is such as to merge these organizations and to assimilate the life of their staff." (1960, 123.)

The growth of technological society also influenced the universities.

"The search for talent to man the economy implies democratization of access to education and the development of selective processes. Schools, colleges and universities become the agencies through which 'achievement' in the occupational role is largely determined and in which the forces of 'ascription' and 'achievement' contend to determine the life chances of individuals."

The educational characteristics of a technological society are clearest where they are most advanced—in America. The explosive expansion which has taken place there in the demand for high scientific manpower has not only created conditions of chronic shortage of supply; it has also transformed the universities. In 1900 the percentage of American 18 to 21 year olds enrolled in institutions of higher education was 4.0. It doubled in the next twenty years and again in the following twenty years to 15.6 in 1940. Since then expansion has been even more rapid until, in 1956 the figure was about one third. Under these circumstances the function of universities as nurseries for elite groups is overlaid by their new function as a mass higher education service in an emergent technological society. The "community of the educated" similarly tends to disappear. Meanwhile it should be noticed that the structure of higher education has adapted itself to the new conditions by forming itself into a status hierarchy or "academic procession" with graded access to "achievement" and power in the stratification system. A comparable development occurred in Russia.

"Russia is the same kind of society in the sense that higher education is geared closely to the economy which, in this case, is controlled centrally in the interests of maximizing economic growth. At first glance the USSR appears to be educationally under-developed. It has proportionately only half as many secondary school graduates as the U.S.A. and only 16 per 1000 of its people have had higher education compared with the American figure of 44. But the essential feature of the Russian case is that the sharp break with earlier social traditions which was made possible by the Revolution resulted in the development of a system of higher education adjusted directly to the demand for technological manpower. Thus in the supply of professional and scientific workers to agriculture, medicine, engineering, etc., the Russian system is as far advanced as the American. For example, in engineering and science the number of graduates per 1000 of the population is 9 in USSR and 10 in the U.S.A.

"The different points reached by these two countries in their advance toward the technological society is indicated by the fact that in Russia the percentage of science and engineering graduates to all graduates is 55 whereas in America it is 21. This certainly does not mean that in America the higher learning either already is or is becoming less closely geared to the economy. On the contrary there is a strong tendency for business to increase its influence over the content of American higher education as is indicated by the decline of the fundamental disciplines and the rise of applied subjects, especially those connected with business administration and commerce. The 'extra' output of American graduates in the humanities and social sciences mainly reflects the professionalization of the tertiary sectors of American industry and may be viewed as an adornment of the affluent society, which Russia has yet to become." (1960, 124–125.)

But in England this development has occurred tardily and at a slower pace. Halsey explained the reasons for this as follows:

"The British case is instructive as one in which the mediaeval and aristocratic traditions of the universities have hitherto acted as a powerful brake against movement toward the technological society. British university life has been dominated by Oxford and Cambridge since the defeat of the migration to Stamford in 1334. On the 14th century Oxford and Cambridge, backed by royal power, established themselves as national institutions with a monopoly over the higher learning. The monopoly was challenged frequently but unsuccessfully until the rise of the universities in the great industrial cities of the 19th century, and even then monopoly only gave way to pre-eminence. The challenge of industrialism and non-conformity was met partly by reform and expansion of the ancient foundations, partly by assimilation of the sons of successful business men through the colleges and the 'public schools' which supply them, and partly by sending staff to the newly created universities.

"As a result a two tier structure emerged in the early 20th century. Oxford and Cambridge were national universities connected with the national elites of politics, administration, business and the liberal professions. The rest were provincial, all of them, including London, taking most of their students from their own region and training them in undergraduate professional occupations created by industrialism such as chemistry, electrical engineering, state grammar school teaching and the scientific civil service.

"Since the war . . . a new wave of expansion, with some emphasis on science and the technologies, has been taking place. But the pace of expansion is much slower than in the U.S.A. or the USSR. The elite conception of the university continues to dominate development plans. Oxford and Cambridge were again expanding to assimilate the rising technological elite through the Cavendish Laboratories and Churchill College. A scrimmage for precedence on the second tier is taking place among the modern universities and the newly emancipated university colleges; and, in the process, the provincial universities are being nationalized. An indication of this trend may be had from the proportion of students drawn from within 30 miles of the university. . . .

"Meanwhile a third tier in the structure of higher education is being formed by Colleges of Advanced Technology and Teacher Training Colleges offering courses of three years duration. The creation of this new level in the hierarchy is to the emerging technological economy what the provincial universities were to large-scale industrialism. (1960, 125–127.)

POTENTIALS OF INSTITUTIONAL ANALYSIS OF EDUCATION

This discussion has attempted no more than to explain what institutions are, and to analyze the American schools as institutions. It has used excerpts from studies of schools not originally made by means of the institutional method to illustrate its main contentions. Now, in conclusion, one may ask, what does the institutional analysis of schools add up to, and to what extent does it increase our understanding of them? And conversely, how does the study of the schools contribute to our knowledge of institutions?

The institutional method aspires, once again, to deal with entire societies, and to analyze the historical development and cultural content of their institutions. It studies institutions comparatively in and between societies in order to discover their universal and unique characteristics as well as their position in the social organization of societies. It considers institutions as cultural solutions to problems of collective life, and utilizes methods of empirical research to learn how societies have arrived at them in their constant efforts to adjust to changing conditions of life. Consequently it investigates institutions in a behavioral or social action context, and fixes on the groups, structures, and social norms involved in institutions.

These last concepts, which are central terms in sociology, synopsize the value of the institutional method. Applied to educational institutions, they signify that institutional analysis is concerned with academic persons and groups, the organization of the schools, their academic practices and policies, and the relations of schools to other institutions and to the society at large. It deals thus with basic issues and problems of the schools.

A corollary value of the institutional method is that it deals with educational institutions as a national system of schools. This is especially important in the case of American schools with their vast number and extreme decentralization. It directs attention to the national traits of the schools, and relates them to the culture and value system of American society. The United States as a nation-state constitutes a national society, and its schools and other institutions must be comprehended in its context. Otherwise studies of schools become parochial in their concern with local schools and with minor issues of academic life.

The institutional method is important also because it studies societies comparatively. It enables sociologists to understand the historical growth and the cultural meaning of institutions, and to achieve a holistic understanding of institutions and societies.

Valuable as the institutional method is, not many institutional studies of schools have been made. Some historians have employed the method broadly—more as a system of precepts than as systematic analysis—in studies of development of the school. Although sociologists study the schools comparatively, they refrain from historical investigations of them, and have preferred functional analysis of schools or have studied them in reference to specific matters, such as stratification.

Were more institutional studies of the schools made, one might wish that they concentrate on these topics, which would increase our knowledge of educational institutions:

1. The national system of American schools, with comparisons with European and other educational institutions.

2. Cultural patterns and complexes of the schools: their practices, policies, structures, and regulations determining the operation of the schools.

3. Cultural goals and values of the schools as institutions, which also relate them to the American society and its system of values.

4. Cultural processes of innovation and change in the schools, and the processes by which practices are institutionalized.

5. The relations of schools to economic, political, and other institutions.

6. The educational problems of the schools, the solutions of which are imperative and may develop into institutions.

Finally, the converse of these assertions should also be said: the study of schools has great promise for increasing our knowledge of institutions. The reasons for this lie in the character of schools and in their accessibility to investigation. Schools multiply and steadily expand their functions of instruction and research, with universities becoming great centers for the discovery and communication of knowledge. Thus they strengthen the society and enrich its civilization, but also instigate profound changes in it which influence all its institutions. They thus play dual roles of stabilizing and changing their societies. For these reasons the schools are exemplary institutions to study in terms of their own development, and their relations to the society and other institutions.

Moreover, the schools, more than other institutions, are available to scientific study of their organization and institutions. Their administrators, faculties, and students are literate and articulate persons who are vastly interested in the educational enterprise which engages them. They are committed to scholarly research and discovery of new knowledge not only of other institutions but of their own also. There exists a vast literature on schools, as well as public records and documents, and other sources of information occur also.

If scholars have not always studied schools scientifically or made many institutional analyses of them, these shortcomings have their remedy. This volume is intended to inform them of their duty and opportunity to do so, and to suggest feasible methods of doing so.

John Sirjamaki is Professor of Sociology at the State University of New York at Buffalo. His Ph.D. is from Yale University, where he has also taught, as he has at the University of Minnesota. His book, *The American Family in the 20th Century* (Harvard University Press, 1953) was selected for the White House Library. He has also published *The Sociology of Cities* (Random House, 1964).

WORKS CITED

Bierstedt, Robert (1957), *The Social Order*, McGraw-Hill Book Co., New York.

Brickman, William A. (1964), *Educational Systems in the United States*, Center for Applied Research in Education, Inc., New York.

Chapin, F. Stuart (1935), *Contemporary American Institutions*, Harper & Row, New York.

Conant, James Bryant (1959), *The American High School*, McGraw-Hill Book Co., New York.

Cremin, Lawrence A. (1951), *The American Common School*, Teachers College, Columbia University, New York.

Crozier, Michel (1964), *The Bureaucratic Phenomena*, University of Chicago Press, Chicago.

Drucker, Peter F. (1959), *The Landmarks of Tomorrow*, James H. Heineman, New York.

Fichter, Joseph H. (1958), *Parochial Schools*, University of Notre Dame Press, Notre Dame, Indiana.

Halsey, A. H. (1960), "The Changing Functions of Universities in Advanced Industrial Societies," *Harvard Educational Review*, 30, No. 2 (Spring) pp. 118–127.

Hertzler, J. O. (1946), *Social Institutions*, University of Nebraska Press, Lincoln, Nebr.

Hobhouse, L. T. (1924), *Social Development*, Allen & Allen, London.

Janet, Sister Mary (1949), *Catholic Secondary Education*, National Catholic Welfare Conference.

MacIver, R. M., and Charles H. Page (1949), *Society*, Holt, Rinehart & Winston, New York.

Martindale, Don (1962), *Social Life and Cultural Change*, D. Van Nostrand Co., Princeton, N.J.

McClusky, Neil G. (1959), *Catholic Viewpoint on Education*, Hanover House, New York.

Parsons, Talcott (1951), *The Social System*, The Free Press, New York.

Parsons, Talcott, and Edward A. Shills, eds. (1959), *Toward a General Theory of Action*, Harvard University Press, Cambridge, Mass.

Schneider, Louis (1964), "Institution" in *Dictionary of the Social Sciences*, Julius Gould and William Kolb, eds.

Spencer, Herbert (1958), *First Principles of a New System of Philosophy*, DeWitt Revolving Fund, New York.

Sumner, William Graham (1906), *Folkways*, Ginn and Company, Boston.

3 Education and Social Change

Reece McGee
Macalester College

There may be no subject more pressing in the field of education to-day than the study of the relation between educational institutions and practices and social change. That change is sweeping our educational systems seems undeniable: riots and student protests at universities, the involvement of students and faculty in national and international affairs and commentary, the increasing political and economic involvement of the public and the government with the schools all attest to a relationship between the educational system and the rest of the society which seems to many of us to be somehow fundamentally different from any we have known before. It is apparent, then, that things are changing: the nature of the schools and some of their functions, the student bodies, and the attitudes of the general society toward them. But the reasons for such changes, and the ends to which they may be leading, and the processes whereby they are coming about or by which they might be directed are considerably less clear.

There are probably many reasons for this unclarity, but a principal one must be our lack of knowledge about change itself. For in reality we know very little of it. There is a plethora of hypotheses to "explain" it (as we will see), but even of these, few have been systematically applied to the study of education. Why this has been so is difficult to say, for in many ways the educational system in the United States is a remarkably available laboratory for social research. Schools (which may be either reservoirs of data or objects of study in themselves) abound in every corner of our nation and are more or less amenable to study since most, in one way or another, are open to constituent publics. They are normally organized in roughly bureaucratic form, further, which means they will have files and records of past action indispensable for tracing change. And finally, of course, many of our citizens are involved with them in some way. But such study is not easy, for examination of the relation between the institution of education and the process of social change, at least within a complex society, inherently involves the student in three subjects rather than the two indicated. Consideration immediately reveals that education can be an *agent* of change in itself, a *condition* of change in the surrounding society, or an *effect* of change in the other institutions with which it is so intimately interrelated.

That education can be an agent of change is hardly a startling proposition; indeed the public educational system of the United States has the accomplishment of social change as one of its fundamental functions and was, in part at least, instituted in its present form in order to effect exactly that end. (How and why this is so is explored later by Brogan.) But for education to be an agent or instrument of social change implies that it is to some extent under the rational control of men who perceive a need for change and are capable of designing tools to accomplish it. Yet it is a truism in sociology that few efforts may be made for the accomplishment of an end without having some consequences unforeseen by the planner or initiator. These sometimes may be of such magnitude as to alter the shape of the result into something rather different from that intended, and may involve latent functions for the society as well. Under circumstances such as these, education may become a *condition* of change as well as an agent of that process. Sometimes, of course, major changes elsewhere in the society necessarily or eventually involve education and have effects on it, in which instances the educational process, if it simply contributes to them along with many other events, might also be deemed a condition of change. (For example, some immense structural changes occurred in American society as a result of the Second World War. One response to these almost geologic shifts was pressure on the Congress from the American Legion and other groups resulting in the passage of what came to be called "the G.I. Bill." Among the provisions of that remarkable law were some financing veterans' attendance in institutions of higher education. Millions of men who might not have attended college except for the accident of the war, and the further accident of that particular response to the war, did matriculate in colleges and universities all over the country, and many of them graduated. Large numbers went on to graduate school. The effects upon the colleges were profound. It seems probable that the effects upon the American nation were even more far-reaching; they persist today.) Finally, education may often be viewed as an *effect* of change. It seems undeniable that profound change in social structures must often affect all the institutions of the society in which they occur, for societies do have what Sumner called "strains toward consistency" so that, in some respects, their institutions appear to reflect the major thrusts and stresses that permeate a social system. Thus the development of co-education in America is often viewed as the consequence of the feminist movement which caused great changes in many aspects of American life. Or, to return to our previous example, many current practices in the colleges and universities may be viewed as the effects of the changes introduced by the G.I. enrollment boom and wartime practices.

These examples of the nature of the relation between social change and the institutions subject to or participant in it illustrate an important theoretical point already implied by discussion of the G.I. Bill. Ofttimes an event appears simultaneously to be an agent, condition, and cause of change, and the student must recognize this as an artifact of the level of abstraction and argument with which he intends to deal. If the subject of our consideration is the G.I. Bill, it is apparent that depending upon how we wish to look at it and what features of its existence in post-war American society we wish to explore, it was an agent, condition, and effect of social change.

Equally, change itself is not a unitary concept. Questions as to what actually constitutes change may be left to operational definition and, perhaps, the quarrels of historians. (Although, obviously, the very notion of "change" necessarily implies temporal dimensions so that the study of social change is always, in this sense at least, historical.) But for social scientists and humanists, if the followers of Hume in the natural sciences may sometimes be excepted, the notion of change usually may be expected to involve questions of cause as well. The universe does not, presumably, work capriciously, so that a change in the state of events is assumed to be the result of other events somehow related to and responsible for the new condition. But the study of social change is remarkably difficult. Most social events of any magnitude have an infinity of relations (of various relevance and congruity) with other equally complex events, and many of *them* will be in flux themselves. Social institutions do not hold still for study and, to further complicate the matter, the act of studying them, in motion or at rest, often introduces changes in their structure and state. For the most part, as a result, we are forced to theorize. The actual measurement of much social change is intolerably difficult and highly qualified at best, and more often than not may be impossible. But with theory we can hold events in motion constant, or discount their influence, or select some aspects of multifaceted reality to focus on while ignoring others which might, in fact, be equally important. This advantage of theory over measurement has meant that although techniques for measurement of social change have necessarily lagged in social scientific development, theories and hypotheses of change have proliferated, some of them surviving for thousands of years. Our purposes do not require us to review them all, since some have no application to education. (There are, for example, no geographic or climatological theories of educational change.) But before review of those pertinent is undertaken, a final observation is required: if theories of social change imply the notion of cause (as we have suggested they almost inevitably do), a further intellectual complexity confronts the student in the problem of first causes. It is not unreasonable to suppose that if change is caused, the explanation of it logically should seek the cause's cause. Of this there can be no ending and so it is avoided for entirely practical reasons. If our interest is the G.I. Bill, we must necessarily examine the lobbies which led the Congress to enact it, and perhaps *their* motivations for their actions. To seek further would be to distract our study from its original consideration and thus, as a practical matter, is abjured. It may be, as White argues (see p. 73), that the introduction of the stirrup at a particular time and place in European history "caused" (or at least made possible) the feudal system there, but if our interest is in that system it will not be served by following the history of the stirrup.

THEORIES OF SOCIAL CHANGE

As suggested above, there has been no shortage of ideas devoted to the explanation of social change, and their history is long. An astonishing array of single and multiple causes for it has been suggested ranging from the significance of rats and lice in human affairs to herring-runs and sunspots. But amid the variety, some stand out for having been appealed to time and again by historians, philosophers, and social scientists. These constitute two major classes of explanation, single-factor theories and multiple-factor theories. The outstanding examples of each are briefly described below.

Single-Factor Theories

While it seems obvious that social change is a phenomenon so complex as to defy explanation in terms of a single cause, it is also true that a number of such explanations have been propounded. It would be unwise to dismiss them, because among that number three have had such intellectual power as to appeal recurrently to sophisticated thinkers and do, in fact, engage the facts of history in such a way as to illuminate brilliantly at least some of them. These are the technological, economic, and ideological theories of history or social change. In each case the students who have proposed them have argued that while of course other variables enter the picture and are contributory, a dominant thrust seems to have been applied to events by one, upsetting old orders through the changes in its wake, eliminating alternatives formerly viable, or making more probable (or even determining) choices for the future.

A recent example of the *technological theory of change* is White's work mentioned earlier. His principal thesis (grossly oversimplified with the attendant violence such treatment deals any complex argument) is that the introduction of the stirrup into medieval Europe was the major cause of the feudal system there.

"The history of the use of the horse in battle is divided into three periods: first, that of the charioteer; second, that of the mounted warrior who clings to his steed by pressure of the knees; and third, that of the rider equipped with stirrups. The horse has always given its master an advantage over the footman in battle, and each improvement in its military use has been related to far-reaching social and cultural changes.

"Before the introduction of the stirrup, the seat of the rider was precarious. Bit and spur might help him to control his mount; the simple saddle might confirm his seat; nevertheless, he was still much restricted in his methods of fighting. He was primarily a rapidly mobile bowman and hurler of javelins. Swordplay was limited because 'without stirrups your slashing horseman, taking a good broad-handed swipe at his foe, had only to miss to find himself on the ground.' As for the spear, before the invention of the stirrup it was wielded at the end of the arm and the blow was delivered with the strength of shoulder and biceps. The stirrup made possible—although it did not demand—a vastly more effective mode of attack: now the rider could lay his lance at rest, held between the upper arm and the body, and make at his foe, delivering the blow not with his muscles but with the combined weight of himself and his charging stallion.

"The stirrup, by giving lateral support in addition to the front and back support offered by pommel and cantle, effectively welded horse and rider into a single fighting unit capable of a violence without precedent. . . . Immediately, without preparatory steps, it made possible mounted shock combat, a revolutionary new way of doing battle. . . .

✪   ✪   ✪   ✪   ✪   ✪

"(The stirrup) must have reached the Franks in the early eighth century. At that moment . . . verbs . . . formerly used for getting on and off horses, began to be replaced . . . showing that leaping was replaced by stepping when one mounted or dismounted. But a more explicit indication of the drastic shift from infantry to the new mode of mounted shock combat is the complete change in Frankish weapons which took place at that time.

"The *francisca*, the distinctively Frankish battleaxe, and the *ango*, or barbed javelin, both infantry weapons, disappear in the eighth century, while the old *spatha* lengthens into a longsword for horsemen. . . . But above all, in the early decades of the eighth century there comes into wide use a spear having a heavy stock and spurs below the blade to prevent too deep penetration of the victim. . . . The generalization of the wing-spear in itself is evidence that under Charles Martel and his sons the meaning of the stirrup for shock combat was being realized . . . the Anglo-Saxons used the stirrup, but did not comprehend it; and for this they paid a fearful price. While semi-feudal relationships and institutions had long been scattered thickly over the civilized world, it was the Franks alone—presumably led by Charles Martel's genius— who fully grasped the possibilities inherent in the stirrup and created in terms of it a new type of warfare supported by a novel structure of society which we call feudalism. . . .

✪   ✪   ✪   ✪   ✪   ✪

"Fighting in the new manner involved large expenditures . . . the great majority could afford to come to muster only on foot. . . . Charlemagne tried to raise horsemen by commanding that the less prosperous freemen should band together . . . to equip one of their number and send him to the wars. Such an arrangement would be hard to administer, and it did not survive the confusion of the later ninth century. But inherent in this device was the recognition that if the new technology of warfare were to be developed consistently, military service must become a matter of class. Those economically unable to fight on horseback suffered from a social infirmity which shortly became a legal inferiority. . . . With the collapse of the Frankish empire, the Feudality which the Carolingians had deliberately created, in terms of the new military method of mounted shock combat, to be the backbone of their army became the governing as well as the fighting elite. The old levy of freemen (although not all infantry) vanished, and a gulf appeared between a warrior aristocracy and the mass of peasants.

By about the year 1000, *miles* had ceased to mean 'soldier' and had become 'knight.'" (White, 1962, 1–2, 27–30.)

Like other single-factor theories of change, this one has the defects of its virtues. Principal among these is that it explains too much. Without in any respect meaning to accuse Professor White of dogmatism (he qualifies his thesis carefully although his work is *about* the influence of technology on change), it is still apparent that if the stirrup was the major cause of feudalism it can also be selected as the cause for any consequences the feudal system had, including the Renaissance, Reformation, Industrial Revolution, and so on. It also suffers from the defect of being untestable: because we cannot say what might have happened, or failed to happen, had the stirrup never been invented, we have no way of assessing the validity of his assertions of its consequences.

Nonetheless, the technological theory of change is remarkably cogent. It is easy to find evidence which seems to support it and, as noted, it is impossible to disprove it. It has proven fertile of hypotheses and viewpoints and illuminative of facts. Although not a scientific theory in the strict logical sense (for reason of its incapacity for test), it ranks high among theories of social change and has much sociological merit.[1]

Another equally popular, single-factor theory of change is the *economic*. The reasons for its popularity are not hard to discern. In the first place, one of the important facts about any individual is how he earns his living and what kind of a living it is, for modes of earning—occupations—and the rewards they bestow do have an important effect upon the quality and character of our lives. Similarly, one of the important facts about a society is how its supply of foods and other necessities and luxuries is produced and distributed. In the second place, of course, the economic theory of change is closely associated in our times with the name of Karl Marx and with Communism and, as such, has had major impact upon the world.

The economic interpretation of social change has become so familiar to all of us that we need not discuss it in detail. The distinctive features of Marx's treatment, perhaps, are its clarity and its power and its influence, and we may therefore quote several of his propositions:

"In the social production which men carry on they enter into definite relations that are indispensable and independent of their will; these relations of production correspond to a definite stage of development of their material power of production. The sum total of these relations of production constitutes the economic structure of society—the real foundation, on which rise legal and political superstructures and to which correspond definite forms of social consciousness. The mode of production in material life determines the general character of the social, political and spiritual processes of life. It is not the consciousness of men that determines their existence, but, on the contrary, their social existence determines their consciousness. At a certain stage of their development, the material forces of production in society come in conflict with the existing relations of production, or what is but a legal expression for the same thing—with the property relations within which they had been at work before. From forms of development of the forces of production these relations turn into their fetters. Then comes the period of social revolution. With the change of the economic foundation the entire immense superstructure is more or less rapidly transformed" (Marx, *Critique of Political Economy*, Trans. by Stone, Chicago, 1904).

"The sociological theory of Karl Marx is an excessive, dogmatic, and radical variant of economic interpretations that are as old as thought itself. . . . Nevertheless, in less extreme and less Marxian terms, there is no doubt that economic factors do play a significant role in social change. Changes in economic variables have been correlated, in specific and sometimes precise ways, with changes in other variables in society. There are thus correlations between economic conditions and the health of a population, mortality and morbidity rates, marriage and divorce rates, suicide and crime, immigration and emigration, and so on. Alternating periods of prosperity and depression—the business cycle in short—affect these variables, and others in manifold ways.

"Attempts to establish correlations between economic factors and social factors of this kind have met with considerable success, and current and future sociological research will continue to explore in these directions. It has also been possible, in many cases, to associate economic conditions with social unrest and political turmoil, with revolution and war. Indeed, the interrelationships between economic and political phenomena, almost of necessity, are so close that in this field the economic interpretation can appear in its strongest light." (Bierstedt, 1963, 543–545.)

It is probably true that any political phenomenon has some underlying economic factor or consequences, but to jump from this fact or probability to the conclusion that economic variables undergird all social behavior is entirely unwarranted. Major political changes have sometimes occurred without any apparent economic shifts of significance (as, for example, in the Middle Ages), and what causal relation there is does not seem to be unidirectional. Political decisions often have economic consequences (as is repeatedly demonstrated in the United States Senate when there are major government contracts or projects to be let).

"Conclusions about the role of economic factors in society, therefore, have to be hedged with caution. . . . If in certain areas of human affairs, such as the political, we watch with alertness the operation of economic forces, in others the influence of these factors, when it is present at all, is likely to be attenuated and incapable of explaining the social consequences in which we are interested. Indeed, to explain the history of music or art or philosophy or science or religion in simple economic terms, as Marxian writers have tried to do, is to indulge in high and unsupported flights of speculation. Homo sapiens is not only *Homo Oeconomicus*. Economic man must eat but the whole man needs also to love and think and create and understand. There is no reason to assume, therefore, in the present state of sociological knowledge, that economic factors have an independent and a universal effect in all the instances of social and cultural change." (Bierstedt, 1963, 547.)

The third major single-factor theory of change emphasizes the *ideological factors* which may cause, accompany, or underlie such historical shifts. The conspiracy theory of the present day American radical right wing which finds subtle Communist ideology and doctrine in schools, churches, Little Golden Books and Bugs Bunny is a current, although ludicrous, example of such thought. It presumes the ideological nature of social change and attaches primary importance to it in the fear that exposure to "Communist" ideas (sic) readies the nation for the day of the "takeover." The assumption is clearly that change is fundamentally caused by ideological events.

Probably the most frequently cited ideological theory of change in sociology is Max Weber's *The Protestant Ethic and the Spirit of Capitalism* (1958). Stemming from the observation that Protestantism appeared in history at approximately the same time as modern capitalism (and apparently from the great social-economist's desire to refute the obvious fallacies in Marxism), Weber argued that Protestantism provided a rationale and source of dedication, a spirit or ideology, necessary to the development of capitalistic enterprise. The "spirit" of capitalism is illustrated through quoting a satirical description of American business maxims: "Remember, that *time* is money . . . that *credit* is money . . . that money is of the prolific, generating nature . . . the good paymaster is lord of another man's purse . . . beware of thinking all your own that you possess . . . for six pounds a year you may have the use of one hundred pounds . . ."

"The peculiarity of this philosophy of avarice appears to be the ideal of the honest man of recognized credit, and above all the idea of a duty of the individual toward the increase of his capital, which is assumed as an end in itself. Truly what is preached here is not simply a means of making one's way in the world, but a peculiar ethic. The infraction of its rules is treated not as foolishness but as forgetfulness of duty. That is the essence of the matter. It is not mere business astuteness, that sort of thing is common enough, it is an *ethos*." (Bierstedt, 1963, 48–51.)

Weber's thesis is that Protestantism provided an essential source for this unremitting pursuit of gain and dedication to work, the unique quality of the capitalist spirit being not just an emphasis on profit, but rather the ethical value which came to be placed upon it.[2] The principal source of this capitalist spirit was to be found in the teachings of Calvin and later Protestantism asceticism. This may be particularly remarked in the doctrine of *calling*, which defined one's occupation as a task set by the Diety, and one, thus, to which one's best energies ought to be directed (in contrast to the Medieval, Catholic, monastic emphasis on withdrawal from the world). This doctrine was further supported by the effect of another Calvinist idea, that of predestination, in which every man's fate was already sealed, directed by God, and unalterable by faith, works, or the Church. The very barrenness of this notion created anxieties in its adherents to know their destinies, and since the "elect"—those divinely selected for salvation—might know of their favor since their worldly efforts would be greeted by success, that success came to be sought as a form of psychic reassurance. Naturally, anyone sincerely believing such philosophies would comport himself according to the moralities of his beliefs, in this instance a morality emphasizing thrift, hard work, sobriety, restraint, and the avoidance of fleshly pleasures. Thus all the elements of early Protestantism (for Lutheran doctrines tended in these directions as well) came to support endeavors that naturally culminated in capitalistic enterprise and gave it a theological rationalization.

"A specifically bourgeois economic ethic had grown up. With the consciousness of standing in the fullness of God's grace and being visibly blessed by Him, the bourgeois businessman, as long as he remained within the bounds of formal correctness, as long as his moral conduct was spotless and the use to which he put his wealth was not objectionable, could follow his pecuniary interests as he would and feel that he was fulfilling a duty in doing so. The power of religious asceticism provided him in addition with sober, conscientious, and usually industrious workmen, who clung to their work as to a life purpose willed by God.

Finally, it gave him the comforting assurance that the unequal distribution of the goods of this world was a special dispensation of Divine Providence, which in these differences, as in particular grace, pursued secret ends unknown to men." (Weber, 1958, 176–177.)

We need not linger further on this particular example. It is, as noted, the best known of its type and has been exhaustively argued and annotated. That there is excellent (if general) evidence to support the Weberian thesis is of interest to its adherents but not relevant to the class of which it is a member.[3] Although Weber made no claim for total causative effect, in this work ideology is described as a major cause of change so we do no injustice by classifying it as a single-factor theory. As such, it has the weaknesses of the type, although it may be the best example of it yet extant. Protestant ideology is certainly closely related to the rise of capitalism and clearly could have had a causal effect upon it. Evidence can be adduced to support the thesis that it did. Again, however, it is a theoretical position impossible to disprove and, to the extent that it is held in a unicausal manner, it is impossible to test and tends to prove too much.

Multiple-Factor Theories

Theories seeking to explain social change as occurring due to a number of interactive causes fall into three general classes, *cyclic, lineal* and what could be called *systemic* or *functional.* In the cyclic type social change is conceived to consist of a pattern of events endlessly repeated, at least in broad form, throughout the tapestry of history. (Both cyclic and lineal varieties of theory tend to address themselves to large-scale historical change in whole societies or civilizations and may actually approximate philosophies of history as an occasional one claims to be.) Hegelian philosophy is an example of the type with its interpretation of history as an endlessly repeating dialectical pattern of change from "thesis" to "antithesis" to "synthesis."

Perhaps more familiar to working social scientists are the cyclic theories of Sorokin (1962) and Toynbee (1946). These may also be classified as "dialectical" in that both authors perceive definite repetitious patterns of social change in cultural history, although neither shares the Hegelian (and, therefore, Marxian as well) view that such patterns are "laws" of change analogous to natural laws. Very briefly summarized, Sorokin's thesis is that there is a pattern of change discernible in western history from a culture form or orientation he calls "Sensate" to another, the "Ideational," (with an intermediate form, the "Idealistic").[4] The pattern of relations between them is cyclic in that the shift from one to the other is several times repeated in history. The distinguishing characteristic of "Sensate" cultures is the orientation or view that reality is what can be perceived by the senses and no more than that. In "Ideational" cultures, on the contrary, ultimate reality is defined as nonsensory or supersensory, a form of transcendent Being. Sensate culture is focused on man, this world, and its goods; Ideational on the things of the spirit. Sensate culture addresses itself to the problems presented or defined by the world and in terms *of* the world; Ideational culture addresses the problems of man *in* the world not through manipulation *of* the world but through address to man who can learn to surmount or transcend it. Neither cultural form is ever perfectly realized and integrated, however, and all culture is always in flux. Change, further, is an "immanent necessity," built-in, as it were, to the nature of things. Cultural systems *must* change, then, but the alternatives possible are limited so that recurrent cycles of events, or pattern, marks history, other alternative forms being impossible.

Toynbee's views being, like Sorokin's, devoted to large-scale theory of social change, are similar in many ways. He tends to focus his attention more, however, upon the mechanics of change rather than the characteristics of society, and proposes a hypothesis to account for the genesis, rise, and fall of civilizations instead of writing such changes off as immanent necessity. Devoting himself in detail to perhaps more conventional history, Toynbee perceives a pattern of change in culture from primitive origins to complex civilizations. While historically recurrent, this pattern is not, however, by any means inevitable in any given culture. For the key to social change, in Toynbee's view, is a litany of challenge (presented either from human or environmental sources) and societal response. Without some challenge there will be no motivation for a primitive society to change at all, and so no civilization will be born of it. If the challenge is too severe for the group to make a satisfactory adjustment to it, however, its resources will be spent in brute survival and again no major development can ensue or it may even be submerged. But within complex civilization itself are contained the roots of destruction, for the more complex it becomes the more challenges with which it presents itself, until finally the possibilities for adjustment run out. At this time the social order will become rigid and with such rigidity its doom is sealed, for it will eventually be disrupted from either within or without by groups or forces with which its now inflexible adjustment formulas cannot cope.

Rather similar in many ways to these two views, and representing yet another example of cyclic change theory, is Spengler, whose *The Decline of the West* was once in intellectual vogue. All cultures, according to this argument, pass through an organic cycle of change from birth to maturity to senility and decline. Each culture is marked by a peculiar style or mentality, or *essence,* and grows "with the same superb aimlessness as the flowers of the field" (Spengler, 1926, Vol. I, 21). But each, by the same "organic" quality of its nature, is doomed to die.

It is not necessary for our purposes to enter into extensive criticism and review of these cyclic theories of social change. All three share the qualities of superb imagination, utility as heuristic devices, and structured explanation (which *does* give an order to the fantastic montage of history). All are also subject to severe criticism as unduly distorting historical fact, superselectivity of facts to be reviewed, and total untestability. We must dismiss them as constituting fascinating speculation and brilliant *tours-de-force,* but also as inadequate for scientific purposes.

Another variety of multiple-factor change theory is the *lineal* in which change is perceived as being nonrepetitive and essentially unidirectional. This class of theory has been productive of hypothesis in social scientific writing and is dominated by that group of theorists and ideas we can label as describing the Great Dichotomy. The theories of the Great Dichotomy are all concerned with one aspect or another of the characteristics of and change from simple societies to complicated ones. Comte (1877) focused on the nature of the development from one condition to the other; Spencer (1892) on the evolutionary nature of that process as he conceived it. Töennies was interested in the characteristic forms and mentalities of the two (1957), while Durkheim (1933) studied the nature of their social organization as constituted by the division of labor. Redfield, the most recent of the Dichotomy theorists (1941), concentrated his attention largely on describing the simpler pole of the two types but attempted to derive empirically valid information about it and the processes of change affecting it. The Dichotomy theories as a class can be described—and criticized—in terms almost identical with those used in summary of theories of a cyclic nature. Of the group (and we have mentioned only the most prominent) Redfield's is the only work with a truly empirical base and the only one for which operational specification of possible tests is easily made (1947). It remains, nonetheless, largely heuristic and involves critical problems of testability.

For serious theoretical use the *systemic* or *functional* theory of change has probably been of more value than either the cyclic or the lineal.[5] It has been generally described (within an institutional frame of reference) by Bohannon:

"Recurrent events can be investigated and recorded. So can rare events or nonrecurrent events. It is also investigable that in the process of recurrence, certain strains may be created within the institution, which ultimately must either be corrected (by recurring events with an atypical pattern of recurrence) and the strain so eased, or which lead to non-recurrent events that make recapturing the older event system impossible, and hence lead to change in all aspects of the institution. The first of these two modes of correction does not lead to change, but merely to what can be called a gyroscopic event, often unrecognized, in the event structure. The second is the very essence of change.

"Some event sequences work smoothly and would seem to proceed over and over again, without noticeable tension or with only self-resolving tension. Yet, there are other event systems which seem to contain elements that so wobble the system as to make exact repetition extremely difficult—events which, even when performed in accordance with the basic ideas and postulates of the accompanying idea systems, throw the institution out of kilter. Such systems would seem to contain the seeds of their own destruction.

"Yet a second event sequence, often called into action by the tension created in the first, is found to be widespread; interestingly enough, these gyroscopic event structures that maintain the operation of the other event structures within the institution are often disapproved by the actors. . . . Thus (witch-hunts in American politics) constantly refortify the middle: the fundamental dynamic of the political process. . . .

*   *   *   *   *   *

"The other alternative is, of course, that the institution will not have such a built-in or even improvised gyroscope which brings it back to its keel of regular events; it will instead change its nature, especially its event system. . . .

"We can say, then, that the repetition of an event system . . . is the dynamic of an institution. It may or may not contain institutionalized correctives. When it does not, or when it suddenly feels an impact from the outside, the events characteristic of the institution may change, and if that is the case, then social and cultural change throughout the society and in all reaches of the culture are to be expected. If the event system, with its repetitive dynamic, becomes wobbly, eventually it will change in such a way that the series of events forming the system are different—and therewith the entire society is different. . . ." (Bohannon, 1963, 369–371.)

Similar notions, stated in the social action frame of reference rather than that of the institutional orientation, can be found in the social change theories of Talcott Parsons. (See his essay in Etzioni and Etzioni, 1964.)

The systemic-functional theory of change enjoys several advantages over other varieties of multiple-factor theory. Being based, in the first place, on what is essentially a theoretical model drawn from observation rather than from interpretations of history, it is more easily operationalized for empirical use. Because it flows from a fairly well-defined theoretical position in the social sciences, its basic assumptions (and their inadequacies) are well-known, often stated, and can be allowed for. It is, finally, a model of change explicitly designed for theoretical use in hypothesis-testing rather than as grand description of the processes of history. The following discussion and readings will be seen to assume that approach as their base of departure.

SOCIAL CHANGE AND THE INSTITUTION OF EDUCATION

To summarize the theoretical discussion thus far, we have seen that (in terms of single-factor theories) social change has been interpreted as fundamentally resident in shifts in technology, economic relations, or ideology. The grand theories of cyclic and lineal change are clearly inapplicable to the analysis of single institutions over limited periods of time and are, thus, of no concern in the examination of education. Systemic-functional theory, however, since it deals with institutions as its universe of discourse, is clearly useful. We have also seen that social institutions may be viewed as agents, conditions, or effects of change. If, therefore, we restrict our consideration to those conceptual tools that might enlarge our understanding and that are applicable to the subject matter, we are left with the ninefold explanatory possibility indicated by the Table 1. A systemic-functional application may be made of any of the indicated categories since any variety of change, regardless of cause, may be viewed as "gyroscopic" if it leaves the institutional event system relatively untouched, or as "wobble-producing" if the reaction to it is such as to introduce permanent deviation from past practice. The table locates the readings to be discussed in the cells in which their dominant themes appear to place them.

TABLE 1   *Some Theoretical Possibilities for Explaining the Relation between Education and Social Change*

| The View of Education as an | The Varieties of Single-Factor Change Theory | | |
	Technological	Economic	Ideological
Agent of change	_____	_____	(Brogan)
Condition of change	_____	(Trow)	_____
Effect of change	(Clark)	_____	_____

Education as an Agent of Social Change

The character of the educational process and educational institutions as agents of social change is expressly considered in the following excerpt. It is also apparent that the main thrust of the author's analysis concerns *ideological* change in the culture of the United States and its citizens.

"The social and political role of American education cannot be understood if it is thought of as being primarily a means of formal instruction. If it is so thought of, it will be overrated and underrated. It will be overrated because the number of college students or high-school pupils will dazzle the visitor used to seeing opportunities for higher education doled out on a combined class-and-intellectual basis. It will be underrated if, at any stage below the highest (that is, below the great universities), the academic standards are compared with those of a good English, French, or pre-Hitler German school. If these millions of boys and girls are to be judged by their academic accomplishments, they will be judged harshly. But they are not to be so judged, for their schools are doing far more than instruct them: they are letting them instruct each other in how to live in America.

"Of those millions, a large section will be the children of immigrants to whom English is still largely a foreign tongue. Of these millions, a very large proportion will be the children of migrants from different parts of the United States. Others will be the children of rural-bred parents, forced to adjust themselves to the new urban world. They have to learn a common language, common habits, common tolerances, a common political and national faith. And they do. It is this aim and this success that justify the lavish buildings of the local high school; not merely the classrooms and the laboratories, but the gymnasium, the field-house where basketball can be played in comfort in the depth of the bitter winter, the swimming pools in which the summer heat can be endured. . . .

❖ ❖ ❖ ❖ ❖ ❖

"The political function of the schools is to teach Americanism, meaning not merely political and patriotic dogma, but the habits necessary to American life. . . . The main political achievement of the high schools and grammar schools is to bring together the young of all classes and all origins, to provide, artificially, the common background that in old, rural society is provided by tradition, by the necessary collaboration of village life. . . .

"Some of that Americanization is, of course, done deliberately and formally. Mr. Carlton Hayes pointed out long ago that the ritual of flag-worship and oath-taking in an American school is a religious observance. Little boys and girls, in a school from which religion in the old sense is barred, solemnly rising each morning and reciting together the 'American Creed' are performing a religious exercise as truly as if they began the day with 'I believe in God the Father Almighty' or asserted that 'There is no God but God.' . . .

❖ ❖ ❖ ❖ ❖ ❖

"(T)he flag in America is more than a mere symbol among many others. It is the regimental color of a regiment in which all Americans are enrolled. Its thirteen stripes and (fifty) stars are symbols far better understood than the complicated heraldry of crosses of Saint George, Saint Andrew and Saint Patrick imposed on each other in a way that only experts understand. . . .

"Thus Americanization by ritual is an important and necessary part of the function of the American School. And because it is best carried out in schools, it matters little that the high-school curriculum has been so widened that it no longer means a great deal that this boy or that girl was graduated from it—if we are looking for proof of academic achievement. But graduation from high school is reasonable proof that a great deal has been learned about American ways of life, that lessons in practical politics, in organization, in social ease have been learned that could not have been learned in factory or office." (Brogan, 1961, 162–174.)

Brogan's view that education is an *agent* of social change in American culture is here apparent almost from the opening phrases. "The social and political role of American education," he says, "cannot be understood if it is thought of as being primarily a means of formal instruction. . . . But (it is) not to be so judged for (the) schools are doing far more than instruct (pupils): they are letting them instruct each other in how to live in America." In the United States, then, the schools are agencies for the creation from immense heterogeneity of a homogeneous citizenry with ". . . a common language, common habits, common tolerances, a common political and national faith" (Brogan, 1961, 162, 167). The analysis of the social and political functions of education which comprises the main body of the material quoted clearly portrays American public education as an agency of social change, in this case in ideological matters primarily. As an *agent* of change (in this view) the institution of education is not itself changed by the phenomena discussed. The functional interpretation, hence, is inapplicable to the understanding of this view of education, although it would, of course, be useful in understanding the *effects* of these educational practices on other institutions, and this is, of course, exactly what the essay does.

Education as a Condition of Social Change

If the preceding reading suggests that education may be an *agent* of social change (in the case in question, of a fundamentally ideological nature), it may also be viewed as a condition of change: either as unanticipated consequences of rational decisions made for other purposes act to shape events, or simply as changes in other institutions of the society influence and affect education and it, in turn, yet other phenomena. The main thrust of Trow's following argument may be interpreted as an example of this theoretical possibility, of the educational institution acting as a *condition* of social change in the society, in this instance one being greatly affected by, and having great effect upon, the economic order.

"The very rapid expansion which American higher education has been undergoing since the end of World War II in many ways resembles the growth of mass secondary education that took place during the first half of this century. As recently as 1940, American colleges and universities enrolled only about 1.25 million students (about 15 per cent of the population of college age, the 18 to 21 year olds). Secondary school enrolments in 1910 comprised the same proportion of the 14 to 17 year olds in that year. By 1963 the number earning credits toward degrees in American colleges and universities had increased to about 4.3 million—40 percent of the age group and increasing at an average of 1 per cent a year (while population of college age was almost exactly as large in 1940 as in 1960).

"The growth in numbers will be even faster in the decades to come, since in addition to rising enrolment rates, the rise in birth rates since World War II will very soon greatly increase the pool of college age youngsters. Estimates of college and university enrolments in 1970 vary between 6 and 8 million; the most plausible estimate, based on projections of present trends, is about 7 million.

"This staggering increase in college going is sending shock waves up and down through the US educational system, and eventually through the whole society of the country.

"The years since World War II are seeing a great change in the occupational structure, one reflecting an enormous growth in demand for more highly trained and educated people of all kinds. Between 1940 and 1950 the number of engineers in the country nearly doubled, and in the two decades after 1940 the number rose from under 300,000 to 800,000. And the careful estimates of the Bureau of Labor Statistics place the number of engineers needed in 1970 at about 1½ million, which would mean an increase of nearly 90 per cent between 1959 and 1970. The rate of increase in the demand for scientists is expected to be almost as great as that for engineers. For all the kinds of educated workers who comprise the "professional, technical, and kindred" category in the census, the growth was 48 per cent during the decade,

1950–60, during which time the whole labour force was growing by only a little over 10 per cent.

"It is clear then that changes in the occupational structure, associated in part with the rationalization of research and its applications in government, industry, and weapons development, are creating demands for a more highly educated population. And it is a reasonable inference that the rapid growth in college attendance in this country is a response to these demands. But other countries have been undergoing similar changes in their economy, without anything like similar consequences for their institutions of higher education. This raises the question of what the connections are between economic and educational changes, and why economic changes have such apparently large and swift consequences for education in the United States, and so much less, say, in Great Britain.

"The commitment of America to equality of opportunity, the immense importance attached to education as an avenue of mobility in a society which holds that status at birth should not be a barrier to advancement—these and other strong historical and social-psychological forces are involved in the extraordinary American commitment to mass secondary and higher education. The role of education as a kind of secular religion for Americans is part of the background against which the current growth in college enrolments is taking place.

"Mass higher education takes the form of some 2,000 colleges and universities, which taken together are far more responsive to social and economic forces than is the case in most European countries. This is a result both of the peculiar historical development and of the present organizational forms of the American 'system.' American colleges and universities have always been relatively free from the direct influence of the Federal government, and thus from central planning of any kind. It is true that the Federal government has indirectly influenced the development of American higher education through various subsidies, as it is doing today in its allocation of research funds. But in the past the government has had virtually no voice in the really critical decisions. The questions of how many colleges there would be, where located, how large, offering what degrees, have been made not in Washington, but by the hundreds of private, state and municipal authorities that govern and support colleges and universities in the United States.

"The radical decentralization of decision-making in American higher education, together with the extreme heterogeneity in the quality and character of the institutions which make it up, make the net effect of their decisions highly responsive to social and economic forces. A given college or university may choose not to grow, but there are ten others that will. The commitment to concepts of 'public service' is so strong in American higher education, both public and private, that the number of places is basically set by the consumers' demand in the market for education, rather than by production agreements among educational producers, as in most other advanced countries. Thus, the effective demand for higher education in the American population is a function of how much people want to attend college (or send their children there) and how expensive a college education is. Educational aspirations are rising, while the growth in the numbers of municipal, state and junior colleges, partly in response to this rise in aspirations, contributes to their further rise by bringing inexpensive nonresidential colleges nearer to many who could not afford high tuition fees or the costs of college residence. In communities where public junior or four year colleges are established, the enrolments of youngsters from working class homes rise spectacularly. In education, supply creates demand in the very act of satisfying it; we see this every time a new junior college or state college opens its doors and is full to the brim before the grass is down.

"But we cannot ascribe to the colleges the chief impulse behind the rising educational expectations. These, in very large part, reflect rational and realistic assessments by ordinary people of the visible advantages of education beyond high school. Let us consider some of those advantages:

"1. First, there is the sheer growth in numbers of jobs for educated people. A college education provides skills, and is a training in flexibility, perhaps the most valuable skill in a society whose economy changes as rapidly as ours. Moreover, a college or university record points to the possession of attitudes and abilities that are needed in a great variety of jobs which do not require high technical skills. And this will be more true the more people go to college: not to have gone to college will increasingly indicate lack of intelligence or ambition or some other defect of character or personality.

"Americans also, paradoxically, take it more casually than do other people. I mean by this that education in the US does not create sharply defined status groups, set off from one another by conceptions of personal privilege and honour. Such conceptions, which we can still see very clearly in most European countries, and even more distinctly in the emerging countries of Africa and Asia, introduce a certain rigidity into the relations of education and the economic structure. For in those countries, educational achievement—degrees, diplomas, licenses and the like—are not only a source of status and privilege to those who earn them, but they also disqualify educated people, effectively if not formally, from holding certain jobs that are 'inappropriate' for people with high levels of education. People will not take jobs that are 'humiliating'; they will remain unemployed rather than do so. These social and psychological links between levels of education and kinds of work in part account for the phenomenon of the 'unemployed intelligentsia' in underdeveloped countries—countries that need all the skills and training they can get.

"In the United States a much wider range of jobs are seen as 'appropriate' for people who have been to college. For example, over a quarter of all Americans employed in clerical and sales work have had some exposure to formal higher education, as have nearly 10 per cent of all foremen and skilled workers. The proportions are much higher among younger workers in those categories, and are rising rapidly. The range of jobs 'appropriate' for given levels of education is also more easily subject to change, as jobs change and are changed by different kinds of people who are recruited to them. This lack of rigidity in the relation of education to job functions is a kind of universal joint between the economy and education, allowing both the easy movement of educated people between different kinds of work, and the educational upgrading of various occupations.

"In the future, enrolments are likely to continue to grow without much reference to the occupational structure; for example, during slumps as well as in prosperous times. Changes in the occupational structure (together with the GI Bill which gave stipends to veterans in colleges) brought educational aspirations and the level of college enrolments to a 'take-off point' after World War II, when college enrolment rates (as a proportion of the 18 to 21 year olds) rose very sharply as compared with the preceding decades. After enrolments passed this period of extreme rise (when enrolments reached about 15 per cent of the age grade), the further rapid growth reflects changes in the educational standard of living of the population.

"2. In addition to the growing demand for educated workers is the clear and visible persistence of differentials in both annual and lifetime incomes associated with greater education. In 1958 college graduates earned on the average nearly 2½ times as much as grade school graduates, and 1.6 times as much as high school graduates. And the differences in income between high school graduates and those who have had some college but are not college graduates is appreciable. Even more impressive is the fact that over the past two decades, while the proportion of college and of high school graduates has almost doubled, and thus while the supply of relatively highly educated labour has greatly increased, their incomes have risen more than those of the less well educated. In 1946 the difference in average income between grade school graduates and high school graduates was 26 per cent; in 1958 it was 48 per cent. And the difference between the average incomes of high school and college graduates was 57 per cent in 1939, 54 per cent in 1946, 65 per cent in 1958. The flood of college graduates has apparently not reduced the income differential accruing to the better educated.

"3. The better educated also have more security in their employment. In March, 1962, six per cent of the American labour force was unemployed. But the proportion varied sharply with educational achievement, ranging from over 8 per cent among those who had not completed high school, to 5.1 per cent among high school graduates, to 3.7 per cent among those who had had some time in college, down to 1.4 per cent among college and university graduates.

"4. One does not need to have easy access to statistical reports to be aware of the objective advantages in job opportunities, security and income, accruing to the more highly educated in the labour force, people see and experience them every day, and say so. For example, a recent national survey asked its sample of breadwinners, "What would you say are your chances for promotion or getting ahead?" Among young men of 25 to 34, the proportion among them with less than a high school diploma who said they had a good chance for promotion was only 27 per cent; among high school graduates and those who had some time in college, it was 59 per cent; among college graduates it was 81 per cent. And the differences are found in every age bracket.

"American economists, most notably Theodore Schultz and his colleagues at the University of Chicago, have begun to look at education as an investment in people, and as an addition to a stock of human capital as important for economic growth as are additions to our stock of material capital.

"The gains of special relevance to economic growth are not merely in the technical skills acquired in schools, but perhaps of increasing importance, in adaptability, to new circumstances, and in general capacities for solving problems and initiating action. We can only get an adequate appreciation of the characteristics of educated men when we reflect on the conservatism, rigidity, and passivity that is characteristic of people with very little formal education, especially in their relations to the formal institutions of the society. There are many such people remaining in our society, and they pose problems in every sphere of social life, problems which are the more severe as the rate of social and economic change increases. It is, for example, not proving easy to retrain workers made jobless by technological developments in coal mining who have little experience with learning, and little of the flexibility or adaptiveness that is partly acquired in school. Flexibility is certainly an important addition to the human resources of the economy." (Trow, 1963.)

To summarize briefly the pertinence of the preceding reading for our purposes, Trow argues that the nature of higher education in the United States has been fundamentally affected by changes in the American occupational structure (themselves, in part, produced and affected by preceding changes in secondary education caused by earlier shifts in economic base and technology). But these shifts in occupational structure, based, of course, in economic phenomena (the increase in demand for educated persons and the upgrading of educational requirements for given positions together with a considerable flexibility in the definition of positions "appropriate" for educated persons), have, in turn, affected the educational institution. Education, then, has been a condition of economic change, while simultaneously economic change has been a condition having immense consequences for education. Although Trow has focused his discussion largely on higher education, he explicitly treats the changes in secondary institutions that preceded and inaugurated changes in the former. It would not be difficult for us to take the argument back to the elementary schools. For before secondary education could reach its "take-off point" in the first half of this century, there also had to be an elementary-school-educated population of sufficient size to produce that secondary one, and reasons for the increasingly universal pursuit of at least elementary schooling. (Reading, writing, and arithmetic, the basic skills transmitted by the elementary schools, have little value for the vast majority of the population of essentially peasant cultures. Only when these skills became essential for large proportions of our population—which implies a certain kind of relatively advanced economic and technological order—could most persons become elementary school graduates and the occupational structure advance to the point where high school skills became essential to it.) Education, thus, may be viewed as a condition of change as well as an agent of it. The processes are simultaneous and nonexclusive.

Realistically speaking they are, in fact, the *same* process, that of social change. The distinctions are only theoretical and, while they are legitimate for analytical purposes—since they call attention to *distinctions* which are real—we should not confuse them with empirical reality.

Education as an Effect of Social Change

In the same way in which education may be viewed simultaneously as both agent and condition of change, both ideological and economic, so it may be an *effect* of prior change in technology as well as in ideas and economics. In the following reading, Clark describes some changes in what may be called the technology of education and the consequences of these *for* education. The initial changes themselves he perceives as stemming from the same pattern of development discussed in Trow's preceding piece.

The Organizational Response

"As modern social forces recast education as part of the economic and political institutions of society, numerous adjustments and adaptations are bound to occur within the single organization, major segments of the educational system, and the system as a whole. For example, there is a move toward alliance among private colleges (Great Lakes Association, Associated Colleges of the Midwest, The College Center of the Finger Lakes). The impulse here comes from the maintenance and enhancement needs of existing organizations. . . . The colleges that move toward confederation are attempting to solve organizational problems: how to grow and yet remain small; how to coordinate across a larger pool of activity while protecting the autonomy of constituent units.

"Other kinds of adjustment can be found within the single educational organization: adaptation of new technologies; the elaboration and professionalization of public relations, fund-raising, and other boundary roles and activities. I will not attempt to catalog the many adjustments, but rather will pursue at some length one major line of adjustment in the educational institution that is fraught with implications for educational administration and for research on organization. That line is the structure of influence and control.

"The decentralized structure of formal educational control in the United States has, through a long history, become tuned to the concerns of the individual school or college, the local community, the separate state. What major responses can we discern in this structure as it comes under increasingly heavy pressure to accommodate to modern social forces, particularly to the concerns that are national in scope and are defined by federal agencies and private national bodies? There is some shift upward in the formal location of educational decision-making, primarily from the local to state level in public education, and secondarily from local and state to the national level in the form of such programs as the National Defense Education Act of 1958. But much of the change taking place is located in arrangements that lie in part outside the hierarchy of public offices. Indirect and subtle means of influence are being developed by many groups, means that we now only dimly perceive. The emerging patterns depend on voluntary relations among public offices and private groups. In some degree, these arrangements serve as substitutes for or as alternatives to formal internal administration, that is, to the national-state-local line of ministerial authority that we find in other countries. The patterns represent ways of influencing the grass-roots level of operation in a field where no formal authority can impose cooperation.

"One pattern is that of the private committee serving as connector between public authorities, notably between federal agencies and local authorities. The curricular reform movement has adopted this pattern. The prototype was the work of the Physical Science Study Committee, the group of professors and secondary teachers of science, under Professor Zacharias of MIT, (which has) done so much since 1956 to affect instruction in high school physics. The Committee was financed by a Federal agency, the National Science Foundation, and review committees of the agency kept an eye on the work of the Committee. The purpose of the Committee was to improve the quality of science teaching in the secondary schools of the nation; the quality at the time was viewed as a national weakness. The granting of funds for this purpose was well within the broad missions of the National Science Foundation, established by Congress in 1950, to strengthen basic research and education in the sciences. The first major component in the pattern of influence, then, was an agency in the executive branch of the Federal Government, an agency whose breadth of mandate allowed initiation of influence within the agency without seeking legislative approval of specific formal programs. Private foundations also soon entered into the financial support of the curriculum reform group.

"The Committee to (which) the problem was delegated and the funds allotted was private and voluntary, having some of the attributes of an independent and impartial group of civic leaders. The Committee, wanting to change what was taught in the high school courses in physical science throughout the nation, set out in effect to write a course for national school use, something that no federal agency could do directly because of Congressional and popular opposition. For a Federal agency to tamper with the curriculum, that sacred domain, would be to send a number of Senators up the wall, and when they came down they would find the budgetary ax. Working away from the political arena, in quiet but hectic offices at MIT, the Committee, in two years' time (1956–1958), provided a 'complex of schoolbooks, homework assignments, laboratory guides, films, teacher's guides, laboratory apparatus, and classroom and college-entrance tests.'

"The Committee then saw to it that these materials would be actively pushed as well as made widely available throughout the nation by putting the materials into normal commercial channels. During the winter of 1959–60, the Committee handed over its printed materials to a schoolbook publisher, its new scientific equipment to a manufacturer of scientific apparatus, and its films to an educational film distributor. In these simple moves, the Committee found an important mechanism of national influence. It had, in effect, made itself a research-and-innovation arm of the textbook industry—more broadly, the course-materials industry—doing the research and development that the industry itself was not doing. No publisher, not even the fat cats of today, has venture capital of the magnitude of three to five million dollars to develop the instructional materials of a course. No publisher is willing to take chances of that magnitude. The course-materials industry has been relatively passive, gearing innovation largely to market research and very little to pure research and development. Thus the commercial market itself provided little money and little impulse for improving courses. In the absence of national standards, where there are no nationwide governmental prescriptions about instructional materials, it is precisely the national market for course-materials that determines the quality of these materials. The Committee affected American education by changing what was available in the market, and, more important in the long-run, by changing the passive relation of the course-materials industry to the market. The Committee, now incorporated as Educational Services, Inc. (an important organizational phenomenon in its own right) promises to revise its materials periodically and thus to remain an active, innovative arm of the industry. It is a national center of textbook revision.

"Teachers also had to be taught how to handle these materials. This task has been performed by another independent party in the pattern.

The National Science Foundation initiated and funded a program of summer institutes that are voluntary throughout, for the colleges that put them on, the professors that direct and staff them, the teachers who come as students. The curriculum and the students of the institutes were made the responsibility of the individual college. The Committee had to convince the directors of these institutes to use its materials. The directors were looking for the latest and best materials, they adopted the new package, and the institutes became part of the implementation of the new physics course.

"Finally, local educational authorities enter the pattern. They retain formal discretion to adopt or not to adopt the new materials. They must voluntarily choose to enter in.

"This pattern of influence sums up as follows: it was set in motion from the top, by a Federal agency and a national private committee. Its object was to affect grass-roots educational practice which was seen as a national weakness. The flow of influence is downward, through a chain of independent groups and organizations who find it to their interest to enter the alliance or compact. A Federal agency provides the funds; a private non-profit group receives the money and develops a new course; commercial firms carry the new materials to all corners of the existing decentralized structure; dispersed universities and colleges train teachers in all regions of the country to the new materials; existing local authorities adopt the materials and allow their teachers to reshape the local courses. Decision-making in this pattern, right down the line, is heavily influenced by the prestige of expertise. The National Science Foundation was expert and prestigeful; so also were the Committee, the Institutes, the teachers trained in the new materials. The very materials themselves traveled under the same aura." (Clark, 1964.)

Clark's interpretation seems a clear example of the view of education as an effect of social changes, some of which are explicitly technological. He describes (in the original from which the quote above is taken) five major "trends" or forces which have influenced the institution: (1) rising levels of educational preparation and repreparation for work; (2) the increasing economic relevance of education; (3) population growth; (4) a growing educational participation by that population; (5) an increasing political concern with education along with its increasing political relevance creating a developing national interest in it in addition to the traditional local interests. The forces influencing education to shape its future in the United States are thus seen as economic, demographic, and political.

The impact of these forces on the educational institution seems to have had three effects: (1) the erection of institutional alliances (particularly between the smaller colleges although not limited to them), primarily for the purpose of solving organizational problems introduced by the new technologies and political concern; (2) the increasing centralization of educational decision-making with the loci of decision moving from local to state levels and from state to national; (3) the emergence of patterns of voluntary relations between institutions, academic disciplines, and various private and public agencies to meet the new need for coordination and action imposed by social change and impossible to resolve within the older structures of authority and initiation. These shifts within American education are seen as fundamental to it and as being largely, if not entirely, the effects of change, much of it technological, from without.

The Paradigm

It has been suggested (p. 84) that for analytic purposes it may be most useful to regard the relations between education and social change as being six-fold and that any major shift is probably multidimensional, being composed of ideological, economic, and technical elements while also, in some senses, being an agent, condition, and effect of change. This pattern for analysis permits us to consider the three preceding readings as a whole and to see relations between them that might otherwise be obscured.

Brogan, the reader will recall, saw American education primarily as an agent of ideological change and acculturation in a heterogeneous society. It is, moreover, an elemental matter to discern that although he focused on the transmission of ideology as being a dominant function of the schools, that transmission has economic and technological overtones as well. For as Trow points out, mass education produces vast economic consequences in a society such as ours, and is a precondition for them. Equally the technology of American education, only hinted at by Brogan (the athletic complex, for example), has social consequences which he suggests but does not detail.

It is also apparent that the relatively unique phenomenon of the education, at least to literacy, of the masses, must be a *condition* of even larger social changes. In the American instance it is one facet of the same political, social, economic, ideological and technological phenomena that have been transforming the nation since the first industrial revolution and the Jacksonian era. It is an effect, clearly, of some of those same changes, of Enlightenment ideologies, the post-Civil War industrialization and immigration, and, more recently, the kinds of economic and technological changes described by Trow.

Trow's essay, in turn, may be viewed in much the same manner. Although our analysis of it specifically concentrates on some aspects of education as a condition of economic change, it is not difficult to discern wherein it is a cause of change or an effect of previous social changes. He gives attention to the ideological character of some of the causes of the events he describes in citing the American ideologies encouraging schooling and acceptance of a wide variety of occupational positions as befitting educated men. The technological aspects of the thrusts analyzed are explicit and, in some instances, explicitly causal as well as conditional. It is apparent that in another sense the shifts discerned are inarguably effects of other change as well.

Clark is concerned with educational effects of certain social forces in the American society, some of them the same as those described by Trow. But the institutional adjustments or consequences of the forces he perceives are themselves conditions of larger changes, economic, technological and ideological, which make them possible, and will be the agents of yet others. (The emerging patterns of cooperation noted, for example.)

Thus the relation between education and social change is not a simple one, and is not susceptible to unilinear analysis. In three quite different papers, written by different authors and at different times with different purposes, we find similar themes woven together and similar reciprocal influences in the variables they describe. That one author sees their significance in one way while another ascribes quite different meanings to them should not surprise us, for this is, of course, an epistemological artifact. It was suggested at the beginning of this discussion that most theories of social change are, in fact, such artifacts. For practical analytic purposes, if we assume that knowledge is for use, we may do best to keep that idea before us. The immense conceptual complexity of the problem of social change argues strongly for multidimensional functional analysis. The sixfold paradigm suggested here is a simple version of what is needed. It seems to serve better than any single-factor theory can, but is not itself a theory in any strict meaning of that word. It may serve to enrich our understanding, however, through forcing our perspective *into* time and history, the matrix in which social change is made.

PROBLEMS FOR THEORY AND RESEARCH

By now it is overwhelmingly apparent that the single most pressing need for the study of social change is adequate theory. None of the unicausal models described heretofore are adequate and, put together in the paradigm suggested earlier, do not constitute a theory at all, but merely a working model for functional analysis. We do not, in truth, know enough of the process of change to make sophisticated theories about it. But if this is so (that present lack of theoretical sophistication is a function of lack of information), then the first order of business must be the collection of relevant data from which to invent a theory of change when our knowledge is more complete. On this argument we pose below a set of empirical questions about the nature of social change which, when answered, might offer materials adequate to at least begin a satisfactory theory. The list, of course, is hardly exhaustive of materials that might be relevant.

Problems for Theory

Following our original suggestion that the institution of education may be an agent, condition, or effect of social change, we may frame four theoretical questions designed to call attention to the functional mechanics, or workings, of change in actual situations. If it were possible to answer them and their subsidiary queries at the present time, we would know a great deal more than we do about social change and the institution of education.

1. *In what ways is change imposed on the institution of education by other institutions and agencies of the society?* Framed in Bohannon's terms (pages 82–83), this asks how "wobble" produced by the adjustment devices of one institution translates into "gyroscopic" adjustments in another. An adequate answer might have to consider the *sources* of pressures for educational change in the community, political process, economic arena, military establishment, etc. It would also need to explore the *reasons* that such pressures develop and the ways in which individuals and groups not involved in education perceive changes there as necessary to their own activities and interests. The possibility of *latent* pressures for educational change developing at various positions in the social structure without the rational awareness of those

involved would also need to be considered. A final consideration would have to be the ways in which pressures for such change, regardless of source, are *manifested*. If valid knowledge is our aim, the theory of change should be able to specify the ways in which such pressures are translated into actual behavior and contact between educational and other institutions and agencies.

2. *In what ways does social change occur from within the institution of education itself?* This, of course, refers to "gyroscopic" adjustments within the institutional event system which may occur without fundamentally altering its past workings. A theory of change such as that we are describing would need to specify the *sources* of such adjustment within the institution and the conditions that generate them.

3. *In what ways does the educational enterprise respond to change?* The answers derived here might concern either what Bohannon has called "gyroscopic" adjustments, or "wobble," depending on the nature of the response. Certainly the reasons why one pressure might call forth an essentially gyroscopic adjustment while another produced wobble and more fundamental and far-reaching change would need to be explored. Such a description of response might also be expected to include *differences in responses* made to pressures originating within and without the enterprise, and why they occur if they do. Finally, consideration might be given to *structures or processes that act to inhibit or retard such responses, or to facilitate them*, and how they operate, and why.

4. *What effects do changes in educational institutions or enterprises have on other institutions or enterprises?* This query could again call forth answers framed in terms of either gyroscopic or wobble adjustments, but in either case a theory would have to describe *how such effects operated* and the *mechanism* with which they are transmitted, facilitated, or resisted.

The foregoing set of queries comprises at least a beginning of the information-collecting enterprise requisite to the construction of an adequate theory of social change in education. On the basis of the answers which might be derived to these and similar questions it should be possible to outline some sort of theory of change. But there are a host of problems and topics specifically educational which such a collection of empirical questions raises but cannot resolve. These involve research problems in educational change in the United States or elsewhere and not the nature of change itself. Some of these might be as follows.

Problems for Research

1. EDUCATION AND POPULATION. We know that the demand for education is increasing both as an increasing number of people consume
schooling in the first place and as increasing numbers of them consume
more of it. We do not by any means know, however, what effects this
accelerating demand is going to have on educational institutions and
systems in the future, nor what qualitative adjustments in their programs might or will be necessitated. In view of increasing costs and
staff shortages it would seem useful to design research aimed at suggesting answers to these questions.

Educational staffing problems *will* increase in coming decades, perhaps most radically in higher education. Severe staff shortages accompanying ever-increased enrollments *will* affect the nature of educational
operations and certainly *may* alter their quality. Little empirical research upon these matters has been conducted, but it would seem
rational to do so before problems become crises.

A different, although related, matter is the problem of financing
increasing levels of education for all segments of the population. A
good many local school boards and districts are experiencing difficulty
in obtaining adequate funds through increased taxation while simultaneously experiencing reluctance to rely upon federal funds even when
available. One reason for this state of affairs appears to be fear of loss
of local autonomy to "federal control." Yet despite increasing federal
participation in education at several levels (most notably in the university) there is little data of a generalized sort to indicate what the
effects of federal financing really are, nor whether the effects may be
different for different kinds of educational enterprises of differing aim
and quality. There is a substantial literature of opinion concerning the
effects of federal funds on higher education but it is largely speculative
in character. Such monies seem to have advanced the sciences, but have
they, as many believe, acted to retard the humanities? It seems to be
generally accepted, again at a speculative level, that federal funding
would improve the quality and quantity of education offered in isolated
or poverty-stricken school systems, but there is little information on the
other consequences which must flow in their wake.

Similarly related is the question of whether the United States *can*
educate its entire population to high school levels, although this has the
appearance of an emergent goal in our educational structure. The ever-

increasing proportions of the population matriculating in colleges and universities raises a parallel question, but there is little empirical information to indicate what effects these practices have upon social structure and educational practice.

2. EDUCATION AND ECONOMICS. That education must have a major impact upon the economic system of the United States we know if for no other reason than that soon approximately one quarter of our total population will be involved in it in some way. Trow and others have given some indications of its effect upon the labor force and occupational structure, but these efforts are hardly more than beginnings. We know also that industrial concentration and dispersion are affected by some aspects of the educational system (as in the concentration of the missile and electronics industries near great graduate centers) and that these, in turn, must have profound effects upon such matters as local tax base. But, again, these are only beginnings.

A different question, more fundamental to education itself, is whether federal and local financial "enrichment" programs can ever permit state and local systems now disadvantaged by inadequate finances to catch up, or whether the increasing growth of educational enterprises (fastest, generally, in the most advantaged areas) will keep them relatively disadvantaged. Neither is there much information to suggest the effects of such programs on a massive scale upon the national economy (for few educational organizations are directly productive of wealth), not to mention such matters as unemployment and fiscal structure at local and national levels. Similarly, there has been little attention paid to the question of whether such programs might work to the disadvantage of areas now educationally affluent.

3. EDUCATION AND POLITICS. The preceding notions necessarily suggest that as education becomes increasingly involved with population and economics it will also become increasingly "political." (For it is through the political process, after all, that every major social decision in the United States is made or ratified.) Yet again there is little empirical information on the interaction of politics and education nor the mutual effects we may expect them to have upon each other as education becomes increasingly expensive, increasingly dominant of the population, and increasingly centralized in varying ways. Perhaps more interesting, but certainly more difficult to answer, are speculative questions about the effect of an increasingly educated population upon the political process itself and upon such immensely significant matters as foreign policy. But we are only beginning to learn today of the politics

of local school boards and their consequences for their districts, and data on these broader matters are totally lacking.

It is easily possible, even on the basis of this brief discussion, to formulate hypotheses and guesses. Some, indeed, have been so formulated and appear scattered throughout the immediately preceding paragraphs. The possibilities for others are literally endless. But they are no more than hypotheses and guesses, however reasonable or probable. These *are* problems for research *because* the information necessary to make our guesses facts either has not been made available or has not been arranged in such forms as to permit it to provide the answers which we need already and may need desperately in the near future. That this is so is no one's "fault" and is, in fact, entirely comprehensible. Our strongly localized systems of education grew up in a very different time and under very different social, economic, political, and educational conditions and assumptions. Much of the "research data" needed for their satisfactory operation might have been contained in the heads and scribbled notes of boards and staff, and the operation of one system or institution had very little effect upon another. But this history and tradition is now invalid for planning the future. The changes which have swept the twentieth century may prove to have been as radical in their effects as those that produced the Renaissance or the Industrial Revolution. If our educational system is to continue successfully to pursue its traditional goals, many of its mechanisms will have to be fundamentally altered, and in the future a better understanding of the nature of social change would seem no longer to be an academic luxury but rather a practical necessity.

Reece McGee is Professor of Sociology at Macalester College. He received his Ph.D. from the University of Minnesota. He has taught at the University of Texas and the University of California, Berkeley. His publications include *Social Disorganization in America* (Chandler, 1962), and (with Theodore Caplow), *The Academic Marketplace* (Basic Books, 1958).

NOTES

1. This critique, like the following, follows Bierstedt (1963).

2. The remainder of this analysis of Weber's argument follows Chinoy (1961).

3. See Bierstedt, *op. cit.*, p. 555.

4. This description follows Louis Schneider in Zollschan and Hirsch (1964).

5. The terms are mine. There is no widely accepted nomenclature for it although the use of "functional" does not imply a strict structure-functional interpretation.

WORKS CITED

Bierstedt, Robert (1963), *The Social Order*, McGraw-Hill Book Company, New York, 2nd ed., Chap. 18.

Bohannon, Paul (1963), *Social Anthropology*, Holt, Rinehart and Winston, New York, Chap. 21.

Brogan, D. W. (1961), *The American Character*, Random House, Vintage Books, New York.

Chinoy, Ely (1961), *Society*, Random House, New York, Chap. 15.

Clark, Burton R. (1964), "Social Trends and Educational Organization," *Proceedings*, Annual Meeting, American Sociological Association, 1964. (Published in altered form as "Interorganizational Patterns in Education," *Administrative Science Quarterly*, **10**:2, September, 1965, 224–237.)

Comte, Auguste (1877), *System of Positive Polity*, Longmans, Green and Co., London.

Durkheim, Emile (1933), *On the Division of Labor in Society*, trans. by George Simpson, The Macmillan Company, New York.

Etzioni, Amitai, and Eva (1964), *Social Change*, Basic Books, New York, Chap. 12.

Redfield, Robert (1941), *The Folk Culture of Yucatan*, University of Chicago Press, Chicago.

Redfield, Robert (1947), "The Folk Society," *Am. Jour. Sociol.*, **III**:4, 293–308.

Sorokin, Pitirim (1962), *Social and Cultural Dynamics*, Bedminster Press, Totowa, N.J.

Spencer, Herbert (1892), *Sociology*, Appleton-Century-Crofts, New York.

Spengler, Oswald (1939), *The Decline of the West*, trans. by Charles F. Atkinson, Alfred A. Knopf, New York.

Töennies, Ferdinand (1957), *Community and Society—Gemeinschaft und Gesellschaft*, trans. and ed. by Charles P. Loomis, Michigan State University Press, East Lansing, Mich.

Toynbee, Arnold J. (1946), *A Study of History*, Somervill Abridgement, Oxford University Press, New York.

Trow, Martin (1963), "The Collegiate Explosion," *New Society*, No. 58 (November 7, 1963), 16–18.

Weber, Max (1958), *The Protestant Ethic and the Spirit of Capitalism*, trans. by Talcott Parsons, Charles Scribner's Sons, student edition, New York.

White, Lynn T. (1962), *Medieval Technology and Social Change*, Clarendon Press, New York.

Zollschan, George K. and Walter Hirsch (eds.) (1964), *Explorations in Social Change*, Houghton Mifflin Co., Boston, Chap. 15.

4 Education, Stratification, and Mobility*

Robert Perrucci

Purdue University

The American stratification system is governed by an open class ideology. This ideology placed great stress upon the Horatio Alger "log cabin to president" success stories which describe the many opportunities for those with ability to achieve higher positions in the society. Individuals are expected and encouraged to aspire beyond their original station in life. Group differences in power, prestige, and wealth are not denied by the ideology, but are viewed as rewards to be earned by using opportunities for social mobility which are allegedly available to all.

There are, however, some contradictions between the ideal of equal opportunity and the existence of established differences in power, prestige, and wealth. The existence of such differences can limit the chances for those with ability, but not advantage, to attain socially valued goals. The recent rediscovery of the poor in American society reflects the growing concern with the manner in which the very existence of a system of stratification may make equality of opportunity a meaningless phrase. Michael Harrington, in his recent book on poverty in America, has chosen to speak of a permanent poor, and, in so doing, to confront the open class ideology with the harsh realities of despair and hopelessness of tens of millions of Americans.

These are important concerns for a society such as ours that places its faith in the openness of the opportunity structure. There is a history of economic expansion and limitless opportunities in America that serves to reinforce such faith and to maintain high expectations concerning the *availability* of opportunity for those with talent and inclina-

* The author would like to thank Robert K. Bain, Richard J. Hill, Reece McGee, and Ephraim H. Mizruchi for their critical reactions to an earlier version of this paper.

tion to use their talent. When such expectations are met, the stability and vitality of a society is reinforced; when they are not met, collective dissatisfaction and political instability are possible.

The purpose of this essay is to examine the factors that aid and inhibit equality of opportunity in American society. The paper has four main sections: A discussion of the nature of stratification; changing patterns of mobility which have brought education to the fore as the main channel for social ascent; the individual and societal conditions which operate to encourage or discourage mobility; and the effect of changing patterns of mobility upon higher education.

THE NATURE AND FUNCTIONS OF STRATIFICATION

Complex industrial societies are distinguished by an elaborate division of labor. Occupational roles requiring extensive amounts of skill, training, and responsibility are found to command disproportionate amounts of income, prestige, and power. The manner in which occupational roles and their attendant rewards are distributed in a society results in a system of stratification which has a particular "shape." The shape tells you something about the proportion of the population holding positions of varying amounts of income, power, or prestige (depending upon which aspect of an occupation is being measured). A pyramidal form, most often used to graphically describe a stratification system, suggests that a small proportion of the population fills occupational roles which yield the highest rewards, and that the proportion of the population increases as you descend the reward hierarchy. American society is often described by a diamond shape which suggests that relatively few persons receive the highest and lowest rewards, with the large majority of the population found in the middle reward groups. This is the so-called middle-class society.

Many occupational roles "hang together" in that they require similar training and skill to fill the occupation, and they share equal or nearly equal amounts of prestige, income, or wealth. Aggregates of persons and families filling similar occupational roles constitute a social stratum. Members of the same stratum, by virtue of their occupations, may share the same style of life, which is reflected in consumption behavior, group membership in the community, and personal values. Some strata may be so distinctive in their style of life that they form separate subcultures within the larger society.

The extent of similarity among persons in the same social strata is a matter of considerable theoretical and empirical interest. The dimensions of stratification such as income, power, and prestige do not necessarily cluster together in a neat fashion. Inconsistencies among these and other dimensions have been found to produce significant within-class variations in political behavior, class consciousness, and individual stress (Lenski, 1954; Centers, 1949; Jackson, 1962). In this same connection, the extent of dissimilarity between members of different social classes is also problematic. Social classes may not necessarily be distinctive subcultures, but may only represent differences in *degree* concerning values and styles of life. Students of mass culture have presented a very convincing case for the broad similarities in exposure and consumption of cultural products among persons variously located in the social structure (Rosenberg and White, 1957; Wilensky, 1964). We will return to this question of similarities and differences among the social classes as an explanatory factor in different educational experiences and patterns of individual mobility.

Given this general outline of the structure of a system of stratification, we may now ask how the positions in the hierarchical structure are filled. What pattern of inducements and constraints motivate individuals to fill different positions? The study of social mobility is concerned with the causes and consequences of individual movement in and out of positions in the hierarchy. We may begin to explore these questions by examining two ideal-type models of society that are concerned with the allocation of persons to positions. The first model is that of a "closed" system in which the range of possible positions available to an individual are fixed by a set of status transmission and marriage rules. In such a system, a person's future rank in the hierarchy is determined by the position of his family, limiting the individual's opportunity to either rise or fall in the hierarchy. The marriage rules operate to designate eligible mates in such fashion as not to disrupt the status transmission rules based upon family position. This model could be represented in a picture of a pyramidal or diamond-shaped stratification system with several solid horizontal lines delineating the two or more "strata" of which the system is composed. Movement across these lines, either up or down, would be virtually absent.

The second model is that of the "open" system in which the only restrictions upon movement in and out of positions are determined by the abilities of the individual himself. Social position at birth is a temporary and relatively unimportant "accident." The system provides a number of avenues of opportunity leading to differentially rewarded positions. All persons have an equal chance to use these avenues so that future positions are a function of natural talents and abilities. This model would be represented by a pyramidal or diamond shape with two or more broken horizontal lines allowing for movement up and down the hierarchy.

There are, of course, certain restrictions upon the full operation of either of these models, and it is these restrictions that give the study of social mobility its theoretical and practical importance. The closed model assumes some balance between positions and people within each stratum. However, differential fertility rates may result in too many or too few persons to fill the necessary positions in certain levels of the hierarchy. An elite group which does not reproduce itself may find it necessary to recruit persons from other strata to fill elite positions. Or, on the other hand, a nonelite group which is producing more people than there are positions in its strata will create pressures for movement between strata. Another restriction upon the closed model is that elite groups do not control all the talent required to maintain themselves as elites. This observation is as ancient as Plato's parable of the metals, ". . . if the son of a golden or silver parent has an admixture of brass or iron, then nature orders a transposition of ranks, . . . just as there may be sons of artisans who have an admixture of gold or silver in them are raised to honour . . ." (Jowett, 1953).

The restrictions upon the open model are those which limit the operation of equality of opportunity. These restrictions are due to the tendency of those persons who at some point in time have gained the most highly rewarded positions to attempt to maintain these positions and transmit them to their offspring. Positions originally won in the free market, where the most talented receive the highest rewards, will be maintained at the expense of equality of opportunity. As Dennis Wrong has observed,

". . . there is a tendency, a result of kinship loyalties, for roles and opportunities to attain them to be passed on from one generation to the next, giving rise to enduring classes or strata monopolizing certain roles and exhibiting a greater or lesser solidarity and a common style of life." (Wrong, 1959.)

The main factor in the development of ascribed advantage is the institution of the family, which transmits greater or lesser opportunity to attain access to the highly rewarded positions. The family also shapes the orientation of its members toward an existing opportunity structure.

Thus it is possible to have an opportunity structure that is potentially available to all persons, while at the same time the very existence of social classes which have persisted over time and have developed their own patterns of responses to their environment may limit an individual from taking advantage of the total opportunity structure. It is important that we maintain a distinction between a characteristic of a society when we speak of the opportunity structure, and an individual's learned patterns for responding to and coping with his environment.

What we have described so far is the structure of a system of stratification and one of its main functions, that of allocating persons to positions. This is often referred to as the *instrumental* function. This allocation function operates through the ascription rules of the closed system as well as the achievement rules of the open system. In either type of system, a critical question is how this allocation function is translated into the behavior of individuals whose actions ultimately give meaning to statements concerning the function of stratification? Surely all persons in a society could not be coerced to undertake positions they had little desire for. The answer to this question brings us to the second major function of a stratification system, its *integrative* function. Although the stratification system allocates persons to more or less desirable positions and provides them with greater or fewer rewards, most individuals tend to respond to their respective fates with the feeling that they have been justly treated. The absence of this sense of justice would throw into question the legitimacy of existing reward distributions. If a stratification system is to fulfill an integrative function, those less favored in the distribution of rewards must respond to those more favored with the feeling that justice has prevailed. It is important to note that when we speak of the need for legitimacy and a feeling of justice, we need not assume that those less favored will be delighted with their less favored condition. What is necessary is that the *explanation* for one's less favored state should not challenge the overall legitimacy of the existing institutional structure. There are a wide range of adaptations available for the expression of dissatisfaction that serves to take the strain off the institutional structure. These may include self-blame, forms of psychological withdrawal, viewing one's position as temporary, transferring aspirations to children, emphasizing the importance of "luck" and "chance" in human affairs, adopting fatalistic ideologies, becoming involved in deviant subgroups, and scapegoating and prejudice as forms of blaming others for one's failures. The importance of these adaptations for the maintenance of order in a society poses a series of yet unanswered questions concerning the relationship between the "looseness" of a system and its stability (Mizruchi and Perrucci, 1962).

With this brief review of the structure and functions of a stratification system in mind, we may now turn to the central concerns of this essay. Given the American stratification system as one governed by an "open class ideology," by an emphasis upon Horatio Alger themes of log cabin to president success stories, by the moral obligation to aspire beyond one's original station in life, and by emphasis upon equal availability of the means to achieve high position, we shall examine the operation of various constraint systems which aid or inhibit equality of opportunity. More specifically, we shall limit our attention to the educational system as a main mechanism for determining the fate of individuals in our society. For education has become the dominant *means* by which the large majority of favored and rewarded positions are attained. The focus will be upon access to this means of achieving mobility, upon the quality and variability of education that is made available, and upon the motivations of individuals to utilize those resources that may be available for social mobility.

The second concern will be upon the distribution of rewards among those persons who have already moved beyond the original hurdle of gaining access to the necessary means for mobility. For it is among this group that we find the highest levels of aspiration and highest expectations concerning rewards. In this connection we shall examine some new dimensions of the American stratification system which may also have implications for the integrative function of stratification.

Let us begin by examining the main outlines of the American educational system in terms of some of the significant changes that have taken place and the implications of these changes for the stratification system and social mobility.

CHANGING PATTERNS OF EDUCATION AND MOBILITY

A simplified view of the American educational system is one of a series of self-contained stages, with each stage a prerequisite for movement to the next. Moreover, the stages are interconnected to the extent that actions, decisions, and performance undertaken in one stage act as constraints upon actions in a subsequent stage. For our purposes, we may further simplify the model by viewing actions within, and satisfactory completion of, each stage as having a probability value that expresses the likelihood that one will "wind up" in one of the more highly valued positions in the occupational structure. Thus, as one moves from completion of grade school through completion of a graduate degree, the probability of a high status occupation is increased.

Prior to the first part of the twentieth century the probability statements generated by such a model would not have been very powerful in predicting future status of persons with various educational backgrounds. Preparation for commercial activities required skills and training that were not necessarily gathered by formal education, and the career of the artisan was often started in the capacity of an apprentice. Even the "older" professions of medicine, law, and the ministry were open to entry through apprenticeship preparation.

Such is not the case in contemporary American society where the revolution in education has paralleled the revolutions in science and technology and their impact upon the occupational structure. Table 1 shows a distribution of the proportion of school-age persons in the population who attended public elementary and secondary schools.

TABLE 1   *Percent of U.S. Population, Aged 5–17 Years, Attending Public Elementary and Secondary Schools*

1870	57.0	1930	81.7
1880	65.5	1940	84.4
1890	68.6	1950	83.2
1900	71.9	1960	82.2
1910	74.2	1962	84.5
1920	78.3		

SOURCE: *Digest of Educational Statistics*, U.S. Department of Health, Education and Welfare, 1964.

The marked increase in attendance rates occurs primarily between 1870 and 1930. The stable and slightly irregular fluctuations in rates after 1930 are in large part a reflection of the changing number of children attending private and religious schools. The rate of increase in attendance in nonpublic schools is much higher than in public schools between 1940 and 1960 (Statistical Abstract of the United States, 1963, p. 113). Of course, growth in population during this same period has resulted in a sizable increase in the absolute numbers of children attending both private and public schools. These relative and absolute increases have also been reflected in the growth in instructional staff in our primary and secondary schools. In 1870 there were about 200,000 teachers in public elementary and secondary schools and

this figure had increased to about 1,500,000 by 1962 (Digest of Educa‹
tional Statistics, 1964).

In Tables 2 and 3 we can see a more dramatic picture of the chang‹
ing pattern of education that has followed the increase in the proportior
of persons attending primary and secondary schools. The increase ir
the proportion of the total enrollment that is in high school indicate‹
that the general trend of universal public education has been extending
the amount of education being obtained by the growing number o‹
students. Table 3 shows a steady increase in the proportion of persons
17 years old who have graduated from high school.

TABLE 2   *Percent of Total School Enrollment in High School*

1870	1.2	1930	17.1
1880	1.1	1940	26.0
1890	1.6	1950	22.7
1900	3.3	1960	23.5
1910	5.1	1962	25.0
1920	10.2		

SOURCE: *Digest of Educational Statistics*, 1964, p. 10.

TABLE 3   *Percent of Persons 17 Years of Age Who Graduated from High School*

1870	2.0	1930	29.0
1880	2.5	1940	50.8
1890	3.5	1950	59.0
1900	6.4	1960	65.1
1910	8.8	1962	69.7
1920	16.8		

SOURCE: Adapted from *Digest of Educational Statistics*, 1964, p. 56.

The trends toward more extensive and intensive use of educaton
have also carried over into higher education. Table 4 shows types of
higher degrees earned in selected time periods. Several trends may be
observed in this table. There has been a continuing increase in the
proportion of advanced degrees awarded in the last several decades
from about six percent to about twenty percent. Most striking is that
aspects of the revolution in higher education have been a very recent
phenomenon. Over 50 percent of all the doctor's degrees awarded since
1870 have been awarded since 1955. A similar pattern may be observed
for other degrees.

TABLE 4 *Distribution of College Degrees in United States*

	1870	1880	1890	1900	1910	1920	1930	1940	1950	1960	1962	1963
Bachelor's	9,371	12,896	15,539	27,410	37,199	48,622	122,484	186,500	432,058	392,440	417,846	447,662
percent	100.0	93.2	93.0	93.3	93.6	90.8	87.6	86.1	87.0	82.3	81.2	81.1
Master's	0	879	1,015	1,583	2,113	4,279	14,969	26,731	58,183	74,435	84,855	91,366
percent	—	6.4	6.1	5.4	5.3	8.0	10.7	12.3	11.7	15.6	16.5	16.6
Doctor's	1	54	149	382	443	615	2,299	3,290	6,420	9,828	11,622	12,822
percent	0.0	0.4	0.9	1.3	1.1	1.1	1.6	1.5	1.3	2.1	2.3	2.3
Total	9,372	13,829	16,703	29,375	39,755	53,516	139,752	216,521	496,661	476,703	514,323	551,810

SOURCE: Adapted from *Digest of Educational Statistics*, U.S. Department of Health, Education and Welfare, 1964.

The changing patterns of education from high school through graduate work have not occurred in isolation from changes in the occupational structure. Since the turn of the century there has been a steady increase in the proportion of the labor force in those occupations requiring greater amounts of education, while the unskilled and farm occupations have declined. It is difficult to forecast future trends in the occupational structure due to technological change, but it is likely that the decline in farm occupations will soon reach some equilibrium point. Although the full impact of automation in production is still uncertain, its effect should be to increase the need for technicians at the expense of the unskilled occupations.

Glick's (1954) analysis of the 1950 census indicates the connection between changes in the educational system and the occupational structure. Comparing the jobs held by persons who did not complete high school, high school graduates, and college graduates, Glick found that the proportion holding white collar occupations was about 25, 40, and 85 percent, respectively. Given these educational and occupational changes, then, it appears crucial to find out who goes to college—for college graduation has become the main avenue for admission to those occupations that provide the middle class way of life. But going to college represents a complex process of motivation and opportunity. The internal constraints of values and aspirations, and the external constraints represented by the social structures one is implicated in, combine to effect the realization of equality of opportunity. One result of the educational revolution has been to make the decisions as well as performance in the eighth or twelfth grade among the most crucial determinants of future status.

Thus one of the effects of these educational and occupational changes has been to make higher education the main avenue for mobility. This fact, however, has put an additional burden upon the secondary schools where the decision to go to college is made and where the curriculum prerequisites for entrance either are or are not obtained. The crucial role played by the high schools in sorting out the college bound from the noncollege bound has increased in prominence as high school enrollments have increased. In 1870 there were only 16,000 high school graduates and 9,371 college graduates, the latter being about 60 percent of the former. A fair proportion of the relatively few people who graduated from high school were likely to continue on to college, thus relieving a good part of the "quality control" function from the high school. In more recent years we have observed that college graduates are only about 20 percent of high school graduates. Since there are about two million high school graduates, the selection process becomes a much more complex problem.

But it is not only the high school that has been affected by expanding enrollments. Because college education has become the royal road to success, increasing college attendance has had the potential effect of devaluing college education. The adaptation to this possibility has been the "Princeton versus Podunk" pattern that was so well documented in the Time magazine study of college graduates (Haveman and West, 1952). What we find here is a growing differentiation in the quality of schools, and more importantly, in the relative success of their graduates (cf. Wilensky, 1964). This increasing differentiation can be interpreted as a transfer of the sorting out process from the high school level to the college level. For as greater and greater numbers of students graduate from high school and continue on to college the quality control function of the high school becomes more difficult to perform effectively. What has been introduced, in effect, is simply another gatekeeper on the road to success. However, this new criterion, namely, the nature of the institution of higher learning one attends, can be viewed as somewhat at odds with normative expectations regarding how avenues of mobility operate in an open class system.

Closely tied to this first set of consequences is our second consideration concerning the effects of these shifting patterns of educational and occupational mobility. Here we face the values and value changes that are associated with mobility, and whether certain value patterns are essential prerequisites for mobility or are a consequence of it. In relatively stable societies with low rates of upward movement the mobility model that is used is one assuming that mobile persons are selected precisely because of their value similarity to the members of·their class of destination. The "mobiles" are viewed as holding those values, aspirations, and characteristics that serve to make them highly "visible" among the other members of their class of origin. The mobility heroes of the Horatio Alger type are often presented as already exhibiting those qualities required for success, such as hard work, thrift, and virtue. All that our hero needs, in effect, is a good scrubbing, a suit of clothes, and a position that will give him a chance to "show his stuff" (Wohl, 1953). Within this framework the move into the mobility channel is the problematic condition, and subsequent success is nonproblematic and relatively automatic.

The changes described above, however, suggest that a good bit of the mobility that has occurred in recent decades—both educational and occupational—has been a result of the "structural push" of expanding numbers of high status occupations caused by technological change. A minimum estimate of the number of new jobs created by technical change between 1920 and 1950 is about eight million (Kahl, 1960, p. 255). Under such conditions of expansion, the stable mobility model of value change or value consonance (in accordance with high status group values) is less likely to be in agreement with the actual mobility process. The great diversity in the ethnic and class origins of persons involved in the upper educational and occupational ranks makes it quite difficult to speak of any kind of value similarity that would play a critical role in the mobility process. An added factor that would tend to support such diversity of basic values is the wide variety of educational programs available as well as the wide variety of occupational destinations for which the mobile person can strive. This does not mean that the educational experience may not lead to greater similarity in values and orientations than existed prior to the educational experience, only that any significant homogenizing effects are more likely to take place within the context of particular colleges and universities. But given the diversity of the schools—created by a combination of the motivations of the students it recruits, the curriculum, the faculty, and the administration—what we would find developing is a certain within-school similarity but between-school diversity. Despite any of these processes, however, the important fact is that the values-mobility sequence has been altered, or at least made a less critical consideration in understanding social mobility.

The important consequence of this shift in the values-mobility sequence, at least from the point of view of this essay, is that the rapid expansion of mobility opportunities has had, above all, the effect of raising expectations concerning the future rewards that higher education will bring. The expectation that higher education will automatically bring money, prestige, power, happiness is probably more appropriate to an age when there were only 16,000 high school graduates a year, and only 9,000 college graduates. Under conditions such as these, higher education would indeed have a very high probability of resulting in success in all its varied forms. It therefore becomes very important to know just how higher education, as the main channel of mobility, operates as a mechanism which either aids or inhibits the free flow of talent to enjoy its "just" rewards.

It is this factor of rising expectations concerning education that brings us to the third effect of the educational revolution. The first two had to do with the instrumental function of stratification, or how people get allocated to positions. Our concern now is with the degree of correspondence between expectations for rewards of occupational and educational mobility and actual rewards realized. Such disparities are important for the integrative function of stratification, for it is under conditions of unfulfilled expectation that the legitimacy of institutional arrangements governing reward structures will be questioned.

There are two different objects or referents for expectations to consider. The first has to do with the distribution of income among various occupational groups. One of the results of the occupational changes described previously has been a growing belief that the upward shift in real income for all groups has been especially pronounced for the blue-collar category, and that such income advances have served to lessen the discrepancy between upper and lower occupational groups. The belief in this shrinking income gap has served as a basis for a number of theories explaining conservative orientations among blue-collar workers who are enjoying both relative and absolute increases in wealth, as well as the anxieties experienced by lower white-collar groups over the status advances of the blue-collar worker. Recent evidence on income distribution among occupational groups suggests that this income gap has not in fact been disappearing as popular belief would have it (Miller, 1962; Hamilton, 1964). Because our estimates of how well we are doing are generally made in relative rather than absolute terms—relative to those groups immediately above or below us whom we may use as standards to evaluate our own income and consumer behavior—the existence of conditions contrary to expectations has the *potential* for inspiring individual and collective dissatisfactions.

The second referent for expectations concerns the view that reward distributions for persons who utilize the legitimate mobility channels will be based on universalistic criteria such as ability and not particularistic criteria such as social origins. Although it is certainly recognized that social origins do affect the likelihood that a person will gain access to the means for mobility, it is often maintained that the negative effects of social origins are "neutralized" among those who manage to complete a higher education. This view has often been expressed in the notion of "careers open to talent," whereby the measure of a man is his ability and performance and his social origins can neither help nor hinder him in the pursuit of such careers. The assumption that the effect of social origins is neutralized in certain careers requires further consideration. This assumption implies that the mobile person does not "carry with him" any of the values and aspirations that are prominently displayed in his class of origin and that might limit his own performance in his career. In order for this assumption to be valid the values-mobility sequence spoken of earlier would have to mean that mobile individuals are selected because of their value consonance with the class of destination, or that they can easily "shed" the values of the class of origin and "take on" the values of their class of destination. Our earlier discussion of the effects of rapid educational and occupational expansion would suggest that the selection process according to value consonance is not in operation; such a process is much too complex to work effectively according to the "natural" operation of the stratification system.

A second question to be raised concerning the assumption that social origins do not affect movement in certain careers is whether or not the environment in which the mobile person operates is in fact neutral or unaware of the existence of the differences in life experiences, values, and style of life that may exist between the new arrival and the old members. Again, to assume that these differences no longer exist, or that if they do, they make no difference, means that persons evaluate each other solely on the basis of technical skills and abilities. We shall wish to examine the facts that bear upon such assumptions and the implications they might have for the existence of order in the stratification system.

The problems that have been identified and the questions that have been raised concerning the instrumental and integrative functions of a system of stratification will form the framework for the remainder of this paper. In looking at the instrumental function (or how people get allocated to positions) the primary interest will be with those factors that aid or inhibit the mobility process in general, and their persistence in the educational system in particular. This is discussed in the following section. In looking at the integrative function of stratification (or collective responses to the manner in which a society distributes its rewards) the concern will be with the rising expectations concerning the rewards of higher education, and the adaptations of higher education to the influx of students from all social levels. This material is contained in the section on mobility and higher education.

INTERNAL AND EXTERNAL CONSTRAINTS ON MOBILITY

Social mobility is best viewed as a result of a complex pattern of relationships between the objective opportunity structure of a society, individual values, beliefs, and aspirations concerning elements of the opportunity structure, and the structural settings within which the individual is influenced, and within which his personal views are reinforced, modified, or challenged. Let us begin with an examination of those elements of the self such as values and aspirations which would induce the individual to undertake patterns of activity that are positively related to mobility.

Values, Aspirations and Personality Patterns

Rather than examine the area of values and aspirations in any general or exhaustive manner, we shall limit our attention to those values and aspirations that have most direct relevance to education as the major means for advancement in our society. The importance of studying the values systems of social classes, which study has a long tradition in sociology, was underscored in an influential paper by Herbert Hyman in 1953. His efforts in the area of class values and mobility can be taken as a crucial point in the development of a large body of systematic theoretical and empirical work.

"The existence of stratification in American society is well known. The corollary fact—that individuals from lower strata are not likely to climb far up the economic ladder is also known. However, what requires additional analysis are the factors that account for this mobility. Many of these factors of an objective nature have been studied. Opportunity in the society is differential; higher education or specialized training, which might provide access to a high position, must be bought with money—the very commodity which the lower classes lack. Such objective factors help maintain the existing structure. But there are other factors of a more subtle psychological nature which have not been illuminated and which may also work to perpetuate the existing order. It is our assumption that an intervening variable mediating the relationship between low position and lack of upward mobility is a system of beliefs and values within the lower classes which in turn reduces the very *voluntary* actions which would ameliorate their low position.

"The components of this value system, in our judgment, involve less emphasis upon the traditional high success goals, increased awareness of the lack of opportunity to achieve success, and less emphasis upon the achievement of goals which in turn would be instrumental for success. To put it simply the lower class individual doesn't want as much sucess, knows he couldn't get it even if he wanted to, and doesn't want what might help him get success. Of course, an individual's value system is only one among many factors on which his position in the social hierarchy depends. Some of these factors may be external and arbitrary, quite beyond the control of even a highly motivated individual. However, within the bounds of the freedom available to individuals, this value system would create a *self-imposed* barrier to an improved position." (1953, p. 426.)

Hyman examined data collected in nationwide surveys concerning class differences in educational values, in motivations for economic advancement, and in perceptions of the opportunity structure. Using a variety of measures of stratification, Hyman finds that the lower socio-economic groups place less emphasis upon college education as necessary for advancement, and are less likely to desire a college education for their children. He also finds that when adult and young respondents are asked to indicate the most important thing to be considered when choosing a life's work, the lower classes emphasized direct economic considerations such as security and wages, whereas the upper classes stressed the congeniality of the career pattern to the individual's personality, interests and qualifications. Concerning these differences Hyman (1953) states:

"It is our belief that this difference in what would be sought in a career would lead the lower class individuals into occupations that would be less likely to enhance their position. Such desiderata will be achieved in a "good job" but not in such positions as managerial or professional jobs. These latter careers have greater elements of risk and are the very ones that would not mesh with the desire for stability, security and immediate economic benefits, but would mesh with the goal of congeniality to the individual's interest." (p. 433.)

Pursuing this line of analysis further, Hyman finds that the lower class individuals are more likely to prefer a low income but secure job, and to have lower aspirations when asked to make projections concerning increased monetary needs. The large body of empirical evidence in which Hyman finds consistent class-based differences is followed by a theoretical coda directed at explaining the cases which do not fit the argument.

"While the evidence thus far presented provides consistent and strong evidence that lower class individuals *as a group* have a value system that reduces the likelihood of individual advancement, it is also clear from the data that there is a sizable proportion from the lower group who do not incorporate this value system. Similarly, there are individuals in the upper classes who do not show the modal tendency of their group. In part, such deviant instances can be accounted for in terms of the crudity of the measurements used. In part, one must recognize that the members of these classes have much heterogenity in such other social respects as their ethnic, religious, and other memberships and have been exposed to a variety of idiosyncratic experiences.

"The value systems would be correspondingly diverse. However, one systematic factor which can be shown to account for the deviant cases which confirms at *a more subtle psychological level* the influence of class factors is that of the reference group of the individual. Some of our lower class individuals may well be identifying themselves with upper groups, and absorbing the value system of another class to which they refer themselves." (p. 441.)

Hyman's results concerning class differences in values and aspirations have also been found in a number of other studies conducted in such varied settings as an industrial plant, rural communities, small cities and urban areas. In a study of high-school-aged adolescents in the middle west in 1941, Hollingshead (1949) found a pattern of vocational choices that roughly corresponded with the job patterns of each class in the adult work world. Sewell, Haller, and Straus (1957) studied the educational and occupational aspirations of a large random sample of public and private nonfarm high school seniors in Wisconsin in 1947. They found a significant association between level of educational and occupational aspirations and social status, with measured intelligence controlled. While their study does not deny the importance of intelligence to aspirations, they do find that status does make an independent contribution. Chinoy (1955) studied the aspirations of automobile workers using data collected by participant observation and prolonged interviews with men employed in one large auto plant. The findings indicate that the auto workers tend to confine their aims to those limited alternatives which seem possible for men with their skills and resources. Of the 62 men interviewed, only eight felt that they had a promising future outside the factory. Within the factory, five men had real hope that they might some day become foremen, while only three semiskilled workers (of a total of 28) felt that it might be possible to move into the ranks of skilled labor. The remaining 46 men restricted their ambitions to such small gains as transfer to a job that pays a few cents more per hour or to one that is easier, steadier, or more interesting. Two interesting patterns observed by Chinoy are the shift of the context of advancement from the occupational sphere to the consumption sphere, and by the moderate tendency to maintain ambitious hopes for their children (cf. Hyman's findings). Chinoy concludes that these automobile workers have retained the form but lost the substance of the American tradition of opportunity.

In addition to the importance of values and aspirations in influencing mobility, there is also the factor of intelligence or ability in undertaking certain mobility-related activities. Intelligence is particularly relevant to mobility within the context of this essay as we are in large part limiting our attention to education as the major means of achieving mobility. In a study of some 3,000 boys in the sophomore and junior years of high school from the Boston area, data were collected which provided estimates of the independent and combined effects of intelligence and social origins upon college aspirations. An examination of these data was undertaken by Kahl, who sought to assess the effects of origins and I.Q. on college plans, and to pursue a question raised earlier by Hyman, namely, what social influences help to explain why students of similar I.Q. and social origins differ markedly in their college aspirations (Kahl, 1960). Table 5 contains the findings from the questionnaire phase of the mobility project and is followed by Kahl's analysis of the interview data for a specially selected number of cases.

TABLE 5   *Percentage of Boys Who Expected to Go to College By I.Q. and Father's Occupation*

Boston Area, 1950—3348 Boys*

I.Q. Quintile (Boys)

Father's occupation	Low 1	2	3	4	High 5	All Quintiles
Major white collar	56%	72%	79%	82%	89%	80%
Middle white collar	28	36	47	53	76	52
Minor white collar	12	20	22	29	55	26
Skilled labor and service	4	15	19	22	40	19
Other labor and service	9	6	10	14	29	12
All occupations	11	17	24	30	52	27

* From Kahl, 1960, p. 283.

"Notice that the combination of I.Q. and social class (in Table 5) successfully predicted college aspiration at the extremes, for a boy with a Major White-Collar father (lawyer, doctor, executive) who was in the top quintile or top 20 percent of intelligence had an 89 percent chance of wanting to go to college, whereas a boy with an Other Labor and service father (semi-skilled or unskilled) who was in the bottom quintile in intelligence had only a 9 percent chance. . . .

"Fortunately, the Boston study had depth in time, for it collected statistics on the performance of the boys from the first grade in grammar school up to the time they answered the questilonnaire in the middle of high school. Boys with high I.Q. scores usually had good marks starting with the first grade, but even more, those with low I.Q. scores had poor marks. Father's occupation did not affect school performance in the earlier grades, but it began to take effect in the fourth grade, and by the time of junior high school was slightly more important than I.Q. in predicting performance.

"The pattern is clear: in the earliest years in school a boy performs according to his native talent and, probably, his general emotional adjustment to the classroom situation. . . . But as he grows older, he begins to shape his performance according to certain values that he learns from his family and friends. Upper-status boys learn that good, or at least adequate, performance in school is necessary, that they are expected to do well enough in secondary school to get admitted to college. . . .

"By contrast, a boy from a lower status home is taught that college is either 'not for his kind,' or at best is a matter of indifference to his parents. The boy's friends are not interested in college nor in high school. . . . Consequently even a bright boy among them gets discouraged. . . .

"What has been said so far concerns boys at the extremes of Table 5; that is, boys with high intelligence and high social status versus those with low intelligence and low social status. . . .

"However, *some* boys of high intelligence and low status do head toward college, even though it be a minority of this group (29 percent of the boys in the highest quintile of intelligence from Other Labor and Service homes). Furthermore, if we look again at Table 5, we can notice that boys from Minor White-Collar or Skilled-Labor homes who have high intelligence have almost a fifty-fifty chance of heading toward college. What differentiates boys in these groups who are interested in college from the majority of their freinds who are not?

"To explore this problem twenty-four boys and their parents were interviewed. . . . All had I.Q. scores in the top quintile; all had petty white-collar, skilled or semi-skilled fathers. Yet almost half were college oriented, the rest were not. . . . The motivation (for college) in these exceptional cases came from four directions:

"1. If a boy had done well in the early years, *and* had built up a self-conception in which good school performance was important, he would work hard to keep up his record. But the idea that school was important occurred only when that early performance was truly exceptional, or if the importance of his standing to him was reinforced by one or more of the other factors listed below.

"2. A boy would sacrifice other pleasures for homework when they were not important to him. If a boy was not good at sports, if he did not have close and satisfying peer contact, or if he had no hobby that was strongly rewarding as well as distracting, then the cost of homework was less and the balance more in its favor. In extreme cases frustration in these alternative spheres motivated a boy to good school performance as compensation.

"3. If a boy's family rewarded good school performance and punished poor performance, and the boy was not in rebellion against the family for emotional reasons, he was more likely to give up some play for homework.

"4. If a boy had a rational conviction about the importance of schoolwork for his future career, he would strive to keep up his performance. But that conviction never appeared unless the parents emphasized it. . . .

"Thus, intelligence and social status account for the major variations in college aspiration, especially at the extremes of the distributions. But in the lower-middle occupational range, and the intelligence range of smart-but-not-brilliant, the prediction is not good, for about half of such boys go to college and half stay away. For those boys the major determining factor is the attitude of the parents regarding the importance of college for occupational success, and the importance of occupational success for personal happiness." (Kahl, 1960, pp. 287–288.)

The important question that remains largely unresolved by these studies which show the lower classes as having low aspirations and mobility-inhibiting values is the extent to which these values and aspirations are simply adaptations to objective conditions or a more fundamental part of the lower class youth's personality system. Whether the apparent absence of motivation to get ahead makes its imprint upon the personality in early socialization processes, or whether this is a more or less realistic response to a restrictive opportunity structure for the adolescent or adult is of considerable significance. It is particularly important in situations where attempts to "open up" the opportunity structure, as in education. are being undertaken.

Concern with this question has led to a significant body of work designed to tap the level of aspiration of the different social classes independent of expectations based upon an appraisal of life chances. Stephenson (1956), in a study of about 1,000 ninth grade students in four, semi-industrial, middle-sized cities in New Jersey, sought to determine the occupational plans and aspirations of his subjects, and, in so doing, to separate out the effect of reality factors upon the aspirations of the lower class students. Each student was asked to indicate his occupational plans for the time after he had completed the level of schooling he intended to complete. He was then asked to make a choice of what he would like to do if his circumstances were different and he could do what he really wanted to do. Stephenson found first of all that both occupational plans and aspirations are positively associated with the prestige ranking of father's occupation. At the same time, however, the discrepancy between the student's plans and aspirations also becomes markedly greater with descent in the occupational hierarchy. Under the assumption that plans, as compared to aspirations, represent an adjustment to the constraints of the real world, these data indicate "that while there is a relatively consistent pattern of high occupational aspirations among these youths, their plans tend to conform to their position in the stratification system" (p. 207). Additional evidence in support of the plans-aspirations distinction is found in Stephenson's comparison of the occupational plans and aspirations of Negro and white children of skilled, semiskilled, and unskilled fathers. Although the Negro students tended to have lower occupational plans than their counterparts from each occupational background, their aspirations were as high or higher. This would suggest that the Negro respondents' plans reflected the double burden of being both lower class and Negro (cf. Parker and Kleiner, 1964).

Stephenson's findings clearly support his conclusions that it is important to differentiate between aspirations and expectations when seeking to establish mobility orientation, since "plans or expectations are more definitely class based and, hence, may reflect class differences in opportunity and general life chances" (1956, p. 212). His data, however, do not support his assertion that "aspirations are relatively unaffected by class," since there was a marked decline in occupational aspirations with lower levels of the occupational hierarchy. Even when given an opportunity to make a fantasy choice, the lower class students tended to make more modest selections. Of course, one could argue that lower class students reduced aspirations in light of lowered occupational plans, but this is exactly what Stephenson tried to avoid in questions asked concerning plans and aspirations. The fact that aspirations are still somewhat related to class origins continues to raise the question of additional class-based factors affecting mobility aspirations.

In discussing class-based aspirations, some consideration should be given to the methodological or theoretical basis of attempts to measure aspirations as a form of a fantasy choice. In other words, should we first seek to establish "reality" choices, and then ask for choices that are based upon very large "ifs"? This does not question the validity of obtaining both reality and fantasy choices in order to show that discrepancies are related to class, as Stephenson did. What is at issue, rather, is whether it is possible to make fantasy choices that do in fact "suspend" the effect of reality plans, and more importantly, even if this assumption is made, whether it is necessary for the theoretical issue under consideration. The problem is not so much to establish that the different social classes have similar aspirations in order to show that their limited educational and occupational attainment is a function of the opportunity structure. Rather, the problem is to establish whether or not the lower classes have any aspirations to move beyond their present situation *regardless of the object of their aspirations*. It is then in the reorganization of an opportunity structure, *not an individual,* that different goal objects are brought into the "reality space" of collections of individuals.

Some of these considerations are to be found in the work of Empey who recognized the importance of avoiding an absolute standard of occupational aspiration as indicative of the desire to "get ahead" (Empey, 1956). Measuring both the relative and absolute aspirations of a state-wide sample of high school seniors, Empey found that while the "lower-class youngsters aspired to get ahead, they aspired to occupations at different status levels than those from higher strata" (1956, p. 708).

Yet while Empey's work was important, its contribution is limited to demonstrating that lower class aspirations did exist if they were measured with reference to their own level as the starting point. The particular *quality* of these aspirations, however, was little explored. Thus, little advance was made toward explaining either the variation in aspirations that occurs among persons with similar values and from similar social strata or the variation that occurs across social strata. The focus upon between-class differences in aspirations resulted in explanatory systems that emphasized a combination of cultural differences and limiting objective conditions. Such explanations proved inadequate in the light of findings of the type obtained by Stephenson, and again by Empey, which did not substantiate the low aspirations of the lower classes. Further inadequacies were revealed when an interest developed in explaining within-class differences, as in the Kahl study.

Much of what has been discussed so far concerning values and aspirations affecting mobility has accounted for only a portion of the variation between the classes. The existence of differential values or levels of aspiration between the classes cannot help to explain the absence of mobility among persons of social classes with values favorable to mobility, nor can it help to explain the presence of mobility among persons in social classes where values unfavorable to mobility predominate. In order to advance our understanding in this connection we shall have to move beyond values, to a consideration of motivations and behavior patterns that may be a basic part of the personality system. An examination of personality differences, if any do in fact exist among the social classes, will help to determine whether the different social classes have "built-in" mobility-enhancing or inhibiting factors. We assume that the factors that we shall speak of here have a "deeper" and more permanent effect upon behavior than values absorbed through the social structures in which one is involved. The factors we speak of are "deferred gratification pattern" and "achievement motive."

Over a decade ago, Schneider and Lysgaard sought to reconceptualize a variety of isolated and unrelated behaviors found in the middle and lower classes along a single meaningful dimension (1953). Many class-related behaviors reported by other investigators seemed to "cluster" according to whether or not they indicated a tendency to postpone or defer immediate gratifications. Schneider and Lysgaard described this clustering as follows:

"The lower-class-characteristic 'impulse-following' (absence of deferred gratification pattern) involves: relative readiness to engage in physical violence, free sexual expression (as through intercourse), minimum pursuit of education, low aspiration level, failure of the parents to identify the class of their children's playmates, free spending, little emphasis on being 'well-mannered and obedient,' and short-time dependence upon parents. On the other hand, the middle-class-characteristic 'impulse renunciation' (presence of deferred gratification pattern) involves the reverse of these traits. . . ." (1953, p. 143.)

Using a national sample of 2,500 high school students, they sought to measure the distribution of class attitudes toward the various dimensions of the deferred gratification pattern. Their findings indicate general support for the hypothesis of a class-related pattern, with those students who identified themselves as "working class" being less inclined to endorse attitudes and indicate behaviors that are dimensions of the deferred gratification pattern. The important question raised by these findings is the extent to which such normatively defined cultural patterns of gratification postponement have their counterpart in personality patterns. Answers to this type of question would have to be sought through psychological tests which might be able to get at a personality configuration going beyond class-based social roles and culture patterns. Such studies are, of course, fraught with methodological and theoretical difficulties. It is difficult to carry out adequate testing with a sufficient number of subjects to make reliable within-class and between-class comparisons.

One of the earliest attempts to use formal psychological testing in stratification research was undertaken by Bernard Rosen (1956) in a study of male sophomores from two large public high schools in New Haven, Connecticut. Rosen's main concern was to explore both the psychological and cultural factors that affect mobility by influencing the individual's willingness to develop and exploit his talents and opportunities. The central factors for Rosen are achievement motive and achievement value orientation. The personality correlate of achievement called "achievement motive" was measured with a Thematic Apperception Test developed by McClelland and his associates (McClelland, et al., 1953). Following standard TAT procedures each subject was asked to tell a story about a set of ambiguous pictures presented to him. The scoring of achievement content in the stories was based upon respondent's story description which discussed an individual's performance in the story within the context of competition with a standard of excellence. That performance is also evaluated by the respondent with a statement showing a positive judgment and approval of the performance in question.

Rosen's findings clearly support his hypothesis that the social classes differ in the strength of the "achievement motive." The mean achievement scores were highest for students in Classes I and II, and declined markedly through Class V (8.40, 8.69, 4.97, 3.40, 1.87. Class I represents the "highest" class and Class V the "lowest." The procedures for classification are reported in Hollingshead and Redlich, 1958). Rosen also reports that over 80 percent of the Class I and II students have high motivation scores, whereas only 23 percent of Class V have high scores. The achievement value orientation scores were also found to decline with social class (4.6, 4.1, 3.8, 3.0, 2.5) and to be quite consistent with the findings of Hyman described earlier. The subjects in higher class groupings were more likely to endorse items showing an activistic, future-oriented, individualistic point of view, which, it is assumed, are most likely to facilitate achievement and social mobility.

Although Rosen clearly established a connection between social class and achievement motive, the hypothesis of a link between achievement motive and mobility remained essentially untested. Since Rosen found some within-class variation in achievement motive, it is possible that this variation is related to the downward mobility of some upper-class individuals and the upward mobility of some lower-class individuals. An exploration of the achievement motive–mobility hypothesis was undertaken by Crockett (1962) in which he closely followed the procedures of Rosen and McClelland in establishing strength of achievement motive. Working with a national probability sample of adult males, Crockett's design allowed for comparisons of high and low achievement motive scores for respondents of four occupational origins (High, Upper-Middle, Lower-Middle, Low) and three mobility levels (occupational prestige below that of father, same as father, and above father). In this way the role of achievement motive can be examined for both upward and downward mobility.

Crockett's findings clearly suggest that achievement motive, as measured by thematic apperception, is an important personality factor related to occupational mobility. Specifically, the findings show "strength of achievement motive clearly related to upward mobility among sons of fathers in the two lower prestige categories but not among sons of fathers in the two higher prestige categories" (Crockett, 1962, p. 203). No relationship was found between strength of achievement motive and downward mobility. Such findings point to the complexities involved in trying to isolate both individual and social fatcors related to mobility. They suggest that achievement motive may be a multidimensional factor in which different dimensions are operative among different social strata (Kahl, 1965). It certainly makes a good deal of sense that the objective conditions of the relatively lower classes are such that exceptional individual qualities are required to move out of such conditions. It is much like the situation in baseball: there should be no great surprise that the first Negro ballplayer had exceptional talent; the nature of the barriers that he had to hurdle required nothing less.

Before exploring further this possibility of a multidimensional nature for achievement motive, let us first consider the extent to which a number of individual factors related to mobility seem to "hang together." Such efforts at seeking patterns of predictors not only attest to the validity of the individual predictors but also provide for greater continuity in research. We have examined the deferred gratification pattern and achievement motive, suggesting their relationship to social class and mobility. What of the relationship between these factors? Are they two different elements involved in mobility or are they two ways of measuring the same thing?

Straus, in a study of 338 high school juniors and seniors in Wisconsin, sought to examine the link between social class, deferred gratification, and achievement syndrome (Straus, 1962). A prior concern, however, was to retest the Schneider and Lysgaard social-class-deferred gratification hypothesis and to see whether "The deferment of such diverse needs as those for affiliation, agression, material goods, independence, and sex fall into a *pattern* . . . [such a pattern would] imply that deferment of any one of these needs tends to be correlated with deferment of the others, particularly in the middle class" (Straus, 1962, p. 328).

A Guttman scale was developed for each of the need areas and these scales were intercorrelated, revealing a tendency for the "deferred gratification scales to fall into two clusters, one representing deferment of interpersonal interaction needs, and the other representing deferment of material needs" (*ibid.*, p. 336). Correlations between deferred gratification and socioeconomic status do not indicate any significant relationships, contrary to the Schneider and Lysgaard findings.

In looking at achievement, Straus used indicators such as academic achievement and occupational aspiration rather than the thematic apperception procedures of Rosen and Crockett. Deferred gratification pattern was found to be related to achievement, as was socioeconomic status. In fact, the correlation between the DGP scale and achievement was found to persist independently of socioeconomic status and intelligence. Thus Straus concludes that "learning to defer need gratification seems to be associated with achievement at all levels of the status hierarchy . . ." (*ibid.*, p. 335).

What, then, may we conclude from the studies relating values, intelligence, aspirations, and achievement motive to social class and social mobility? Beliefs and values that are assumed to have a positive effect upon social mobility have been found to be class-related. The lower classes are described by Hyman as placing less emphasis upon success and upon those patterns of behavior that are likely to result in success. This view would tend to locate many of the causes of immobility within the individual himself. There are others, however, who have preferred to emphasize similarities in values and aspirations among the social classes while pointing to the objective conditions that inhibit their attainment (Merton, 1957, Chap. IV). A recent study by Mizruchi has pointed to the fact that while the goals of "success" and "education" are equally shared throughout the class hierarchy, there are different meanings attached to these goals (Mizruchi, 1964). The classes differ in terms of the symbolic indicators of success valued, and in terms of their view of education as having intrinsic value or as an instrumental means for advancement.

The *pattern* of the relationship between social class and success found by Mizruchi—that the same variable, i.e., success, has different meanings at various levels of class—is similar to that found in other studies discussed in this section. We found, for example, that intelligence and social status provide a good prediction for college aspiration; this is especially the case for both the extremes of intelligence and social status where predictions regarding college aspirations were best. For persons in the middle status and middle intelligence groups, however, prediction of college aspirations on this basis were no better than chance (Kahl, 1960). A similar pattern is revealed when trying to relate personality variables to social mobility. Achievement motive, achievement values, and deferred gratification were all found to be related to social class and to each other. However, when relating achievement motive to occupational mobility we find strength of achievement motive related to mobility among the lower strata but not among the upper strata. In addition, achievement motive is not found to be related to downward mobility.

The "uneven" nature of the findings discussed above attests to the complexity of social data. Simple main effects of one variable upon another neither explain a significant amount of variance nor accurately represent the real world. In explaining social phenomena we often find that two variables in combination (interaction effects) produce consequences that are quite different from each variable taken singly (main effects). In addition, the interaction effect is "uneven," in that it produces certain effects only at specified levels of a variable. Thus, achievement motive was significantly related to mobility at certain levels of social class.

There are several methodological and theoretical steps that can be taken to cope with the apparent complexity of the phenomena of mobility. First of all it appears that many of the things we have been talking about and measuring as achievement orientation and deferred gratification are not unitary but multidimensional phenomena. This is certainly suggested by Straus (1962), who showed that the component parts of the deferred gratification pattern actually form two clusters rather than one, and more recently by Kahl (1965), who factor-analyzed achievement-type items from a number of studies. This being the case, it might help to explain some of the inconsistencies in findings from different studies, and in the "uneven" nature of these findings.

With methodological refinement may come theoretical explanations of mobility that are specific to persons located at various levels of the social structure. Youth from upper strata, for example, may not need strong personal motivation for mobility because they often operate in quite structured and determinate careers that are more a function of factors external to the individual. They are, so to speak, carried along by wise decisions, each of which provides an increment to the probability of achievement of high position in the occupational hierarchy. Such decisions as going to college, type of college, type of career, what fraternity, and the like, are more related to the general way of life of one's environment than personal drive. The lower class youth, on the other hand, must learn to make these decisions, and the very process of learning itself may eliminate their possible effectiveness. The "naturalness" of the behavior of the high status person in contrast to the self-conscious striver is well put by Kahl:

"Those with more education strive less openly and vigorously, but they have other values that in fact aid them in reaching or maintaining a level of occupational success higher than that obtained by the 'striver.' They trust in people and are thus able to develop long-term relationships that aid their careers, particularly in bureaucratic structures where the judgments of peers are so crucial. They believe that planning for the future is possible and fruitful; thus not only people but 'destiny' can be relied upon. They are willing to move away from their parents in order to accept career advancement, and in general put efficiency ahead of nepotism. These values are more subtle than open striving, yet are more directly connected with success." (Kahl, 1965, p. 677.)

With the general tendency toward greater cultural homogeneity among persons throughout the social structure, as well as the increasing number of persons from low status origins who go on to college and fill high status occupations, research concerning values and motivations related to mobility will have to delve for the more subtle differences and dimensions of values and motivations that have generally remained hidden in earlier efforts.

The Structural Context of Mobility

The role of values, aspirations, and motivation as positive or negative factors in the mobility process is clearly of considerable importance. But it is only a part of the story. Values and aspirations have their origin within specific group contexts, and they are encouraged, nourished, or extinguished in these same contexts. Networks of social relationships, or social structures, are the paths through which ideas concerning mobility are transmitted. Yet social structures do more than simply channel and transmit values to those persons implicated within them. They also generate their own peculiar set of inducements and constraints upon the mobility process. Families of varying size and composition can create bonds of kinship so strong as to inhibit any motivation to "leave" one's family of origin. Community size and structure can affect the existing opportunity structure and, as a result, the individual's perception of and aspiration for occupational mobility. School climates, in terms of pupils, faculty, and curriculum, are also a significant set of constraints upon the mobility process. In this section we shall examine some of the structural contexts in which the desire, expectation, and opportunity for mobility are found.

Let us begin with a view of social structure as a set of channels for the transmission of mobility-relevant values and aspirations. Since social structures represent patterns of social relationships that persist over time, the information transmitted through the relationship networks will have a tendency to maintain and reinforce established patterns of living. In the case of the social structure of stationary lower class families, for example, we may offer the following structural explanation for intergenerational immobility: Given unfavorable conditions for real improvement, individuals will adapt in such fashion as to reduce occupational and educational aspirations. These initial adaptations develop supportive values and norms which take on their own reasons for existence and are transmitted through established networks of social relationships. With this separate existence as cultural patterns, values and norms which emerged as adaptive responses now function to perpetuate immobility.

Stated in this form, such a description of intergenerational immobility does not provide a good fit to reality. There is enough upward and downward mobility in all classes to indicate that social structures must also transmit values and aspirations that are not in keeping with the dominant values of a particular class. How is it that some lower class youth endorse values and aspirations that are the modal patterns of another social stratum? What are the mechanisms by which values which move through one social structure are transmitted through another social structure? Are there particular persons in a social structure who are the "carriers" of foreign values and who provide the necessary support for the maintenance of these values?

One of the main channels for the transmission of mobility values to lower class youth is to be found in families characterized by "status discrepancies"; a situation where either the wife is of higher status than her husband, or where the husband has been downwardly mobile. In either case, a "tension" is set up whereby dissatisfaction with present conditions is of such dimension as to impel parents to teach their children about the importance of education and self-advancement. In the work of Kahl discussed earlier, the father was singled out as an important factor in determining whether boys from minor white-collar or skilled labor families were interested in college.

"In most instances the parents who believed in getting ahead were somewhat frustrated in their own degree of success: father had not reached the place in the hierarchy that he had expected and desired. *He blamed his failure on insufficient education, and was determined that his son would do better.* By contrast, the parents who believed in merely getting by were adjusted to their way of life and saw no reason to influence their sons to live differently." (Kahl, 1960, p. 287.)

The father, however, has not enjoyed the same position of importance concerning his children's mobility as has the mother. This is likely due to the greater amount of time available to the mother to influence her children. In examining studies concerning the role of family size, sibling position, and relations with parents in mobility, Lipset and Bendix (1959) state that "one might summarize the implications of these studies for social mobility by saying that all factors which intensify the involvement of a child with his parents or other adults, and reduce his involvement with other children, increase the likelihood that he will be upwardly mobile" (p. 239).

The mother has been found to be much more influential in the decision to attend college among lower-status males and females (Ellis and Lane, 1963). In over one-third of these same lower-status homes, the mother's education was found to be markedly superior to the father's. (p. 774). In this same connection, working-class high school students (in terms of father's occupation) are more likely to have college plans when the mother is employed in nonmanual work than if she is unemployed or employed in manual work. Similarly, when the mother's educational attainments are higher than the working-class father who has completed high school, the child's positive interest in college is markedly affected. This pattern has much greater influence upon college plans than if the mother has married "up" or if father and mother are both high school graduates (Krauss, 1964).

Kahl's findings that the father was the most significant figure in mobility aspirations are not necessarily contradicted by those reported by Ellis and Lane, Krauss, and Lipset and Bendix. Both sets of findings may be seen as part of a general feature of dissatisfaction with present status conditions. The father who is frustrated by his own failures may be even more painfully aware of them when his wife's higher status origins or educational attainments stand as a constant reminder. In other words, it may be much less important which family member is the prime carrier of achievement values than that some family member performs this function.

In addition to discrepant status conditions within the family as producers of "deviant" values, relationships with members of high status groups can also operate as channels for mobility values. Contact with a wide range of persons outside the family has been shown to be of considerable importance in the mobility plans of lower status youth. Nonfamilial influences of adults in general, and high school teachers in particular, were very strong among low status college students as compared to high status youth (Ellis and Lane, 1963). College-oriented working-class youths were also found to have college-oriented friends, to be active in school activities, and to have greater exposure to middle-class youth than were noncollege-oriented working-class youth (Krauss, 1964).

Simpson (1962) sought to examine the effects of parental and peer influence upon the aspirations of working-class and middle-class boys. Both parents and peers were found to independently influence mobility aspirations among working-class boys and less strongly among boys from the middle class. In examining the relative influence of the two factors, the parents seemed to be much more important than peers.

The structural patterns suggest a very interesting tendency among mobile lower-class youth, as compared to middle-class youth, to look outside the family for information, advice, and support for upward mobility. This tendency seems to be related to the functional role played by loose family ties in the process of mobility. Strodtbeck (1958), for example, has pointed to the manner in which "familism" values interfere with mobility values and result in lower achievement among Italians as compared to Jews. Involvement in extended family relationships and concern with leaving the family as a result of job mobility has also been found to limit mobility and migration among persons in rural depressed areas (Perrucci and Iwamoto, 1966). Thus it appears that structural supports for mobility outside the family may also reinforce the need of the mobile person to leave behind old established ties and take on new ties (Lipset and Bendix, 1959, p. 249; Blau, 1956).

To this point in this section we have stressed the significance of social structure for mobility in terms of the capacity of various social structures to provide channels for transmitting mobility-oriented values and aspirations. However, structural contexts are important for understanding mobility not only from the point of view of value transmission, but for their capacity for providing personal qualities, skills, self-confidence, personal control, and independence as a function of the type of relationships that children are exposed to. A family structure, for example, can become the "small society" in which the child learns the rules for coping with, adapting to, or mastering relationships in the larger society. As Strodtbeck has put it in his study of mobility among Italians and Jews:

"The general question is: what is the arrangement of power and support among the three roles of father, mother and son which is maximally related to attitudes for achievement and to subsequent adjustment to success outside the family? . . . .

"Two possible ways in which power relationships may affect a boy's subsequent achievement immediately suggest themselves. The first involves the ease with which the son identifies with his father. Proper father-identification, which is probably related to adequate performance in the male role, could very well be facilitated or inhibited by different power relationships among father, mother and son. The second concerns the fact that the power distribution in the family will condition the way a boy expects power to be distributed in the outside world, and that his adjustment to family power will, therefore, generalize to external systems." (Strodtbeck, 1958, pp. 147–148.)

Strodtbeck's findings on the role of family relationships in mobility are most revealing. Italian and Jewish boys who were more likely to believe the world was subject to rational mastery and independent achievement were those who reported democratic relationships with their father and equalitarian relationships between parents. Perhaps even more interesting is the finding that the son's achievement and mastery values are correlated with the nature of the power relationships but not with whether the father held the values of mastery and achievement. In effect, the father's pattern of relationships with other family members—in this case, father domination—serves to negate the very values he might seek to transmit in his relationships with his son. As Strodtbeck most pointedly puts it: "The son is more likely, at least in this stage of life, to resign himself to the notion that there are forces beyond his control—in this instance, father" (Strodtbeck, 1958, p. 189). Such findings are not only suggestive for understanding upward mobility among lower status sons, where equalitarian family relationships are less likely to occur, but also for understanding downward mobility among sons of high status parents. The successful and demanding father can be a forbidding figure more likely to encourage withdrawal from the game rather than active involvement in the pursuit of success.

More general support for these findings is found in a study of the effect of parental dominance upon educational attainment of persons in the United States, Great Britain, West Germany, Italy, and Mexico (Elder, 1965). Parental dominance in adolescence was found to reduce the likelihood of secondary school attendance in all five nations. Important limitations on these findings were found under conditions of a limited opportunity structure as in rural Mexico and Italy. In addition, the application of a controlled analysis with the U.S. sample (controlling by social class, religion, and region of birth) results in no relationship between family structure and educational attainment. Thus, Elder's analysis suggests the need for further work in order to establish the generality of Strodtbeck's findings.

The final structural context related to the encouragement and transmission of mobility-related values and aspirations is that of school climate. In speaking of school climate we are interested in two things. The first is the normative climate of the school, which in large part is related to the characteristics of the student body. Does the particular social composition of the student body provide a normative environment that becomes a constraining force on the values, aspirations, and performance of individual students? Our second interest turns attention away from the student, to the teachers and type and quality of curriculum and instruction.

One of the most extensive and systematic investigations of school climate and its effects upon education is Coleman's study of the social structure and value climate of ten high schools in northern Illinois (Coleman, 1961). Among the more important findings was that school climates, as exemplified by those students who were the social elites and members of leading crowds, contained a strong emphasis upon social activities, sports and popularity as contrasted with intellectual activity. Such value emphases were found to exist in the working-class school and the upper-middle class school as well. To quote Coleman:

"As has been evident throughout this research, the variation among schools in the status of scholastic achievement is not nearly so striking as the fact that in all of them, academic achievement did not 'count' for as much as did other activities in the school. Many other attributes were more important. In every school the boys named as best athletes and those named as most popular with girls were far more often mentioned as members of the leading crowd, and as someone to 'be like' than were the boys named as best students. And the girls who were named as best dressed, and those named as most popular with boys, were in every school far more often mentioned as being in the leading crowd and as someone to be like, than were the girls named as best students.

"The relative unimportance of academic achievement, . . . , suggests that the adolescent subcultures in these schools exert a rather strong deterrent to academic achievement." (Coleman, 1961, p. 265.)

The existence of such adolescent subcultures in high schools is important for understanding mobility. For the lower-class youth, such an environment simply becomes an added barrier to his own mobility. For if he relies more heavily upon sources outside the family for support of mobility aspirations as suggested earlier, the nonintellectual high school climate operates as a mobility inhibiting factor. Or to put it another way, if he is to get support for intellectual values through involvement with others of similar inclination, he does so at the expense of lowered status within the school status system. As a double burden, he would probably also lose status among his lower-class peers outside the school for his interest in things intellectual.

The middle-class youth, on the other hand, may not "suffer" as much from such a school climate. It is possible that the adolescent subculture is a luxury he can afford, at least from the point of view of the likelihood that it will lead away from a college career. Since he is more likely to have mobility-inducing support from the family, not to mention the economic resources which make higher education an established expectation, there will be a discrepancy between the adolescent and adult world in which mobility-inhibiting values are not reinforced. And perhaps most important is that Coleman's findings refer to the pursuit of high standards of academic achievement which, while important for the encouragement and fostering of exceptional talent, is not necessarily related to expectations regarding college attendance and occupational aspirations. Thus, the middle-class boy can devalue intellectual pursuits without impairing his desire to go to college (for he may find the college and high school environments to be quite similar), but the lower-class youth who devalues intellectual pursuits is too apt to find ready sources of support and reinforcement for devaluing education.

If we turn to the effect of high school climate upon college aspirations, we can see how the social milieu of school exerts a thrust upon educational and occupational aspirations which is independent of an individual's social position. The importance of the social class composition of the school has been found to affect educational aspirations very dramatically. In a study of thirteen California high schools which were grouped according to dominant class composition, Wilson found students with similar I.Q., grades, and social backgrounds but in different schools expressing different college aspirations (Wilson, 1959). Sons of professionals in upper-white-collar schools are more likely to aspire to go to college than sons of professionals in blue-collar schools. Similarly, sons of manual workers in upper-white-collar schools are more likely to aspire to go to college than sons of manual workers in blue-collar schools. Perhaps even more significant is the fact that manual workers' sons in upper-white-collar schools aspire to go to college in the same proportions as professionals' sons in blue-collar schools. This suggests that the normative climate of the school with reference to college aspiration operates to "neutralize" the effect of social class origins upon aspirations expressed.

The same pattern is found for students of different achievement levels (grades and I.Q.). Aspirations of high-achievers decline as the class composition of the school goes from predominately upper white collar to predominantly manual.

That a normative climate is apparently based upon the social majority in a school was also established by Coleman's work. Coleman contrasted two different theories to explain the emergence of high school leaders and heroes of different social origins; the "majority-group" theory and the "privileged-class" theory. If the former were true, then working-class schools would choose their elites from among these with working-class backgrounds, and middle-class schools would choose elites with middle-class backgrounds. (As Coleman put it: "The elites would exemplify in the extreme the characteristics of the dominant group in the population"). In "privilege-group" theory on the other hand it is assumed that students would tend to select their elites from social levels higher than their own.

Coleman's data tends to support majority-group theory in that leading members are more likely to be selected from the group with the characteristics of the majority whether low class or high. As Coleman states:

"The leading crowd of a school, and thus the norms which that crowd sets, is more than merely a reflection of the student body, with extra middle-class students thrown in. The leading crowd tends to accentuate those very background characteristics already dominant, whether they be upper- or lower class. A boy or girl in such a system, then, finds it governed by an elite whose backgrounds exemplify, in the extreme, those of the dominant population group. In particular, a working class boy or girl will be most left out in an upper-middle-class school, least so in a school with few middle-class students." (Coleman, 1961, p. 109.)

The tendency to extend majority-group characteristics into established normative climates is apparently a condition that is most likely to be produced by relatively homogeneous schools. Patterns of residential segregation which have their counterpart in socially segregated schools greatly encourage the trend toward homogeneity (Rhodes, Reiss, and Duncan, 1965).

What of the second aspect of school climate that we set out to examine? Do socially segregated schools do more than affect the normative climate of a school regarding educational aspirations? It is highly likely, of course, that school climate is related to the character and quality of education that a school provides. If a shabby curriculum and poorly motivated teachers coexist with a student-based normative climate which does not value education, then there are present all the ingredients for "vicious circles" and "self-fulfilling prophecies" concerning poor motivation, poor education, and poor performance. There is, unfortunately, very little direct evidence concerning variations in the character and quality of instruction of schools of different socioeconomic composition. However, some indirect evidence on the point is suggestive.

The quality of instruction provided by a school is a result of the combined contribution of physical facilities, teachers, and curricula. One crude way of indexing the quality of physical facilities is through the age of school buildings. The age of buildings is, in turn, a geographic accident, related to the patterns of growth in an urban area. The central areas of the city are most likely to be the oldest sections, as well as the place of residence of low income groups. Patricia Sexton, in her examination of school facilities in a Midwestern city, indicates that the age of school buildings is associated with the level of income in an area. School buildings in low income areas are almost twice as old as the buildings found in higher income areas (Sexton, 1961, p. 124). In addition to the relation of age of buildings to income, there is a suggestion that the facilities of the school—such as those related to curriculum, recreation, and health—are also associated with income.

Poor physical facilities in a school can have a greater negative effect upon quality of instruction through its effect upon the teachers recruited to teach in such schools. Sexton reported that low income schools had a higher proportion of the total teaching time carried by "substitute" teachers. Although substitute teaching does not imply lower standards of teaching competence, it may be related to motivational levels concerning such things as commitment to teaching and identification with students. And if, as has been suggested, teacher-pupil relations are more difficult with children from low income areas, the teacher with low motivation is most likely to perpetuate patterns of differential treatment by following the path of least resistance in contacts with pupils (Becker, 1953).

In addition to the effect that low income areas may have on the quality of instruction, we also find such areas related to variations in curriculum emphasis and the availability of college-oriented curricula. A content analysis of textbooks in civic education programs in three schools revealed different views of the political process associated with the socioeconomic composition of the schools. Most significantly, the material presented in the working class school did not "encourage a belief in the citizen's ability to influence government action through political participation" (Litt, 1963, p. 74). The material in middle class schools, on the other hand, stressed political participation as a means of influencing political processes and political decision-making. The implications of such findings suggest a perpetuation of the problems of low income areas that are related to indifference to the community and low political involvement.

The characteristics of schools in low income areas lead to a series of problems in meeting the educational needs of deprived and segregated children. These problems were presented by David Street as follows:

"a. A shortage and inflexibility in the use of resources, which limit many school systems in providing adequate remedial and counseling services, sufficiently decreasing or varying class size, instituting new programs, or taking other needed actions.

"b. The general tendency toward traditionalism and inflexibility in school system operations. In the big cities, administrative organization and bureaucratic control often limit the possibilities for creative innovation. In all systems there is a tendency to rely on traditional practices; for example, the recruitment criteria for school personnel are defined narrowly, usually so that professional educators are the only adults allowed inside the classroom, and teachers spend almost all of their in-school time teaching, with little time for planning, contacts with colleagues or in-service training.

"c. Curricula and teaching often are inadequate. Teaching tends to be formally academic and restricted by rigid concepts of graded materials and course work, and teachers often spend their time 'presenting material' rather than stimulating the development of inquiry, initiative, interest, courage, and industry among the students. Textbooks and other curricular materials frequently fail to capture the imagination of the students, many of whom simply find school a bore.

"d. The school is especially inadequate in adjusting to lower-class children. The expectations of the school are middle-class, involving the application of tried-and-true teaching techniques to 'normal' children. Because the difficult 30 percent are not normal in terms of school's expectations, the result is often simply to lower standards and to assume that the school can produce only poorly with such poor students. The lower-class child may have verbal virtuosity in the language of his own culture and may have high imagination, creativity, spontaneity, and aggressiveness, but there is little opportunity for him to use these attributes in the school. When the gap between cultures is not bridged, the child often fails to have any substantial success in school as a basis for the development of attitudes of trust and self-respect.

"e. The school's relationship to the community often is inadequate. Frequently, there is weak coordination between the school system and those community agencies that are also involved with the child and family. Further, the school often is unable to communicate effectively to parents and help educate them in ways to make the total environment of the child more supportive of the goals of education." (Street, 1965, pp. 9–10.)

Educational innovations in organization, personnel, curricula and community participation are required to meet some of the special problems of the child from lower socioeconomic areas. Different strategies will be required for different problems, but effective solutions will in large part depend upon the coordinated activities of programs directed to various levels of the problem.

STRATIFICATION AND HIGHER EDUCATION

Up to this point we have limited our attention to those factors that aid or inhibit a person's access to education, the major means for social mobility in American society. In particular, the focus has been limited to socioeconomic effects on persistence and performance in secondary schools in terms of their relationship to gaining access to higher education. The intention at this point is to continue to examine the effects of socioeconomic factors upon persistence in college, the character of college environments, and postcollege performance in terms of success. A half-century ago, it would have been unnecessary to continue our analysis at this point since the relatively small numbers of high school graduates and college admissions almost guaranteed persistence in college and postcollege success. In recent decades, however, we have witnessed a marked expansion in college attendance, especially among youth from socioeconomic strata that formerly did not have access to college.

This expansion in college enrollments has had one effect in introducing great diversity into the college environment. It is probably safe to assume that in the era of small enrollments, the college population was composed of persons of similar social, economic, and intellective characteristics. With expanding enrollments has come greater diversity in levels of aspiration, motivation, economic level, and social level of students. It is this diversity which has also altered the values-mobility sequence that we spoke of earlier, so that it is no longer possible to infer certain values from knowledge of college attendance. The added burden of the "screening function" of the present-day college has been a partial response to expanding enrollments and has also shown a class-related pattern. Students who leave college early before obtaining the degree are most likely to be students from lower socioeconomic origins (Eckland, 1964).

The Paradox of Expanding Educational Opportunities

The main thesis of this section is that while expansion of enrollments at the college level have resulted in larger proportions of working-class youth in colleges and universities, we have at the same time moved to a more rigidly class-based system of stratification *within* the framework of higher education. The stratification has manifested itself in the overinvolvement of working-class college graduates in certain occupations as well as in certain types of colleges, and in the combined impact of both social origins and the nature of college attended upon postcollege performance and success. That this more subtle type of stratification takes place within the general trend of expanding opportunities in higher education is what accounts for its relative "invisibility." The consequences of a class-based allocation system *within* higher education are as serious in terms of wasted human resources as a class-based allocation system for entering higher education.

Evidence from a number of studies indicates that college students of certain social origins are differentially recruited into certain occupations (Charters, 1963). A rank ordering in terms of prestige and income of professional occupations such as medicine, law, college teaching, engineering, nursing, secondary teachers reveals an inverse rank ordering of the same occupations in terms of proportion of practitioners coming from working-class origins. The highest prestige and income professions have the smallest proportions of persons from blue-collar origins. Two recent national studies of college graduates provide general support for the correlation between social origins and field of study. A National Science Foundation study of 40,000 persons who received their degrees in June, 1958, from 1,200 degree-granting institutions revealed that major field of study and father's occupation were associated for male students (1963). Sons of white-collar fathers were more likely to be found in natural science and business and commerce majors, while sons of blue-collar fathers were more likely to be found in education majors (*ibid.*, p. 28). These patterns of undergraduate majors are also reflected in type of school attended. Boys from lower occupational origins were more likely to be found attending teacher's colleges, while those of higher occupational origins were more likely to be found attending universities or liberal arts colleges for men. No consistent differences are found between father's occupation and attendance at coeducational liberal arts colleges or universities. This last category is the largest one and in its present form is too gross a classification to be of any meaningful value for our purposes.

These class-based career choices which, as we have just seen, begin their development at the undergraduate level (although they obviously have their roots in quality of high school attended and curriculum selected) also continue to shape career plans at the graduate level. A National Opinion Research Center study of some 34,000 June, 1961, graduates from 135 colleges and universities reports that plans for graduate study are significantly associated with father's income, occupation, and education (Davis, 1964, p. 105). Curiously, the effect of social origins upon plans for graduate work are most pronounced among students in the top fifth on an academic performance index. Among the top students, about 25 percent more sons of professionals plan to do graduate study than sons of unskilled workers. This difference drops to 16 percent among "above average" students, and further declines to only six percent among students from the "bottom half" of the academic performance index (*ibid.*, p. 108).

Among students who do plan to go on to graduate study, the choice of graduate field is related to social origins. The graduate fields with the highest proportion of students from high socioeconomic backgrounds were law and medicine, while the lowest proportions of such students were in engineering and education (*ibid.*, p. 188).

It is difficult to give a satisfactory explanation for the emergence of class-based career decisions in undergraduate and graduate schools. One thing apparent in the Davis study is that class-based career choices do not develop because of class differences in ability. Students with high academic performance were drawn in almost equal proportions from high and low socioeconomic origins (*ibid.*, p. 30). Thus the class-based occupational streams must be related to such things as financial obstacles that certain fields of study present (and this may again be reflected in school attended) and in motivational factors. Davis suggests that his data point to financial obstacles as one of the most important deterrents to immediate advanced study (*ibid.*, p. 118).

Closely related to class-based careers, and perhaps in large part responsible for them, is the existence of great prestige differentiation among institutions of higher learning and the possible relationship between this differentiation and the social origins of their students. This prestige differentiation among schools has served to produce an "institutional effect" which makes an independent contribution, either positive or negative, to the postcollege performance of their graduates. This "institutional effect" may either enhance individual factors such as ability and motivation in contributing to successful postcollege performance, or it may "neutralize" the contribution of individual factors to individual success.

The first systematic examination of the role of the institution attended in effecting a graduate's success was undertaken by *Time Magazine* and The Bureau of Applied Social Research at Columbia University, and reported by Havemann and West. In a chapter entitled "Princeton Versus Podunk," the authors group schools in a rough prestige ranking represented by the Big Three (Harvard, Yale, Princeton), other Ivy League (Columbia, Cornell, Dartmouth, Pennsylvania), Seventeen Technical Schools (California, Carnegie, Case, Detroit, Drexel, Georgia, Illinois, Massachusetts, and Stevens Institute of Technology; Rensselaer, Rose Virginia, and Worcester Polytechnic Institutes; Clarkson College of Technology, Cooper Union, Polytechnic Institute of Brooklyn, Tri-State College), Twenty Famous Eastern Colleges (Amherst, Bates, Bowdoin, Brown, Clark, Colby, Franklin and Marshall, Hamilton, Haverford, Hobart, Lafayette, Lehigh, Middleburg, Rutgers, Swarthmore, Trinity, Tufts, Union, Wesleyan of

Connecticut, Williams), The Big Ten (Chicago, Illinois, Indiana, Iowa, Michigan, Minnesota, Northwestern, Ohio State, Purdue, Wisconsin), all other Midwest Colleges, and all other Eastern Colleges (Havemann and West, 1952, p. 178). The median incomes of the male graduates in each group is positively associated with the prestige ranking, reaching a maximum differential between the top and bottom schools of about $3,000. The same pattern of relationship is found to hold even for specific occupations; business graduates from high prestige schools earned more, as did education graduates.

Even individual characteristics such as academic achievement and social origins were found to be influenced by the "institutional effect." Concerning the relative importance of academic achievement and institution attended, the authors state:

"Although we have noted that good grades may at least sometimes lead to good incomes, it develops that even the poorest students from the Ivy League share in the general prosperity—and do better than the best students from other schools. Of the Ivy Leaguers who just got by— the C and D students—42 percent had reached the $7,500 level. Of the A students from the Big Ten only 37 percent had hit that mark, and only 23 percent of the A students from 'all other Midwest' colleges. Even the great financial disadvantage of a general education, rather than a specific one, does not seem to hold back the Ivy Leaguers. Of the Ivy League humanities majors, 46 percent had reached the $7,500 bracket, and of the social scientists 50 percent. But even among the Big Ten's engineering graduates, with their highly specific training and all the advantages that . . . go with it, only 23 percent had reached the $7,500 level.

"What all this amounts to is that the differences in earning power between graduates of rich and famous schools and those from small obscure schools are so great that they override everything else. Earning power rises steadily with each increase in wealth and prestige of the school. At the extremes, the Ivy League graduates do best of all financially even when they make poor grades and take a general rather than specific course, both of which are ordinarily handicaps—while the graduates of the smallest schools do not get up to the averages even when they make fine grades and take the type of specific courses which ordinarily produce the biggest incomes." (*Ibid.*, p. 180).

It also appears that the different types of institutions select students from different social and economic origins. If the proportion of graduates who earned more than half of their college expenses is used as an index of the socioeconomic composition of a school, we find that the prestige ranking of Havemann and West's closely corresponds to the proportions of students who work their way through college. The proportion for the Ivy League is about one-fifth; about one-quarter for the eastern and technical schools; over one-third for other eastern colleges; over two-fifths for the Big Ten schools; and about one-half for the students from other Midwest colleges (*ibid.*, p. 182). When the earning power of students of similar economic backgrounds who go to different schools is compared, it appears that the "institutional effect" again influences earnings. Students of lower economic backgrounds (earning more than half of their college expenses) from higher prestige schools earn more than their counterparts from less prestigious schools. The independent contribution of economic background and school prestige to earning power reveals some mixed findings. Low economic status and high prestige school attendance predicts earning power better than does high economic status and low prestige school attendance. This is especially true for the extremes of prestige (Ivy League versus all other Midwest and Eastern colleges); but the pattern is not true for middle prestige schools, where little difference in earning power can be attributed to economic background over school prestige.

The findings of Havemann and West are most important for what they may tell us about the changing nature of stratification in the United States, and for what they do not tell us about the relative ability of successful and unsuccessful graduates. On the one hand, such findings can indicate a lack of correspondence with the open-class ideology that ability and effort lead to success regardless of social origins. The inclusion of particularistic criteria, such as school attended, would challenge the open-class ideology and erode the integrative function of stratification which requires the supporting belief that a reward distribution is "just." However, the Havemann and West study can give little help here, since it is quite possible that the students from lower prestige schools were also less able in their respective fields. What is required to estimate the "workability" of the open-class ideology is occupational achievement data from students of varying social origins, varying ability levels, who attended schools of varying prestige. In this way we could determine whether ability is the main factor determining rewards in one's career.

While such data are not now available we can seek good approximations in trying to establish the chances for mobility through higher education. One of the problems in trying to assess the extent to which college "levels" the socioeconomic differences with which students start college is due to the fact that students of different class origins tend to make class-related occupational choices. As we indicated earlier, students from lower socioeconomic origins tend to be partial toward the lower paying professions, such as teaching, as compared to higher paying occupations, such as business. One solution to this problem is to try to estimate the effects of origins and ability upon success *within the framework of specific occupations.* The choice of occupation for such an estimate of equality of opportunity is vital, for it has been shown that the greatest inequality in earning power between students of lower and higher socioeconomic origins has occurred in business as compared to the professions (West, 1953). And even within the professions it is possible to select occupations that are "free" from the influence of social origins in determining relative success. In the professions of medicine and law it is possible that family background may influence success by being able to provide financial assistance for establishing a practice or having social contacts that can be converted into clients. The particular professions that seem to be most free of these influences are the salaried professions of science and engineering. These are occupations that best fit the characterization of "careers open to talent."

A recent study of intra-occupational mobility among engineers sought to estimate the openness of the opportunity structure by measuring whether or not rewards in an occupation are differentially distributed according to the social origins of the persons in the occupation (Perrucci, 1961). The sample for the study consisted of engineering graduates of 1911 to 1950 from a large Midwestern university. Such a sample has several advantages deriving from use of a single occupation and university. The effects of differential preparation and institutional prestige are partially eliminated. In addition, any general changes in the economy or the occupational structure—that might raise or lower the prestige and income of occupations over time—are also controlled.

The engineers were grouped into three eras of graduation, 1911 to 1930, 1931 to 1940, and 1941 to 1950. Within each period the degree of association between the engineer's father's occupation and the job position held by the engineer himself was determined. In all three time periods there was a significant relationship between father's occupation and the job position of the engineer. Engineers of higher social origins were more likely to be in a position of higher prestige, power, and income. More important was the finding that social origins were more closely associated with the engineer's job position among the more recent engineering graduates than among the earlier graduates. Considering the measure of success used in this study, the data indicate that engineering graduates from lower social origins are less likely to be found in higher administrative and technical job positions.

A similar study was conducted among engineering graduates between 1947 and 1961 from two large Pacific universities (Cummings, 1965). Several important differences in this study from the Midwest study were that the author used several success measures, and was also able to control for ability, career-related values and the organizational setting in which the engineer was employed. The most important finding for our purposes was that social origins of the engineers were *not* related to any of the measures of success of income, high administrative positions, high technical positions, and professional performance.

A comparison of these two studies raises a series of questions concerning how an institution can affect the postcollege performance of its graduates. Why are social origins positively related to success in one institution while in another there is no such relationship? It is possible, for example, that the admission procedures in the Pacific universities were more selective, thereby admitting students of higher ability from *all* social origins, while the Midwestern university admitted students of lesser ability among those of lower social origins. It is also possible, however, that the prestige of the Pacific universities provided a "halo" effect for their graduates which minimized the influence of social origins upon their postcollege performance.

But these are only competing speculations for which we have no comparative data. In each case, however, there is an institutional effect operating either through selection criteria or through the relative prestige of the diploma. The patterns observed in comparing the mobility of engineers from Midwest and Pacific universities are also reflected in a comparison of the channels of higher education in the United States and British systems, in which it was found that success among British engineers is more independent of social origins than among Americans (Gerstl and Perrucci, 1965). In interpreting the findings the authors state:

"As access to the means for mobility . . . becomes wider, differential rewards are more likely to be related to social origins. For access to training operates as a screening mechanism which, if highly vigorous, is more likely to result in equal treatment once the initial hurdle is passed. Since university entrance is much more selective in Britain than in the U.S., we would expect that this is the stage at which the crucial sorting out process takes place. Just as almost all British entrants to university survive through their final year while Americans do not, so the success of the British graduates . . . should be more independent of their social origins than it is in the U.S." (*Ibid.,* p. 229–230.)

A rapid expansion of the educational system such as we have observed in the United States brings to the colleges and universities a student body with great diversity. Such diversity is seen not only in ability, which may or may not be related to social origins, but more importantly also in values, aspirations, educational attitudes, and behavior. The impact of college life does not necessarily reduce this diversity, for colleges may maintain quite distinct class-based sub-cultures. These subcultures may serve to reinforce the values and behaviors that the student brings to the college with him, thereby influencing the impact of college life upon him and upon his subsequent career performance (Trow, 1960).

Under such conditions of expansion and diversity we find the emergence of class-based occupations and colleges. It would also appear that under such conditions criteria other than ability may enjoy greater prominence in evaluating the performance and rewarding the achievements of college students and college graduates.

A Final Note on Opportunity in American Society

In looking at the American opportunity structure concerning social mobility several emerging patterns were discerned. The role of formal education in attaining relatively high status occupations has become more important in recent years. Long-established channels for achieving fame and fortune outside of formal education are slowly disappearing. Business opportunities for the independent entrepreneur are vanishing as rapidly as mobility through sports and entertainment is vanishing for working-class persons. The entrepreneur has been replaced by the manager with educational credentials; the sandlot player by the college star; and vaudeville by the school of performing arts.

Expanding high school and college enrollments have followed the increasing importance of education for placement in the occupational structure. Expansion in higher education has pointed to greater opportunities for large segments of the population that were formally unable or unwilling to attend college. With the greater availability of education, however, we have observed the emergence of a pattern of stratification in higher education which does not lead to expansion of equality of opportunity. Selected colleges become the province of students from different social origins. This selectivity may be due to educational costs which are prohibitive for those not of the upper-middle class, or it may be due to academic selectivity which operates against those who come from less adequate high schools with poorer academic preparation. When entrance requirements in terms of money and academic standards are raised faster than the ability of parents and schools at lower socio-economic levels to meet these requirements one of the results is highly stratified colleges and universities.

Screening according to ability to pay and academic preparation also results in career choices that are influenced by social origins. The more prestigeful professions of medicine and law with a period of preparation demanding time and money are less compatible with the resources of those from modest origins. The blue-collar student with demonstrated ability in the sciences and mathematics in high school is more likely to find himself enrolled in an engineering school. Even here, however, the sorting out does not stop. Those with better preparation in science and mathematics will be found in those schools emphasizing the engineering-science disciplines, while others will find themselves in more traditional programs which will prepare them for a career as a "nuts and bolts" engineer-technician. Blue-collar students without science interests or abilities will most often find their career paths from the teacher's colleges and schools of education that provide teacher training. The great pressure of money and time often turns the blue-collar college student into that vocationally oriented, single-minded person who cannot afford the luxury of enjoying his education and partaking of those "frills" which are not centrally related to his future job.

What we find, then, is the paradoxical situation of great expansion of educational opportunities accompanied by a restriction of choices within that expanding framework. Asymmetrical patterns such as these revealed by a stratification system make it difficult to make definitive statements as to the expansion or contraction of the opportunity structure. We need to know more about where high school graduates of different economic and ability levels go to college; about selection procedures used by colleges and universities; about how the characteristics of students, faculty, and administration create a distinctive campus climate; and about how the settings in which college graduates are employed are influenced by school reputation in their selection and promotion procedures. Answers to these and similar questions will give us a better understanding of what the changing patterns of education mean for the stratification system and the opportunity structure.

Yet despite the increasing number and proportion of persons who are finishing high school and gaining access to higher education, there is a sizable segment of the American population for whom there is little hope for a better life. The greater the expansion and growth of the larger society, the more restricted the avenues for change available for these impoverished groups. These are the people that Harrington has spoken of as the permanent poor. They are clustered together in urban areas in a manner that maximizes the negative effects of their condition. The framework of constraints upon mobility that we used earlier in this paper serves to highlight the low motivation and despair of the urban poor. Even among the young whose aspirations still run high, the object of such aspirations may be such available careers as pimp, pusher, runner, or bookie. The increasingly rigid patterns of residential segregation create a social structure which does not transmit more legitimate goal-objects to the attention of those that have not yet given up. The schools in the urban slum have little chance of influencing the young as long as they are run in the traditional manner. Although Operation Head-Start does represent an attempt to interrupt the vicious circle, it must be combined with more far-reaching programs of educational reform.

Thus, we can observe an emerging set of conditions which limit the instrumental and integrative functions of stratification. The existence of stratification itself hampers the identification of talent in society and the allocation of the most talented persons to the most rewarding positions. Not only do some persons never have the opportunity to discover their talents, but others who have discovered and demonstrated their talents are limited by restrictive patterns in higher education. Finally, the feeling of justice which is attributed to a stratification system by legitimizing the distribution of rewards will more likely be withheld when large segments of the population are denied full participation and enjoyment of the opportunities available to most.

Robert Perrucci is Associate Professor of Sociology at Purdue University, where he received his Ph.D. in Sociology. He is author of numerous articles in the areas of social stratification and complex organizations. He is currently research director of a study of engineers in industry and government, and, with Joel Gerstl, is editing a symposium, *The Engineers and the Social System*.

WORKS CITED

Alexander, C. Norman, Jr., and Ernest Q. Campbell (1964), "Peer Influences on Adolescent Educational Aspirations and Attainments," *Am. Sociol. Rev.*, **29** (August), 568–575.

Becker, Howard S. (1953), "The Teacher in the Authority System of the Public School," *J. Educ. Sociol.*, **27**, 128–141.

Blau, Peter M. (1956), "Social Mobility and Interpersonal Relations," *Am. Sociol. Rev.*, **21** (June), 290–295.

Bowerman, Charles E., and Glen H. Elder, Jr. (1964), "Variations in Adolescent Perception of Family Power Structure," *Am. Sociol. Rev.*, **29** (August), 551–567.

Centers, Richard (1949), *The Psychology of Social Classes*, Princeton University Press, Princeton, N.J.

Charters, W. W., Jr. (1963), "The Social Background of Teaching," in N. L. Gage, *Handbook of Research on Teaching*, Rand McNally & Co., Skokie, Ill.

Chinoy, Ely (1955), *Automobile Workers and the American Dream*, Doubleday and Co., New York.

Coleman, James S. (1960), "The Adolescent Subculture and Academic Achievement," *Am. J. Sociol.*, **LXV** (January), 337–347.

Coleman, James S. (1961), *The Adolescent Society*, The Free Press, New York.

Crockett, Harry J., Jr. (1962), "The Achievement Motive and Differential Occupational Mobility in the United States," *Am. Sociol. Rev.*, **27** (April), 191–204.

Cummings, Carolyn L. (1965), *Social Origins and Success: A Study of the Individual, Social and Organizational Factors Related to Intra-Occupational Mobility Among Engineers*, unpublished doctoral dissertation, Purdue University, Lafayette, Indiana.

Davis, James A. (1964), *Great Aspirations*, Aldine Publishing Co., Chicago.

Eckland, Bruce (1964), "Social Class and College Graduation: Some Misconceptions Corrected," *Am. J. Sociol.*, **LXX** (July), 36–50.

Eckland, Bruce (1965), "Academic Ability, Higher Education and Occupational Mobility," *Am. Sociol. Rev.*, **30** (October), 735–746.

Elder, Glen H., Jr. (1965), "Family Structure and Educational Attainment: A Cross-National Analysis," *Am. Sociol. Rev.*, **30** (February), 81–96.

Elder, Glen H., Jr., and Charles E. Bowerman (1963), "Family Structure and Child-Rearing Patterns: The Effect of Family Size and Sex Composition," *Am. Sociol. Rev.*, **28** (December) 891–905.

Ellis, Robert A., and W. Clayton Lane (1963), "Structural Supports for Upward Mobility," *Am. Sociol. Rev.*, **38** (October), 743–756.

Empey, Lamar T. (1956), "Social Class and Occupational Aspiration: A Comparison of Absolute and Relative Measurement," *Am. Sociol. Rev.*, **21**, 703–709.

Flanagan, J. C., F. B. Davis, J. T. Dailey, M. F. Shaycoft, D. B. Orr, I. Goldberg, and C. A. Neyman, Jr. (1964), *The American High School Student*, Project Talent Office, University of Pittsburgh, Pittsburgh.

Gerstl, Joel, and Robert Perrucci (1965), "Educational Channels and Elite Mobility: A Comparative Analysis," *Sociol. Educ.*, **38** (Spring), 224–232.

Glick, Paul C. (1954) "Educational Attainment and Occupational Advancement," in *Transactions of the Second World Congress of Sociology*, International Sociological Association, London.

Hamilton, Richard F. (1964), "Income, Class, and Reference Groups," *Am. Sociol. Rev.*, **29** (August), 576–579.

Haveman, Ernest, and Patricia Salter West (1952), *They Went to College*, Harcourt, Brace and Co., New York.

Hollingshead, August B. (1949), *Elmtown's Youth*, John Wiley and Sons, New York.

Hollingshead, August B., and Frederick C. Redlich (1958), *Social Class and Mental Illness*, John Wiley and Sons, New York.

Hyman, Herbert H. (1953), "The Value Systems of Different Classes: A Social Psychological Contribution to the Analysis of Stratification," in Reinhard Bendix and Seymour M. Lipset, eds., *Class, Status and Power*, The Free Press, New York.

Jackson, Elton F. (1962), "Status Consistency and Symptoms of Stress," *Am. Socio. Rev.*, **27**, 469–480.

Jowett, B. (1953), *The Dialogues of Plato*, Clarendon Press, New York.

Kahl, Joseph A. (1960), *The American Class Structure*, Holt, Rinehart, & Winston, New York.

Kahl, Joseph A. (1965), "Some Measurements of Achievement Orientation," *Am. Jour. Sociol.*, **LXX** (May), 669–681.

Krauss, Irving (1964), "Sources of Educational Aspirations Among Working-Class Youth," *Am. Sociol. Rev.*, **29** (December) 867–879.

Lenski, Gerhard (1954), "Status Crystallization: A Non-Vertical Dimension of Social Status," *Am. Sociol. Rev.*, **19**, 405–413.

Lipset, Seymour M., and Reinhard Bendix (1959), *Social Mobility in Industrial Society*, University of California Press, Berkeley.

Litt, Edgar (1963), "Civic Education, Community Norms, and Political Indoctrination," *Am. Sociol. Rev.*, **28** (February), 69–75.

McClelland, David C., John W. Atkinson, Russell Clark, and Edgar Lowell (1953), *The Achievement Motive*, Appleton-Century-Crofts, New York.

McDill, Edward L., and James Coleman (1963), "High School Social Status, College Plans, and Interest in Academic Achievement: A Panel Analysis," *Am. Sociol. Rev.*, **38** (December), 905–918.

McDill, Edward L., and James Coleman (1965), "Family and Peer Influences in College Plans of High School Students," *Sociol. Educ.*, **38** (Winter), 112–126.

Merton, Robert K. (1957), *Social Theory and Social Structure*, The Free Press, New York.

Miller, Herman P. (1962), "Is the Income Gap Closed? 'No!'," *New York Times Magazine* (November 11).

Mizruchi, Ephraim A. (1964), *Success and Opportunity*, The Free Press, New York.

Mizruchi, Ephraim H., and Robert Perrucci (1962), "Norm Qualities and Differential Effects of Deviant Behavior: An Exploratory Analysis," *Am. Sociol. Rev.*, **27** (June), 391–399.

National Science Foundation (1963), *Two Years After College*, U.S. Government Printing Office, Washington, D.C., 63–26.

Parker, Seymour, and Robert Kleiner (1964), "Status Position, Mobility, and Ethnic Identification of the Negro," *Jour. Social Issues*, **20** (April), 85–102.

Perrucci, Robert (1961), "The Significance of Intra-Occupational Mobility: Some Methodological and Theoretical Notes, Together With a Case Study of Engineers," *Am. Sociol. Rev.*, **26**, 874–883.

Perrucci, Robert, and Kichiro Iwamoto (1966), "Work, Family and Community in a Rural Depressed Area," in Hanna Meissner, ed., *Poverty in the Affluent Society*, Harper & Row, Publishers, New York.

Ramsøy, Natalie Rogoff (1965), "College Recruitment and High School Curricula," *Sociol. Educ.*, **38** (Summer), 297–309.

Rhodes, Albert L., Albert J. Reiss, Jr., and Otis D. Duncan (1965), "Occupational

Segregation in a Metropolitan School System," *Am. Jour. Sociol.*, **LXX** (May), 682–694.

Rosen, Bernard C. (1956), "The Achievement Syndrome: A Psychocultural Dimension of Stratification," *Am. Sociol. Rev.*, **21**, 203–211.

Rosen, Bernard C. (1961), "Family Structure and Achievement Motivation," *Am. Sociol. Rev.*, **26** (August), 574–585.

Rosenberg, Bernard, and David M. White, eds. (1957), *Mass Culture*, The Free Press of Glencoe, New York.

Schneider, Louis and Sverve Lysgaard (1953), "The Deferred Gratification Pattern: A Preliminary Study," *Am. Sociol. Rev.*, **18** (April), 142–149.

Sewell, William H. (1964), "Community of Residence and College Plans," *Am. Sociol. Rev.*, **29** (February), 24–38.

Sewell, William H., Archie O. Haller, and Murray A. Straus (1957), "Social Status and Educational and Occupational Aspiration," *Am. Sociol. Rev.*, **22**, 67–73.

Sexton, Patricia C. (1961), *Education and Income*, Viking Press, New York.

Simpson, Richard L. (1962), "Parental Influence, Anticipatory Socialization, and Social Mobility," *Am. Sociol. Rev.*, **27** (August), 517–522.

Stephenson, Richard M. (1956), *Mobility Orientation and Stratification: A Study of One Thousand Ninth Graders,* unpublished doctoral dissertation, Columbia University, New York.

Straus, Murray A. (1962), "Deferred Gratification, Social Class, and the Achievement Syndrome," *Am. Sociol. Rev.*, **27** (June), 326–335.

Street, David (1965), "Summary Report of the Seminar," in *Education of the Deprived and Segregated,* Bank Street College of Education, New York.

Strodtbeck, Fred L. (1958), "Family Interaction, Values and Achievement," in David C. McClelland et al., *Talent and Society*, D. Van Nostrand Co., Princeton, N.J.

Trow, Martin (1960), "The Campus Viewed as a Culture," in H. T. Sprague, ed., *Research on College Students,* University of California, Center for the Study of Higher Education, Berkeley.

U.S. Department of Health, Education and Welfare (1964), *Digest of Educational Statistics,* Washington, D.C.

West, Patricia S. (1953), "Social Mobility Among College Graduates," in Reinhard Bendix and Seymour M. Lipset, eds., *Class, Status, and Power,* Free Press of Glencoe, New York.

Wilensky, Harold L. (1964), "Mass Society and Mass Culture: Interdependence or Dependence?" *Am. Sociol. Rev.*, **29** (April), 173–197.

Wilson, Alan B. (1959), "Residential Segregation of Social Classes and Aspirations of High School Boys," *Am. Sociol. Rev.*, **24** (December), 836–845.

Wohl, R. Richard (1953), "The 'Rags to Riches Story': An Episode of Secular Idealism," in Reinhard Bendix and Seymour M. Lipset, eds., *Class, Status and Power,* The Free Press, New York.

Wrong, Dennis H. (1959), "The Functional Theory of Stratification: Some Neglected Considerations," *Am. Sociol. Rev.*, **24**, 772–782.

5 Education and the Sociology of Complex Organizations*

Ronald G. Corwin

Ohio State University

THE STUDY OF SOCIAL ORGANIZATIONS

"Authors are often convinced," March and Simon (1958) have observed, "that the particular subjects with which they are dealing are more significant than the world has acknowledged. We cheerfully make this claim for organization theory." The claim may be valid, for the growth of complex organizations appears to be a critical determinant in the future of society. Drucker (1953) refers to an "employee society" in which the vast majority of adults in the labor force make their livings as employees in large-scale organizations. To Presthus (1962) it is an "organization society" in the sense that the fundamental power no longer belongs to individual families or communities, but to giant corporations, 500 of which are responsible for two-thirds of the nation's production.

These men are not alone in their interest and concern. Indeed, in the past twenty years the study of large-scale, complex social organizations has emerged as a central interest of scholars in several disciplines, including sociology, psychology, political science, economics, and even mathematics.

Approaches to the Study of Organization

These interests represent a confluence of two streams of thought. One stream developed in the action-oriented industrial workplaces

* The assistance and comments of Dr. J. Eugene Haas, Dr. Virgil Blanke, and of several graduate students at the Ohio State University, especially those of Mr. Phillip Schlechty and Mr. Jack Foster, have been helpful.

during the first half of this century; the other earlier emanated from the more scholarly interests of European sociologists, notably Weber, Marx, Durkheim, and Simmel. It will be necessary to carry the reader over only enough of these well-worn accounts to review some of the intellectual legacy.

SOCIOLOGICAL THEORY. In Weber's studies of the rationalization of the Western world, bureaucracy plays a central role. Bureaucracies of Weber's Prussia were products of a quest for rational efficiency, which in practice became translated into rule by experts under law. His bureaucratic model consists of specialized jurisdictions of activity governed by rules and documents; a system of graded levels of authority based on strict compliance of subordinates to the commands of their official superiors; appointment to office on the basis of expert competence for a lifetime tenure; and guarded separation between the bureaucrat's personal life and his official vocation (Gerth and Mills, 1958; Bendix, 1962).

These bureaucracies, though big, were not as complex as many modern ones; and perhaps because the bulk of the personnel who staffed them were lesser functionaries with skill levels below those of the professionals who staff many of today's organizations, they seemed more interdependent, stratified and unified. Then, too, Weber's model was for the purpose of comparing broad cross-cultural and historical trends, not for making refined analyses of particular organizations. For these and other reasons, Weber's model has become the object of much criticism. It is maintained that the ideal model confounds two opposed characteristics—bureaucracy and rationality (Udy, 1959); that it incorporates inconsistent types of authority, one based on technical competence, the other based on the power derived from the position itself (Gouldner, 1959); that it ignores the role of personal, informal relations and power struggles while overemphasizing rationality and the infallibility of rules; and that it assumes a unity of direction and purpose which obscures the autonomy of subparts and the prevalence of intra-organization conflict.

The modifications of the original model implied in these criticisms are reflected in the writings of sociologists during the past two decades. Writing of bureaucracy's "other face" in the military, Page (1946) among others, observed how informal work group relations in organizations compensate for problems created by certain rigidities of formal organization, such as the "chain of command"; Sykes (1956), on the other hand, describes how the authority of prison guards becomes corrupted by informal friendships with inmates. Other writers have analyzed the functions of lenient enforcement of rules (Gouldner, 1954), and the dependence of formal authority on bases of power outside the organization. Some studies have emphasized the process by which organizations maintain and replace their goals. Sills (1957) studied the dilemma faced by the National Foundation for Infantile Paralysis when it became apparent that its major objectives would be realized. Only a few studies, however, have been concerned with the very crucial topic of conflict and boundary maintenance, although most authors recognize its importance; Dimock (1952), as one example, provides one of the few descriptions of the efforts of work groups (in a maritime branch of the military) to expand their jurisdictions of authority.

INDUSTRIAL MANAGEMENT. While these theoretical developments were fermenting and unfolding the general context, the affiliated field of industrial management had formed and begun its development through what were to become three phases dominated at first by the scientific management approach, followed in striking contrast by an emphasis on human relations, and most recently by the personality and organization approach.

Studies in the early part of this century by F. W. Taylor (1911) emphasized "scientific" *industrial management.* This perspective fixated on the techniques of impersonally controlling workers from the top, especially by manipulating such characteristics of the formal organizational structure as the optimum "span of control" for supervisors. This approach christened a battery of time-and-motion studies, and the science of aptitude testing matured. Because of the emphasis on impersonal control during this period of development, showing as it did disregard for the values and interests of the workers, it has been referred to as the era of organizations without people (Peabody, 1964).

By contrast to this early "formalistic" phase of organization theory, the 1920's and 1930's were dominated by an emphasis on people without organization, known as the *human relations* approach. The personal elements of work groups, such as friendship cliques, job satisfaction, and group morale, are central to this approach. Decision making and control at all levels of organization are emphasized, and the manager's job is considered to be one of eliciting cooperation, a conception of management that turned the attention of students to the motives behind subordinates' acceptance of authority.

The now classic experiments during the 1930's at Western Electric's Hawthorn Works in Chicago by a group of Harvard social scientists represents a turning point at which both approaches became fused.

Initiating their experiments with little appreciation for the significance of informal principles of organization, they attempted to determine the effect of lighting, length of workers' day, etc. upon productivity. It was not only demonstrated that any change in the physical working conditions produced favorable effects, but upon return to the original conditions, productivity often reached a new high, all of which indicated that productivity was being affected less by the working conditions themselves than by the workers' personal involvement in the experiment; they were taking more pride in their work because they had been singled out to participate. These findings precipitated a rediscovery of informal organization in industry documented by a flurry of studies and essays hailing the important role that workers' motivations play in modern organizations.

Both of these traditions still are a prominent part of organization theory. Formal decision-making theory represents a logical outgrowth of the scientific management school of thought. That theory, which delineates the logically available alternatives for solving a problem and fixes the probability of their outcomes, has reached its most elaborate form in game theory based on mathematical models. The underlying assumptions are that the "players" will seek to maximize their gains and reduce their risks of failure, that they will have the rational capacity to visualize the consequences of the alternatives, and that they will have the power of choice (Latane, 1963).

The human relations approach, too, was updated in a recent publication by Likert (1961), reporting the results of research on management procedures over the past 15 years. Compared to low-producing managers in American industry, there is a tendency for high-producing managers to be more interested in the personal problems of employees and less interested in the logical distribution of jobs and tasks; to exert less, rather than more, pressure on personnel to produce; to supervise less closely; to be more understanding of poor work performance.

Despite apparent dissimilarities between these schools, until recently at least, both usually have satisfied the same objective—which is not to *understand* organizations *per se*, but to improve their productivity and efficiency. The variables that are preferred for study are those which can be manipulated by management. While an organization usually provides the *setting* for studying supervision and work groups, then, seldom has understanding the organization, its structure and functioning, been the primary *objective*.

A concurrent stream of thought now is emphasizing the conflict between *personality and organization*. From his studies of a bank

(1954), hospitals (1956), and industrial organizations (1957), Argyris concludes that the inherent personality needs of "mature" individuals for independence, variety, and challenge are suppressed by a general preference in organizations for placid, dependent, and submissive employees. This development resembles the earlier morale studies in that the central focus is on how individuals cope with organizations rather than on how organizations, *per se*, function. While this approach illuminates the nature of organizations, then, again they are not the primary focus of analysis, but are treated as a setting, this time for the study of personality problems.

In attempting to integrate personality theory with organization theory, in attempting to maintain a "true" balance between people and system, the theoretical focus is split between two sets of variables (personality and organizational structure). These diverging perspectives create a critical strategic problem, for they have tended to compromise theoretical consistency, diluting the student's efforts and distracting his attention. The prominence of this approach has been partly responsible for the strong element of reductionism that has intruded into organization theory, whereby organizations are explained in terms of the social psychology of individuals. The central problem of organization has been obscured in the midst of philosophical speculation about the nature of persons. Although this development has been noted with favor by Homans (1964), the fact that people comprise organizations does not seem to be a sufficient reason for concentrating on the motives and attitudes of individuals.

The history of a science is one of oscillation between facets of the subject matter. Even at the risk of some distortion, this oscillation permits students to concentrate alternately on oblique perspectives, developing each at different periods without distraction. At the present time, it does not seem that the analysis of organizations profitably can proceed much further without reemphasizing the structural components of organizations. This chapter is written on that assumption.

What Is an Organization?

Many students of "complex organization" have been casual about defining the term. It is usually easier to illustrate it. Despite the fact that theirs is one of the most comprehensive treatments of organizations in the literature, March and Simon (1958) do not offer a definition. Other authors have dismissed the definition with a sentence. Etzioni

(1961, p. 79) asserts that "organizations are social units oriented toward the realization of specific goals."

Authors who have provided definitions seldom agree completely on the priority of different organizational characteristics. Moore (1951, p. 125) states that "organization in the social sense refers to either the patterns or structure of relations among a number of persons oriented to *a set of goals or objectives,* or to the group as a whole viewed as a unity" (italics supplied). On the other hand, Barnard's (1938, p. 65) definition of formal organization as "a system of consciously coordinated activities" avoids imputing to workers common motives and common goals. Caplow's (1964, p. 1–3) definition is more specific, "An organization is a *social system* that has an *unequivocal collective identity, an exact roster of members, a program of activity, and procedures for replacing members.*" Since a definition points to the characteristics which a particular author is concerned about, it will be defined here for purposes of this discussion.

DEFINITION. The following statement, in attempting to integrate some of the characteristics common to several definitions, will provide guidelines for sampling from the broadly ranging, if sometimes sparse, literature on organizations: *A complex organization consists of (1) stable patterns of interaction, (2) among coalitions of groups having a collective identity (e.g., a name and location(s), (3) pursuing interests and accomplishing given tasks, and (4) coordinated by power and authority structures.*

Patterns of interaction among people are determined partly by their positions in their organizations. These positions, and the relationships among them, form the power and authority *structures* which are largely responsible for coordinating an organization's primary activities. Positions are comprised of work *roles,* consisting of related norms, which are maintained in part by common expectations and in part by sanctions imposed for conformity and deviation. Responsibility for performing the key processes (to be described) is allocated *via* these roles.

Among the most vital relationships are those which define the system of *control* over work and of one member over another. The control system, in turn, includes three components. The first is the *official status system* by which the authority to issue commands is delegated to a hierarchy of positions. *Informal prestige* and *power* also accrue to each position in the official hierarchy. The *prestige* hierarchy, an expression of the value system, reflects the relative importance assigned to each position by organization members; the *power* hierarchy reflects the actual opportunity which positions provide to members for controlling others. The distribution of power and authority determines the degree of centralization and decentralization of the decision-making process.

Rules and Procedures are the second component of the control system. They provide guidelines for coordinating the organization's parts and for regulating the conduct of its members. The number, scope, specificity, and enforcement of rules and regulations establish the degree of standardization throughout the organization.

The third component, *the division of labor,* is partially produced by and supplements the first two. Whereas the status system refers to hierarchies of power and authority, the division of labor is determined by assignments of responsibilities laterally to distinct units (positions) at the same level in the hierarchy. It establishes "who does what." In fixing responsibility, however, the division of labor also assigns prestige and power to positions, often on a basis somewhat different than dictated solely by the status hierarchy. For example, although English and shop teachers are peers in the official authority system, in fact English teachers usually have more prestige, and in some upper-middle-class communities they also have more influence because of the importance of their jobs for getting children into college.

These characteristics are dynamically commingled. The division of labor produces specialization, or the process of breaking work down into spheres of responsibility, some of which are officially designated as *offices.* It sets in motion the counterprocess of coordination, which is accomplished through centralized positions of authority and standardized work procedures. Specialization and centralization present a picture of complex organization in a state of simultaneous expansion and contraction of responsibility, a repetitious process of delegation and recontrol.

ORGANIZATIONAL PROCESSES. For an organization to maintain this structure and to perform its tasks, several functions, or processes, necessarily must be fulfilled—coordination, allocation, replacement, decision making at the policy level, and boundary maintenance. More specifically, to function over a period of time organizations must:

1. Coordinate the division of labor.
2. Allocate power and authority in a generally stable way, and devise procedures for regulating conflict.
3. Replace members and procure other resources.

4. Regulate output and direction by constant readjustments in policy.
5. Establish and maintain boundaries against outside control.

However, while it is essential that organizations maintain these processes at some *minimum*, the precise level at which each must be maintained presently is not known. When organizations fail, or lose effectiveness, it is probably because any one or several of these processes have not been maintained. On the other hand, it is certain that most successful organizations do not regularly maintain each process at an optimum level. In fact, it seems plausible that an *over*emphasis on any one process can be as detrimental as failure to perform it at all, and that during certain periods a degree of conflict, ambiguity, scarcity of labor supply, and floundering may be as beneficial as it is normal. It seems especially notable that organizations normally are conflict-ridden, and that they vary considerably in the degree to which their policies are "goal-directed." Moreover, it is plausible that the ineffective performance of some functions can be compensated for by emphasizing the others. In those cases where goals (such as citizenship training) are so abstract, or an organization's practices are so remote from the stated goals that for all practical purposes the organization has little control over its direction or the nature of its product, exceptionally effective authority structures or boundary defenses, for example, can help to maintain its effectiveness.

To summarize, a complex organization is an arrangement for coordinating the activities of subdivisions having a common identity, which consists of a status system, rules and procedures, and a division of labor. The way it functions somehow depends upon its recruiting practices, how it deals with nonmembers, the allocation of status and the division of labor, and the degree of stability and control it is able to maintain over its direction. Responsibility for these processes is assigned to various roles.

The preceding definition does not specifically refer to individuals because a theory of organization need not (and perhaps it cannot) be derived from an aggregation of the principles of individual behavior. Organizational properties are assumed to represent an independent form with a uniquely characteristic logic and dynamic. Each organization represents a single unit of the total population of organizations.

The conceptual boundaries of the field of organization can be clarified by distinguishing organizational variables from three types of personal ones (Barton, 1961, pp. 1–5): (1) psychological attributes (such as attitudes toward mobility), (2) personal behavior (such as the number of previous jobs a person has held), and (3) a person's demographic position in the social structure (such as his age, sex, and marital status). Organizational variables, on the other hand, refer (1) to variables based on organizational attributes which cannot be derived from data on individuals (such as the number of department heads or the number of levels of authority), (2) to stable relationships between positions (such as the average frequency of contact between teachers and principals), or (3) to the distribution of individual characteristics throughout an organization, derived from individuals but indicative of organizational properties (such as the proportion of freshmen who drop out). The psychological and social psychological variables are, of course, important for a complete understanding of everything that takes place within organizations, but priority will be given here to the organizational variables.

Why Study Educational Organizations?

Sociologists study educational organizations for the same reasons that they study other organizations—to improve them, to understand how they function, and to determine the implications of organizational principles for personality and behavior. The same schools of thought which have dominated the study of industry, in other words, are found in this field also.

First, sociologists are beginning to appreciate the relevance of educational organizations for extending and testing theory. Within this century, educational organizations have become one of the most prominent parts of the organizational society. Schools are mammoth and costly, and concentration in education is as real as it is in industry. Twenty-five percent of the public schools educate nearly 80 percent of the school children. Public education is an 18 billion dollar enterprise, one of the nation's largest capital investments, and according to some estimates one of its most productive (Schultz, 1961, pp. 50–52). More than one-fourth of the nation's population is involved in educational organizations in one capacity or another, and the first major organizations outside of the home with which children have extensive contact are schools.

Educational organizations are so much a part of the social fabric that it is safe to say that one's understanding of society is incomplete unless he understands them. This large-scale growth and transformation of educational organizations provides a natural setting in which to study the sociological consequences of such world-wide, tension-producing institutional developments as bureaucratization, professionalization, the rise of semiautonomous groups, and the growing interdependence, subordination, and dominance of groups within large-scale systems.

In addition to these theoretical interests, because of the practical functions which educational organizations perform, many students have studied them in order to improve them. Educational administrators, in particular, have drawn upon social science to improve the efficiency and effectiveness of schools and colleges. Their interests seem to have paralleled those of students of industrial organizations. Textbooks in educational administration traditionally have stressed the scientific management concepts, being largely descriptive and emphasizing the mechanics of running schools rather than the general and theoretical principles by which organizations function. As late as 1952 Miller and Spaulding, the authors of an otherwise excellent textbook in the field who treated topics such as the nature of culture, cultural conflicts, the interaction of school and community, and the decision-making process and leadership, also seemed compelled to discuss at length personnel record keeping, trends in schoolhouse construction, efficiency and safety in school transportation, and purchasing and accounting practices.

Since the late 1950's several educational administrators oriented toward the social sciences have written on *human relations* in education (Griffiths, 1956; Campbell and Gregg 1957; Halpin and Croft, 1962). Like their colleagues studying human relations in industry, these men have been concerned with the problems of morale, the logic of decision making, and styles of leadership and supervision of personnel. They generally have neglected the informal organizational structures, the essential organizational processes, and especially the way in which the variety of structures and functions of organizations may affect the learning process.

On the one hand, then, lies the theoretical approach, and on the other hand are the more pragmatic interests of many educational administrators and of some social scientists who primarily seek to use social science knowledge for improving schools and colleges. However, an interesting synthesis between the two perspectives is now becoming more explicit, especially in certain attempts to link forms of educational organization to a sociological theory of learning. Since the writings of Dewey, it has been apparent to some sociologists and educators alike that the way schools are organized plays an important role in the way people learn—progressive education was a reaction to scholasticism and authoritarian methods employed at the turn of the century. Now, organizational theory promises to germinate an *organizational theory of learning*, a theory in which the premises are organizational principles rather than psychological ones.

Of course, for years learning theories in education have been concerned with the dynamics of individual growth and development *within* organizational settings. Attention was concentrated on what goes on in classrooms—democratic teaching, reading readiness, pet teaching methods, tracking and ability groupings, and teacher-induced rewards and punishments (Gordon and Adler, 1963). Social psychologists, too, have called attention to the influence of peer group pressures in the classroom, on the playground, and in the home. Years ago teachers began to revise seating charts, to make sociograms, and to chart the interaction patterns of students. In all of this, like the studies in industry, only the behavioral variables that could be manipulated were considered, while the organization itself was taken for granted most of the time. The learning theory was addressed to human relations within *given* organizational settings. But the consequences of those settings themselves for learning were for the most part ignored—except when the traditional organization was threatened by change. Usually at these crisis periods a catalogue of ideologies, grounded in rural tradition, is suddenly announced: small classrooms and small schools are less efficient than larger ones; small classrooms are more effective than larger ones; neighborhood schools are more effective than schools which recruit students from throughout the city. Team teaching, the effectiveness of large lecture classes, and the feasibility of administrative decentralization are all examples of issues having fundamental implications for an organizational theory of learning.

Such a theory is far from being explicitly formulated, but it is in the air. Little is yet known about how organizations influence the learning climate, but that they do influence it is now almost certain. The beginnings of such theory are implicit in some of the research comparing organization size with the intellectual achievements of students. For example, there is evidence from Ohio that two-thirds of the winners of Ohio State General Scholarship Tests in 1952 and 1957 came from large and average size schools, and four-fifths of the 1959 and 1962 group came from large schools (although the comparable proportions of students attending these schools are not given) (Neff, 1964). The opposite conclusion was reached about colleges by Stern (1963) who, comparing colleges which scored very high and very low on a measure of the "intellectual climate" of schools, found that schools low on intellectual climate had on the average six times as many students as the schools which demonstrated a high intellectual orientation among the student body and faculty. The same study showed that the source of control over colleges also was associated with their learning climates. Private, nonsectarian schools exhibited high intellectual orientations, while most of the schools with low intellectual climates were public institutions, with state institutions overrepresented among schools with average learning climates.

Organizational theories of learning need to go well beyond crude comparisons between size and output. Cicourel and Kitsuse (1963) have broken ground to a promising line of inquiry by suggesting that bureaucratic principles determine the way in which students are classified by schools. In limiting the kind of programs available to specific students, the classification system influences the way they are treated and evaluated by teachers. Following parallel reasoning Goslin (1963) suggests that tests may have similar consequences.

Bonjean and McGee's (1965) study of cheating among college students reinforces the proposition that organizational characteristics play an important role in student behavior. Comparing students in a university using the honor system with one relying on "external" controls, they report that there were fewer actual or potential violators in the honor system, and that the differences apparently are more closely related to the risk of punishment than to any other single factor. They explored the question of whether cheating can be better explained by situational-organizational characteristics and informal peer group norms than by the personal backgrounds of students.

There seems to be a relationship between a school's source of financing and students' attitudes and values. Although a comparison of Catholic children attending parochial schools with those in public schools revealed no observable differences in attitudes toward the virtues of honesty, gratitude, and obedience, parochial school pupils were more liberal than those in public schools toward certain social problems (Fichter, 1958). Miller's (1958) analysis of the Cornell Values Survey also suggests that students attending private Ivy-League Colleges are more liberal toward civil liberties than students attending state schools. Not only are the richest and upper-middle-income freshmen more liberal upon entering Ivy-League schools than their counterparts entering state supported colleges, but within each of three economic groups, seniors in Ivy-League Colleges are (or presumably have become) more liberal than freshmen, and the change is greater than in state colleges. It is conceivable that privately financed and controlled schools are less effective in achieving their official commitments (e.g., teaching religious values) than in achieving such latent secondary objectives as reinforcing liberal social attitudes.

In conclusion, although the danger exists that a theory of learning based on principles of organization will deflect theoretical concerns away from the organizational problems to learning problems, this synthetical approach, if used with discretion, can illuminate principles of organization, for they are certain to be reflected in the way people learn.

Educational organizations have properties in common with organizations having different purposes; by studying them, hopefully, more can be learned about the functioning of organizations in general. The section following immediately is written with this hope. However, the fact is that before the knowledge accumulating on educational organizations can be actually extended to others, a vehicle, in the form of a conceptual model facilitating comparative studies and regulating transfer of knowledge, must be evolved. That will be the concern of the last section.

THE SCHOOL AS AN ORGANIZATION

With the context established, attention now can be turned more profitably to the task of describing schools and colleges as complex organizations. Regrettably, the study of complex educational organizations is a relatively neglected topic, for sociologists, like educators, have been so impressed by the teaching function itself—the characteristics of teachers and students, the teaching methods, and face-to-face interaction in classrooms—and they have been so concerned with the values that schools teach, that only rarely have they shown genuine interest in the theoretical issues connected with the organization of educational systems.

Nevertheless, evidence has begun to accumulate. This discussion will weld available evidence with conjecture in an attempt to isolate a few selected structural properties which promise to be of more general relevance for describing many types of organizations in addition to schools. These "elementary properties," as they will be called, can be identified through the way organizations function; or, more specifically, their *dys*functional reverberations may be the key. For, like the pressure applied by physical scientists to metals in order to determine their structural properties and hence their tensile strength, organizational problems produce tensions which, in exposing weaknesses in organizational structure, illuminate the essential properties that always are in operation, though less apparent under normal conditions.

The first problems to be treated—coordination and allocation— originate from the internal principles of organization, the complex system of authority and division of labor. Principles of organization not only prevent conflicts, they often are responsible for them. The tendency for divisions of an organization to become self-sufficient (functionally autonomous) and the corresponding tendency for its parts to change at different rates (structural lag) are prime problems of internal coordination.

Organizations are even less in command of the outside pressures, and for that reason most of their problems concern ways of accommodating to and resisting social forces that eventually impinge upon them. The *recruiting process* represents one mechanism linking them to fluctuations in the environment.

Internal conflicts and inconsistencies, and the precarious balance between organizations and their environments, diminish their ability to control their own *direction,* which is a problem deserving separate treatment. Official goals tend to be replaced by other objectives and unofficial commitments. The comprehensive scope of most public schools has increased their resiliency, but in comparison to more specialized ones, comprehensive schools cannot hope to achieve all their goals with equal effectiveness.

The importance of the intruding environment explains the enormous energy that organizations devote to defining and defending their *boundaries.* Although recruiting practices afford a long-run defense against outsiders (by keeping certain types of people out), more direct strategies are available. The crucial problem of boundary maintenance is how to enlist the aid of outsiders without succumbing to their influence. The capacity to do this depends in part upon the financing procedures employed and the control structure. This problem will be considered at the end of this section.

Coordination Problems

Coordination is the act of unifying the responsibilities of lower echelons. Coordination problems increase with organizational complexity, which in turn is a function of the number of subparts and the degree of consistency among them. It should be noted that school administrators derive power from a complex administrative system. For, in the first place, complexity increases the available alternatives; a wide range of alternatives increases the ability of administrators to bargain for the loyalty of members and to win outside support. Band, chorus, football, and dramatics all contribute to a school's community support, and the availability of these activities increases the likelihood that most students will find something of interest in school. Second, the more complex an organization becomes, the more control it can develop over its noninternal functions and the less dependent it must be on outside assistance. Because they have their own research, testing, and public relations departments, the largest school systems in the country can be impervious to outsiders who may approach them to do research or testing. Similarly, the full-time public relations officers found in the more complex systems protect the organization by serving as permanent watchdogs screening information that might otherwise leak to the public as well as concentrating on favorable publicity.

Yet despite these advantages, a major share of the problems of school systems can be attributed to their complexity. Problems develop because work flow has not been well planned and priorities not assigned to scarce resources; grade levels are improperly arranged so that the work of students does not accumulate progressively; football teams compete with the band for use of the practice field; overlapping basketball and drama schedules create problems in scheduling the use of the auditorium. To counteract this divisiveness, administrative systems are established to coordinate the separate functions. The difficulties likely to be encountered, and the consequent size of the administrative system, increase with complexity. Complexity, in turn, is a function of several characteristics: (1) the division of labor, (2) specialization of personnel, (3) hierarchy of authority, and (4) standardization, or the system of established rules and regulations governing work. Each characteristic will be described briefly.[1]

DIVISION OF LABOR. The way work is divided and allocated determines the number of divisions at each level of the organization. The number of separate education programs in the educational "track" system (e.g., vocational, college prep, and general programs) and the number of separate academic departments and special administrative units are indices of the extent of division of labor in schools.

The division of labor probably tends to increase with organizational size. However, larger organizations do not necessarily have more varied *kinds* of parts than small ones. In this regard, Barker and his colleagues (1962), exploring the relationship between size of high schools and the opportunity of students to participate in extracurricular activities, found that large schools which have 25 times as many students as small ones have only five times as many "behavior settings" and 1.5 times as many varieties of setting (although the schools were not as large as many metropolitan schools, and community size was not controlled). In other words, although small schools have fewer replications of some of their parts, they do have similar parts. The proportion of participants was three to twenty times as great in smaller schools as in larger ones, while the kinds of activities in which students engaged was twice as great in larger schools. (Schools differing in enrollment by 100 percent permitted only 17 percent [median] difference in variety of instruction.) Proportionately more behavior settings were devoted to operation (administration) in larger than in smaller schools. The authors conclude that when better facilities are purchased at the expense of large size, the facilities are likely to be discounted by lower participation rates of students, and hence, that it may be easier to bring specialized and varied behavior settings to small schools than to raise the level of individual participation in large ones.

The distinction between distinctively different parts and those which are merely replicated may prove to be important for estimating administrative complexity and for evaluating the learning experiences that schools provide. For, as this study suggests, the amount of sheer replication can alter learning opportunities.

SPECIALIZATION OF PERSONNEL. Whereas the division of labor is a property of organization, the kind of specialization being referred to here is a personal characteristic: the level of training required of employees. An index of specialization of teaching personnel might include the formal training of a school's faculty and the proportion teaching courses in which they majored in college. It is possible for an extensive division of labor to be implemented by relatively unspecialized personnel; assembly lines, for example, require very low degrees of specialization, whereas highly specialized personnel, such as lawyers, can function outside of complex organizations.

STANDARDIZATION. To the overlays of structure already mentioned must be added the system of standards embodied in rules and standard procedures. Seeking order and consistency among subordinate units and overall predictability, the administration spins a web of rules and regulations and establishes standards. An index of standardization might include measures of compliance with standard lesson plans and curriculum guides, and the uniformity of tests and textbooks in use in the system.

Standardization produces a number of latent, often ignored side effects. For example, although teachers frequently complain about the constraints of rules and regulations, standardization can increase their power if they are in otherwise insecure positions subject to the caprice and arbitrary judgments of administrators. The way rules compensate for power unexpectedly became apparent in Moeller's study of teachers' sense of power in twenty school systems rated by eight judges on the bases of specified bureaucratic characteristics. (Midwest Administration Center, 1962) The original hypothesis was that bureaucracy is responsible for teachers' feelings that they are powerless to affect teaching policy (as measured by a scale developed for the purpose), but it was not confirmed. On the contrary, teachers in bureaucratic systems sensed more power than those in less bureaucraticized systems, where particularism and lack of policy were more typical.

Perhaps only in an orderly, understandable, and predictable organization can individuals expect to have influence. If a subordinate knows the prescribed course of action, the lines of communication, and the policy on a particular issue, he is at least protected from the caprice of the administration, and rules actually may permit him to make demands which he could not make in the absence of policy. For example, when rules regulate the use of the auditorium, a teacher using it out of turn has some idea of the risk involved, and the authorized party has the recourse of demanding that the rules be enforced. If nothing else, explicit rules can be evaded more easily when the reaction of the administration can be foreseen. Teachers benefit especially from rules governing the behavior of *other* people. For these reasons, teacher organizations are a major force behind certain types of rules.

However, the same uniformities that support *teachers* can jeopardize the interests of some of their *students*. In their quest for a fully coordinated system, administrators and teachers have attempted to apply uniform methods and curricula to diverse types of students, even when they have not been uniformly relevant. Moreover, the uniform status system which has evolved from the use of homogeneous evaluation criteria throughout the system has lowered the effectiveness of teachers with some types of children. Teachers are rewarded for complying with standards applicable to middle-class-oriented schools, even when assigned to situations where these standards cannot be achieved with normal efficiency. Faced with the same evaluation criteria applied to teachers in middle-class schools, slum school teachers are compelled to impose system-wide standards on slum school children for whom they are less relevant. Teachers who modify the curriculum to fit the interests of lower-class children or those who do not require their children to "keep up" with the system-wide rate of progress are likely to be treated as failures.

Becker has observed that because teachers feel successful when they are able to observe changes in children's skills and knowledge, they prefer to work with the more interested middle-class children. As one teacher told him:

> "Well, I would say that a teacher is successful when she is putting the material across to the children, when she is getting some response from them. I'll tell you something. Teaching is a very rewarding line of work, because you can see those children grow under your hands. . . . You can see the difference in them after you've had them for five months. You can see where they've started and where they've got to. And it's all yours. It really is rewarding in that way, you can see results and know that it's your work that brought those results about." (Becker, 1952, p. 453.)

Because children in slum areas of the cities are the most difficult to teach successfully in this sense, teachers feel less competent with them. They compare the performance of their lower-class children to system-wide standards, and invariably feel that they are "falling behind."

In other words, in the face of uniform criteria of teaching success, some teachers cannot excel. And this situation, with its emphasis on standard lesson plans, is maintained because it is convenient and efficient from the standpoint of administering the system, not because it is effective with lower-class people. The fact that valid principles of coordination, so convenient for the organization, can be detrimental to the education of lower-class children again illustrates how organizational principles affect the learning process.

STRUCTURAL LAGS. Social changes create serious handicaps for coordination. Because organizations have only incomplete control over their subparts, some parts will adapt to changes differently than others; hence, organizations can adapt to change only imperfectly. A social change tends to divide the membership into separate coalitions, some of whom welcome it, while others, who owe their positions to the existing system, resist it. Consequently, most complex organizations experience some degree of *structural lag*, that is, an inconsistency throughout the organization due to the fact that the subparts change at different rates. As a result, the organization has difficulty performing its new functions.

The concept of structural lag is illustrated in Gross' analysis of American universities. Although some details of the discussion are distinctive of the university setting, the major issue is relevant to public schools and other complex organizations as well. Acknowledging that colonial colleges were single-purpose institutions, he notes that American universities today obviously offer a variety of specialized services:

"The basic approach adopted by most American universities has not been a functional division of labor among the members of its faculty— different portions of its *permanent* staff assigned to the teaching of undergraduates, to training graduate students, to research activities, and to the service function. Rather, the basic pattern has been the gradual redefinition of the professor's role to include all of these tasks. Although there are some notable exceptions, most professors on tenure in the faculties of arts and sciences are expected to teach graduate and undergraduate courses, carry out research or scholarly inquiries and write them up for publication, provide consultant, advisory or other service functions related to their specialities, as well as advise undergraduate and graduate students, supervise doctoral theses, and serve on departmental, graduate faculty, and university committees. . . .

"In short, the academic role has been gradually redefined to embrace the variety of diverse tasks that the university has assumed. Whereas other establishments have characteristically met similar situations with increased specialization and further division of labor, the university has primarily chosen the path of adding function after function to the tasks of the same personnel.

"*The Reward System.* As the universities assumed new organizational objectives and enlarged the scope of the role of academic man to cope with them, there seems little question that . . . although multiple functions are expected of academic man, the reward system of the universities gives research productivity and scholarly publication the highest evaluation in the assessment of a man's worth to his institution.

"*Organizational Substructure.* . . . Although the value and reward system of the university now gives highest priority to the advancement of knowledge among its several objectives, the organizational setup as it relates to *the great majority* of the permanent faculty members in most universities is one that is still basically geared to function as an agency whose primary function is the transmission of knowledge. . . .

"Caught in this nexus of multiple expectations and demands something must give. The patterns of response to these incompatible expectations are undoubtedly diverse, but my own observations lead me to suspect that the modal pattern for senior professors is to give minimum effort and time to their teaching responsibilities and greater attention to their research obligations and outside activities such as consulting. . . .

"But although the reward system of the university stresses research and scholarly productivity the social arrangements of the university for *most* faculty members are not conducive to the effective accomplishment of this objective. . . . Its budgets are basically teaching budgets and so the faculty members are forced to go outside the university—to the foundation, to industry or to the federal government primarily—for support of their research activities. And this has many interesting consequences. One is that since most foundations, industrial supporters of research and a number of government agencies have clearly developed notions of areas they are interested in, and since the university looks with favor on a man with a research contract, many academics are involved in inquiries that frequently do not represent their basic research interests. A second consequence is that although the universities proclaim that one of their major objectives is to advance knowledge they have in large part allowed external agencies to determine the problems to be investigated. A third consequence flows from the fact that *most*, although not all, contractors of university research will support only short term research." (Gross, pp. 61–63, 67–69, 1963.)

The passage shows again that organizational arrangements help to determine the type of education students can receive. State universities, acting on the assumption that their primary function is teaching, admit masses of students who cannot possibly have regular contact with the limited number of over-burdened professors. The situation is aggravated by the growing acceptance of the ideal that everyone has the right to a college education. The situation that is developing has intriguing parallels in the transformation of public high schools around the turn of the century as enrollments soared. As more children from nonintellectual backgrounds entered public schools, the traditional college-oriented curriculum was adapted to their demands and interests; progressive education reflected growing concern for the "average" masses of children who were not intellectually inclined. The complaints which college students and administrators presently are making about poor teaching and the unwarranted priority given to research echo similar concerns. Complaints that professors are not spending enough time in the classroom, that they are uninterested in students, that they are too concerned with publications, and with merely dispensing ideas in lectures, while showing too little concern for slower students who are having difficulty, all seem to imply that universities should modify their intellectual standards and gear their programs to the average students who are beginning to flood universities.

Charges that professors are uninterested in students and in teaching and are too involved in research and writing are misplaced, however. For, in adapting to increased enrollments, with only limited resources, the system simply has become displaced in other ways; the problems are produced by the resulting structural strains, not by negligent professors. Herculean efforts of individual faculty members will not compensate for the fact that the *system* itself is maladapted to the variety of demands being made of it. The very principle of mass universities is opposed to personalized teaching, and even if legislatures were willing to pay higher salaries to attract more professors into teaching, there would be an acute shortage of Ph.D.'s in the foreseeable future. That the problem is aggravated by pressure to do research does not alter the fact that this nation's economy—and higher education itself—is now so dependent upon research that it must be performed. The evaluation system mentioned by Gross has its source in an economy that requires research for its growth, and our understanding of the problem is hardly increased by blaming professors for adapting to these demands.

High schools, facing similar problems forty years ago, "solved" them by increasing the teacher's time in the classroom and working directly with students. As a result, most high school teachers officially have less than five hours a week for preparation and reading. However, professors of higher education, being responsible for developing ideas and for training graduate students as well as for transmitting knowledge, cannot afford to reduce their research and reading time without eventually seriously impairing the advance of their disciplines, the economic growth of industries that rely on university research, and, ultimately, the quality of their teaching because of lack of opportunity to keep up in their fields. These issues will be important sources of contention between students, administrators, professors, and between research professors and classroom teachers during the next decade. But it now appears that most undergraduates will be in classrooms with teachers who are only a few years advanced of them in preparation and experience.

Allocation of Power and Authority

The division of labor and standardization represent "horizontal" systems of control, the results of allocating responsibility among peers. Complex organizations also have a vertical division of responsibility, the hierarchy of authority (or the chain of command). The official authority system is an organization's moral spine. Before work can be coordinated and before outside changes and pressures can be accommodated, at least the blueprint of an authority system must be established.

HIERARCHY OF AUTHORITY. The prominence of administration (i.e., activity devoted simply to maintaining the day-to-day operation of the organization) can be expressed as a ratio of the number of administrators in the system to the number of teachers. In one study, it was found that administrators increased disproportionately with the size of the school system (Terrien and Mills, 1955). This tendency may be explained, in part, by the fact that school systems consist of a number of schools at different locations, each requiring separate administrative staffs (Anderson and Warkow, 1961); it also may reflect a particular stage of growth of public schools in this country. A related dimension is the time lapse that occurs before a request by a teacher is acted upon by the administration; the time required increases with the amount of consultation that administrators must do among one another.

Perhaps the most important fact about the hierarchy is the way authority and power are *distributed*. This distribution can be measured along several dimensions (Tannenbaum, 1961). First, the total number of levels of authority can be counted. For example, the authority structure of a system having only a principal and a superintendent differs from one with department heads responsible to a series of assistant principals, curriculum coordinators, and assistant superintendents. Second, the amount of control exercised at *each level* relative to the other levels determines the "slope" of the structure. For example, in one school department heads exercise more control than either teachers below them or the principal above them; while in another, both teachers and the principal exercise equivalent influence in excess of that of department heads. Finally, the *total amount* of control can vary between systems. Two organizations with similar distributions of authority can differ because in one there is more power at every level than at comparable levels of the other. Tannenbaum (1961) reports that the effectiveness of local Leagues of Women Voters studied was related to the distribution of control within each league; in the more effective locals, control was distributed in a more "democratic," less centralized way. It would be instructive to examine the quality of schools from the same standpoint.

Although they represent an organization's moral system, authority structures are challenged by the tendency of subordinate groups to develop more power than authorized. The problem assumes three forms, which will be discussed: (a) functional divisions having officially equivalent status develop differing amounts of power; (b) subordinates develop informal power structures among themselves, irrespective of their formal status; and (c) subordinates as a group become professionalized, claiming the technical competence that enables them to challenge official authority.

FUNCTIONAL AUTONOMY. The hierarchy of authority produces "social distance" between strata, and thereby reduces the interaction between levels of the hierarchy, hence limiting the opportunity for conflict between supervisors and their subordinates. To a lesser extent, divisions of labor and rules, such as the separation of classrooms and scheduled time periods for particular activities, help to reduce ambiguities which are sometimes a source of conflict in organizations.

However, the two major principles on which cooperation in large-scale organizations is based—hierarchy and division of labor—are responsible for tensions as well. For segments of organizations which perform different functions tend to compete, and become semi-autonomous. Katz postulates that forms of autonomy in school systems develop systematically from patterns of specialization and interaction, including affiliations of members with outsiders (Katz, 1964). Thus, rivalries arise between teachers of academic subjects and athletics and between teachers of "fundamental" and "practical" fields. In many communities athletic programs achieve a degree of autonomy because of their independent income from public attendance and from support of adult-sponsored booster clubs. Katz contends that a group of teachers can accomplish its functions more effectively if it has developed a degree of autonomy from the rest of the system. Similarly, "the school requires a degree of autonomy from local pressures if it is to accomplish its cosmopolitanizing tasks, such as weaning the child from his specific family context.

The fact that teachers are less subject to direct community pressures than school administrators, who work directly with the school board, perhaps puts teachers under less direct pressure than administrators to bargain away the interests of their students. However, it is administrators who often have the primary responsibility for developing and enforcing professional standards.

INFORMAL POWER STRUCTURES. In addition to being segmentalized by official lines of authority and divisions of labor, the organization is further differentiated by informal power structures, or, in other words, cliques of influential teachers and their followers. These leaders derive unauthorized power from their positions and their contacts and use that power in turn to increase the autonomy of their positions. The importance of contacts and the unauthorized influence[2] that subordinates sometimes are able to derive from their positions both are illustrated at one school where a teacher developed an informal arrangement with the secretary to call ahead and warn of the principal's unannounced classroom visits. She also had persuaded the secretary to reschedule her classes for a more desirable time, without the principal's knowledge. An informal power structure which seems to derive its influence from outside contacts is described by Kimbrough:

"Two informal clusters of persons interested in influencing administrative policy decisions were identified in West Town School. The Old Guard or Lounge Group was largely comprised of women faculty members. Although the Men's Group, as the name of the group suggests, was masterminded by men faculty members, some women faculty members were definitely associated with this cluster. . . .

"There was no question of the influence these two basic informal clusters had on the faculty. . . .

"The discovery of a number of these small groups led one to suspect that the two basic structures were made up of leaders associated with smaller satellite friendship groups . . .

"Interestingly enough, Emily Thadum was consistently mentioned by members of the Lounge Group as having influence with an official high in the central administrative offices and with certain community leaders. Informants also reported that Mrs. Thadum 'was in with some prominent families' or 'knows everybody in town.' Also mentioned as having influence outside the school staff were Emma Lucky, Dorothy Smith, and Mildred Steffens. Among the latter, Emma Lucky was said, most frequently, to have influence with someone at the superintendent's office. Mrs. Steffens was said, a number of times, to have ties with certain local community citizens. Mrs. Lucky was also described as close to a member of the board of education.

"Of interest . . . is the immediacy with which certain persons of influence on a school faculty are associated with influential persons and groups outside the individual school. In a number of preliminary trials of instruments in other schools, the interview conversation inevitably moved to how a certain influential staff member *was close to* someone outside the staff. Some staff members are often perceived to have ties with prominent persons, board members, or someone in the superintendent's office. This gives them power advantages, just as the superior interaction position of men of power in a community power structure is an advantage.

"The Old Guard had direct communication with Mr. Traxler (the principal). Most informants reported that the person in the Lounge Group most often in communication with the principal was Emma Lucky. As one person expressed it, 'They jest a lot with each other. She is the one in the Old Guard closest to Mr. Traxler.' Another reported, 'Emma (Lucky) has influence with Mr. Traxler. She can talk to him.' . . .

"Some writers have assumed that the so-called informal organization is a response to the impact of formal organization. There is reason to question whether this stimulus-response model accurately explains a large number of schools, especially in view of the public nature of education, as opposed to the more private control over the resources of a business organization. Informal influence structure, as illustrated in the above studies, is often a source of power in initiating important actions through the formal organization. The informal groups often generate enough power to bring about significant changes in the nature of formal organization itself. Thus it would be feasible to view the formal organization as reacting to the impact of the informal organization in such instances." (Kimbrough, 1964, pp. 242–243, 247, 253–254.)

Organizations whose informal power structures are monopolistic can be distinguished from those with competitive power structures. In more complex organizations, perhaps power cliques are unusually competitive. The distinct and competing objectives that semi-autonomous segments sometimes develop are illustrated in the following quotation of a high school drama teacher:

"Mr. A. would not allow anybody on his team to work in any of the other areas. It wasn't really a friction between personalities; he wanted a winning team, and we wanted a winning team. Practices came at the same time. Coaches then saying that the individual is not considered a member of a team if he misses the practice; the dramatics coach saying that the individual can't be considered for a part in the play if he misses practice. So there is a conflict there that puts the student in the middle. . . . he gets bawled out by both individuals concerned. If he doesn't do too well, he drops out of one or the other." (Corwin, 1965a.)

In the preceding example, the teacher describes a situation which, as she says, "Wasn't really a friction between personalities." What was involved was the relative status of different extracurricular activities;

the two teachers represented *groups* in conflict—a point often neglected by those students of organization concentrating on conflict between the "individual and the organization."

PROFESSIONALIZATION. As school systems become larger and more influential, as pressures for more efficient decision making increase, and as the gap between pedagogical theory and public understanding grows, the staffs and administrators of public schools seem intent on demanding more discretion to exercise their professional viewpoints. The ideological conflict over the role of teachers as employed professionals is expressed by Solomon:

"With the growth of urban centers and the consolidation of rural districts, the proportion of teachers who work in sizable organizations is large and growing larger. In these school systems teachers are subject to the exigencies of the big institution as well as to the traditional paternal authority of the superintendent. . . .

"Large, centralized organizations are often associated with undesirable bureaucratic tendencies. Rules may become ends in themselves; administrators may pursue such goals as larger empires, greater security, administrative convenience, or smooth operation; control systems may frustrate creativity and initiative; and the rewards may go to conformists. . . .

"A crucial characteristic of school systems is the lack of consumer control. The absence of such control stems from the intangibility of the product of the school system: education or learning. The recipients of the educational service, students (or their parents), are not able to properly evaluate the educational process. Teachers could do so, but the influence they exert on standards may be slight because of their position as subordinate employees and the character of their group morale. Intangibility of product thus provides the opportunity for administrators to pursue bureaucratic goals at the cost of the educational process. In a school system where such displacement of goals takes place, many children may pass or graduate each year even though much less than the desirable, or the potentially achievable, amount of learning has taken place. . . .

"Perhaps the most crucial fact to be reckoned with in public education organization is the contradiction between the teacher's role as a subordinate employee and his role as a professional person. This contradiction affects significantly the teacher's relationships with administrators and with fellow teachers. . . .

"A bureaucratic system tends to foster a controlled, routinized work

situation, one that is not compatible with notions of professional autonomy or responsible participation in decisions relating to the work process, and certainly not compatible with the exercise of creativity or
initiative. Thus the teacher, lost in the rule-bound system and having
access to few effective channels by which to influence the remote (as
well as the near) sources of authority, may eventually retreat to a more
or less unhappy accommodation to the realities of his position. . . .

"As professional people, teachers have the need to secure conditions
under which their profession could meet its corporate responsibilities
and under which the individual teacher could achieve maximum professional growth. As employees, teachers have the need to protect and
advance such common interests as adequate salaries, fringe benefits,
and job protection.

"These important interrelated needs would seem to supply a sufficient
basis for strong teacher organization. Nevertheless, the traditional
orientation of teachers, reinforced by the structure of administrative
controls, appears to be one that rejects responsible powers for the
profession. . . .

"We thus come up against the harsher realities from which responsibility cannot be disassociated: the imperatives of power and conflict.
These are stark matters for teachers, a white-collar and mainly female
group. They shy away from power and find the prospect of conflict an
even more unpleasant notion. Teachers seem little aware of the vital,
constructive role that conflict, properly channeled, can play in relationships between groups." (Solomon, 1961, pp. 287–290, 294–295, 297.)[3]

Solomon distinguishes between the somewhat inconsistent professional and employee obligations of teachers, and suggests that if teachers had more professional authority, they would be in a better position
to improve the quality of education and to counteract the temptations of
administrators to implement bureaucratic principles at the expense of
educational ones.

Several crucial differences separate the ideal-type professional from
nonprofessional employees. The nonprofessional employee (even
though he may be an individualist) is unlikely to distinguish closely
between his work responsibilities and his obligation to obey supervisors. He may object to uses of authority that infringe on his personal
rights as a citizen (such as no smoking rules), but he is willing to accept
supervision over his job. A good employee is obedient; he has been
hired to "do what he is told." Therefore, when he does disobey, he must
be ready to sabotage his work and the organization's clients; employees

sometimes do disobey with that intent (as in the case of "slow downs" in factories).

The professional employee, on the other hand, denies the principle that his work always must be supervised by administrators and controlled by laymen. Because of his training, pressures from his colleagues, and his dedication to clients, the professionally oriented person considers himself competent enough to control his own work. Hence, he sometimes must be disobedient toward his supervisors precisely in order to improve his work proficiency and to maintain standards of client welfare—especially if there are practices that jeopardize the best interests of students.

Caught in political crossfire, under public scrutiny for efficiency, sensing a need for good public relations, and under daily pressures to act expediently, administrators probably sense less pressure than teachers to resist detrimental administrative practices in the name of client welfare, especially since they are designed for their own administrative convenience. They are more likely to favor good employees, and to forget the special problems of clients. Hence, school administrators, vulnerable to the demands of middle-class parents, until recently at least, have neglected the education of slum school children. By contrast, slum school teachers, who see these special problems constantly, are under daily pressure to adapt the middle-class program to the needs of these students, the reward system notwithstanding. In one exceptional case a slum school teacher devoted three-fourths of the class time to reading, far more than the usual time allotted, because she considered it to be the students' major weakness. She was able to succeed only by hiding the fact from her principal and by falsifying school reports.

A survey of English, science, and industrial arts teachers in ten junior high schools tends to support this thesis (Anderson, 1964). It was found that although rules regulating curriculum, lesson plans, tests, selection of textbooks, and other teaching materials were more emphasized in slum schools, teachers in them reported treating their students with *less* impersonality and were more willing to experiment with new procedures than teachers in middle-class schools. Despite greater pressure on them to follow standard teaching procedures, then, slum school teachers were more obliged to adjust their teaching to the varied needs of their students. Probably middle-class teachers are able to be effective without providing as much individual attention precisely because their students' skills, objectives, and motives are more homogeneous.

Most schools probably need mavericks to manipulate the system in defense of students. It is conceivable that counselors and some types of professionally oriented teachers are beginning to institutionalize such a role.

Some of the major struggles now going on in educational organizations involve the efforts of teachers to obtain more responsibility for certain types of decisions. In most schools, at least some teachers are attempting to increase their control over the classroom. Sharma's study suggests the norms which are developing. He found sharp differences between what teachers desired and current practice with regard to participation in decision making by groups of teachers. In thirty-two of the thirty-five activities, the percentage of teachers desiring participation in decisions was significantly *higher* than the percentage reporting participation by such groups. They especially wanted responsibility for activities concerning instruction, and they wanted more autonomy for the individual schools in which they teach; the role of citizens in the community, they believed, should be limited to participation in policy making in areas other than professional matters (Midwest Administration Center, 1955).

The struggle of teachers to govern their work necessarily involves militancy, as Solomon has suggested. The more bureaucratized the school, the more resistance they are likely to encounter. Hence, it can be expected that conflict will increase simultaneously with bureaucratization and with professionalization. Comparing seven public schools of varying size, the writer found a positive rank order correlation between the professional climate of the schools (as reflected in the faculty's endorsement of professional norms) and the number of reported conflicts in the school between teachers and administrators and the proportion of teachers in the school reporting that contacts with the principal or his assistants involved disputes. Other evidence collected from interviews also supported the contention that professionalism is associated with conflict between teachers and the administration (Corwin, 1965b). If this evidence is indicative, teachers seem to be exercising more than the traditional amount of leadership in education.

IMPLICATIONS. Concerns of some students (Argyris, 1957, pp. 50–51) about incongruities between the mature adult individual's needs (for initiative, independence, variety, deep and common interests) and pressures on him stemming from the organization's authority system to exhibit infantile characteristics (such as passivity, dependability, shallow, casual interests, and subordination) can obscure the conflict integral to the organizational pattern itself, i.e., conflict stemming from inconsistent *principles* of organization. For, the same system of organization that is designed to prevent conflict is largely responsible for it.

Stress on efficiency on the one hand and on democratic debate and dissent on the other exemplify inconsistent principles of organization found in many bureaucracies (Blau, 1956). Parallel inconsistencies have been noted between the principle of expertise and the principles on which the democratic decision-making process is based (Laski, 1960). For example, the expert opinions of teachers concerning the appropriateness of certain library books, the validity of personality tests, or the feasibility of a certain curriculum for specific students at times are seriously at odds with the opinions of laymen in the community. Ultimately, the character of public education will be determined by the outcome of conflicts involving these principles.

To summarize, it is difficult for an organization to maintain its integrity in the face of internal, semi-autonomous coalitions, each with its own interests and goals. Outside social changes are equally upsetting. This last observation directs attention to the problem of the organization's relation to its environment. The remaining functions of organizations are centrally concerned with regulating and maintaining that relationship.

Recruitment Problems

Balances between coordination and incoordination and between accommodation to change and structural lag can be altered in at least two ways by the recruiting process. First, the type of leaders recruited can influence the rate of change and the stability. Second, certain procedures for recruiting rank-and-file members can protect organizations against their own recalcitrance to change.

TURNOVER OF LEADERSHIP. Carlson's (1962) discussion of school superintendents who come from "inside" and from "outside" the system reveals the instrumental role that turnover plays in promoting or retarding organizational adaptation and lag.[4] The insider, attached to a specific place, his home system, puts place of employment above his career as a superintendent. By contrast, the outsider is career bound and willing to leave the system for a job elsewhere. From his observations of four school systems, Carlson concluded that school boards appoint outsiders when they are dissatisfied with the present administration and want creativity; insiders are appointed when boards are satisfied with the *status quo*. In an analysis of thirty-six successions no insider reported that the school board was unhappy with the way the schools were being administered at the time he was appointed. Carlson reports on ways in which insiders and outsiders differed in their administrative practices and their possible effects on their schools:

"Even though superintendents, new to the particular position, tend to become preoccupied with rules, their preoccupations take on varied forms relevant to the origin of the successor. The place-bound superintendents observed, gave attention to old rules. Publicizing and reinforcing old rules and assessing the extent to which old rules were being taken into account by those to whom they applied, are illustrative of their activities. The insiders' preoccupation with rules did not include a reassessment of rules nor any extended work with new rules. The rule activities of insiders tended to tighten what existed, rather than to alter or redefine either the internal commitments or the external ties of the school system.

"On the other hand, the outsiders observed devoted about 85% of their rule-making activities to rules that filled in gaps or supplanted old rules. They did modify and redefine the commitments of the school system.

". . . When the insider advanced a new rule, it typically related to the technical or managerial aspects of the system. The following are examples: 'All individuals responsible for making classroom observations will turn in a weekly report stating the number of such observations and follow-up conferences.' 'Decisions regarding promotion in questionable cases will be made by the child's teacher, the building principal, the elementary supervisor and the home and school visitor.' This is not to say that outsiders did not make this kind of rule. Outsiders did make new rules in the technical and managerial aspects of the school. But, in addition, they were more prone than the insiders to make new rules at the institutional level of the organization. Rules at the institutional level are those that go beyond technical and managerial concerns and modify or change the character of the organization and its relation to the environment. Examples of this kind of new rule are the establishment and integration of a kindergarten and the employment of social workers to serve the school in relating individual pupils with the law, the courts, welfare agencies, and psychiatrists. . . .

"If the insider does attempt dynamic changes, he does so with two strikes against him which have not been called on the outsider. One is the constraining influence of his friends and enemies in the organization. The other is that the conditions under which he was hired indicate that change is not necessarily wanted nor expected of him, and if change is proposed, all sorts of questions are raised. In this sense the changes of the outsider are not questioned, for change is expected and encouraged. . . .

"The differences found between the ways in which insiders and outsiders relate to their containing organizations are sufficiently marked to suggest the proposition that a school system cannot afford two insiders in a row in the superintendency. With two insiders in a row, a school system would experience, on the average, about twenty years of leadership which operated in a manner designed to maintain the system as is. This would seem to be a longer period of this type of leadership than a school district could afford. During such a period, adaptation and development would be lacking and the school district would come to face many problems. Study of 103 successions taking place over about 32 years in 48 city school systems in California revealed that the least frequent pattern of succession was from insider to insider. This pattern occurred only seven times among the one hundred three instances of succession. A study of succession patterns in school districts of Pennsylvania replicated the finding." (Carlson, 1962, pp. 29–30, 39, 72.)

The relative influence of successive leaders is likely to depend upon the system's complexity. In more complex organizations, subunits are likely to gain more autonomy, which not only puts subordinates in a better position to resist changes proposed by the chief executive but also creates incentives for them to propose their own innovations (Wilson, 1966). In complex organizations, therefore, rates of turnover among subordinates may produce as much ferment and change as turnover at higher levels.

In any event, a practice seemingly so remote from the classroom as the replacement of superintendents can have a vital effect on the kind of education that people eventually obtain.

PROCEDURES FOR RECRUITING MEMBERSHIP. The recruitment of rank-and-file members can be as important for an organization's character as the replacement of administrators. The more stringent the recruiting standards, the more control an organization can exercise over its members' values, a fact documented in a study of four sororities and six fraternities at the University of Colorado (Scott, 1965). These organizations were so effective in selecting their members that each new generation reaffirmed the dominant organizational values (e.g., social skills, group loyalty, tolerance of cheating and dependency) more strongly than the senior members. The new members, rather than the older ones, were responsible for maintaining the value system. This perhaps represents a unique case where recruiting procedures were so effective, and the period of membership so short, that a socialization process that had the effect of undermining the value system could be tolerated.

The ability to select new members represents one form of protection to an organization. At the other extreme, even an organization unable to fully regulate its goals by controlling the actual selection of its members, has some assurance of at least survival when membership is compulsory for certain persons. This organization, certainly, is in a less precarious position than one which can neither select its members nor compel them to join. In the public schools, as suggested in the following excerpt by Carlson, the compulsory attendance of students is an especially significant feature which permits schools to operate and flourish with less than perfect efficiency or effectiveness.

"If we put the variables of selectivity on the part of the organization and on the part of the client together, we get the possibility of four types of service organization-client relationships as seen below.

Selectivity in Client-Organization Relationship in Service Organizations

		Client Control over Own Participation in Organization	
		Yes	No
Organizational Control	Yes	Type I	Type III
over Admission	No	Type II	Type IV

"Most of the service organizations we know in the United States are probably Type I organizations: organizations which, either by formal or informal means, select the clients they wish to deal with and are participated in by clients on a voluntary basis. The private university is a good example. Hospitals and doctors' offices also are of this type. In addition, many of the public welfare service units belong to this type. They apply stringent criteria in the selection of clients, and the potential client is not compelled to accept the service.

"Type II service organizations do not select their clients, and participation in the organization is nonmandatory. The state university whose charter specifies that it accept (but not continue to serve) all high-school graduates who are at least 17 years old and who wish to enrol fits this type, for it is not mandatory for high-school graduates to attend college. In addition, most junior colleges and adult-education units fit within this type.

"Service organizations of Type III are seemingly very rare or non-existent. This type of organization selects clients and is one in which clients are compelled to participate. An organization which has such a relationship with its members (not clients) is the citizen army, but it is not a service organization. When laws specify that individuals having certain characteristics must embrace a given service, it seems that the service is always provided by an organization that has no control over admission of clients.

"There are a number of service organizations of Type IV, such as public schools, state mental hospitals, reform schools, and prisons. The clients of these organizations receive the service on a mandatory basis, and prisons, public schools, and state mental hospitals cannot exercise choice in the matter of clients. . . .

". . . Though all service organizations, by general definition, establish a social relationship with their clients and thus face a motivation problem, the typology makes it clear that an equal necessity to motivate clients is not placed on all service organizations. It may perhaps be unnecessary to remark that the problem of inducing clients to participate would seem to be most pronounced in Types III and IV, because these organizations are most likely to be in contact with some clients who have no real desire for their services. This factor undoubtedly has many organizational ramifications. To mention only a few, it would seem to bear upon the attitudes which staff members and clients hold toward each other, personality make-up of staff, prestige of the work, and deployment of organizational resources.

"Further, it seems appropriate to call Type IV organizations 'domesticated.' By this is simply meant that they are not compelled to attend to all of the ordinary and usual needs of an organization. By definition, for example, they do not compete with other organizations for clients; in fact, a steady flow of clients is assured. There is no struggle for survival for this type of organization. Like the domesticated animal, these organizations are fed and cared for. Existence is guaranteed. Though this type organization does compete in a restricted area for funds, funds are not closely tied to quality of performance. These organizations are domesticated in the sense that they are protected by the society they serve. Society feels some apprehension about domesticated organizations. It sees the support of these organizations as necessary to the maintenance of the social system and creates laws over and above those applying to organized action in general to care for domesticated organizations.

"Type I organizations, on the other hand, can be called 'wild'; they do struggle for survival. Their existence is not guaranteed, and they do cease to exist. Support for them is closely tied to quality of performance, and a steady flow of clients is not assured. Wild organizations are not protected at vulnerable points as are domesticated organizations. . . .

". . . Of particular relevance to this discussion is that the research has pointed out the tremendous importance and the occurrence of adaptation by wild organisms to their changing environment.

"This suggests the proposition that domesticated organizations, because of their protected state, are slower to change and adapt than are wild organizations." (Carlson, 1964, pp. 265–67.)

The typology is a simplification, of course, and is subject to several reservations. The parents of public school students do have something to say about where their children will attend school, as they can move, pay tuition to another district, or attend private schools. Schools likewise can gerrymander district lines, expel certain students, and send others to special agencies. Moreover, schools do compete for favored students, as well as faculty, do struggle to perpetuate a favorable reputation. The distinctions are based on official characteristics which do not recognize the informal influence that some administrators in Type IV organizations can have in securing favored clients. In fact, the distinction between wild and domestic seems analogous to the difference between industrial and governmental organizations.

Nevertheless, the scheme is provocative. It can be speculated that bureaucratic regulations will be prominent in Types II and IV, where the organization does not control admission, as a means of controlling members who do not share similar values and who are not involved with the organization's objectives. Type I organizations, by screening out undesirable clients, perhaps tend to have higher social status and more influence than comparable Type IV organizations; the relatively high status of some private schools attests this, although the existence of less influential, low status private colleges also suggests the presence of other factors.

Domesticated organizations, having little opportunity to regulate values, then make structural adjustments to relieve some of the tensions produced by the heterogeneous membership:

". . . Type IV organizations have goals to which they are committed and their achievement is hampered by the presence of the unselected clients, and . . . in the course of day-to-day operations there emerge within these organizations adaptive mechanisms which tend to minimize the disruptive factors presented by the unselected clients.

"The first adaptive response of domesticated organizations to the environmental condition of unselected clients is *segregation*. Segregation takes several forms. 'Dumping ground' is a term well known to educators; it signifies that some part of the school program constitutes a place where students are assigned or 'dumped' for part of their program, for various reasons, to serve out their remaining school days. Students do not get dumped into the academic areas of the program but, most frequently, into the vocational areas. This practice gives clues as to the type of student the school system is most anxious to serve. . . .

"Frequently a more extreme form of segregation takes place. In California, in some school systems, there are continuation schools for those students who have proved to be too disruptive for the regular high schools. And New York City has its '600' schools. In a sense, they are the dumping grounds' dumping ground. . . .

"Segregation in domesticated organizations frequently may lead to or is accompanied by goal displacement. Goal displacement is a process whereby the original or overriding goal is abandoned (completely or partially) and another goal substituted." (Carlson, 1964, pp. 268–269.)

Recruiting practices, then, can protect an ineffective organization. Partly because they are guaranteed students and a minimum level of support, schools can endure for long periods of time without improvement. This "kept" status provides security, but permits them to avoid change. Thus, schools continue to stress ancient languages, English literature, and the history and values of the local region in a nation increasingly caught up in a world society, the demands of which logically dictate more modern languages, European and Asian literature, and world history. For similar reasons, until recently, schools have avoided making adjustments necessary to appeal to the one in three high school students who drops out.

At the same time, this protection has permitted educational organizations to subtly transform their objectives, compromising their official goals, for with a guaranteed clientele, it is less essential to be completely effective in fulfilling any given objective. This fact complicates the already difficult problem of setting and maintaining direction in organizations. Attention now will turn directly to this problem.

Policy Problems (Direction)

In the process of regulating their precarious relationships to changing environments, in contending with partially autonomous subunits, and in adjusting their structural lags, organizations eventually can lose sight of their objectives, some of which become modified as a result.

GOAL DISPLACEMENT. Social change produces a dilemma, with respect to organizational objectives, which eventually must be faced: if organizations do not adapt their objectives to changing circumstances, they are likely to be judged ineffective; yet, in adapting their objectives, they violate prior commitments.[5] Many organizations do violate old commitments and replace them with new ones. This goal displacement and replacement occurs because they are unwilling or unable to resist new demands made upon them.[6]

An organization's direction is the result of compromises between its acknowledged objectives and the actual circumstances it confronts. It follows that cultural trends and shifts can have enormous influence on those objectives. Largely because they depend so on other social institutions for moral support and direction, the objectives of schools have been sensitive to social changes. In fact, until recently at least, their mode of organization has perhaps changed less than their major objectives, which have readily adjusted through the years to such diverse purposes as training theologians, scholars, businessmen, technicians, immigrants, and factory workers. Laymen perhaps have had more interest in controlling the objectives of schools than in how schools are run, while educators have had more vested interest in their internal positions than in resisting new demands; indeed, they have strengthened their positions precisely by accommodating those demands. The existing structure of schools therefore has provided a convenient means for indoctrinating each generation with whatever value system is current.

As nonlocal groups (such as the federal government) with less interest in maintaining the local status quo have become interested in education, the educational structure itself has shown more signs of change. It might be noted parenthetically that the growing interest of outsiders in the internal structure helps to explain the dramatic transformation that has begun to take place in educational organizations in recent years. During the 1930's Mort and Cornell (1941) estimated that it took a practical invention like the kindergarten nearly 50 years to become completely diffused after its introduction; 15 years typically

elapsed before 3 percent of the school systems had adapted an innovation. By contrast now, largely from nonlocal pressures and incentives,
within five years after their introduction 17 percent of the school
systems adopted language laboratories; in eight years 18 percent
adopted teachers' aids in the high schools; 12 percent adopted team
teaching in five years, and 20 percent adopted PSSC physics in four.
By the earlier formula less than 2 percent of the systems would have
adopted these innovations within five years (Miles, 1964).

Because organizations tend to adopt the values and practices of
dominant institutions, changes in patterns of institutional dominance
are of consequence; shifts in the major institutions are of supreme
importance. The likelihood of schools borrowing practices from other
organizations increases as the prestige of the latter ascends. For as
long as religious leaders dominated the Colonial period, schools re-
sembled puritan churches in their rigid disciplinary practices, authoritarian teaching procedures, and religiously based curriculum. But later,
as business became predominant, schools shed their churchlike missions
to appropriate the values and practices used by successful businesses.
By the turn of the century, the influence of business on education was
evident; by the end of the first decade it was nearly complete.

By subscribing to good business practices, schools were able to
secure backing from the most powerful groups in the country; but the
coalition with business not only had minor effects on the procedures of
organization, they corrupted some of the very educational objectives
that educators previously had endorsed. Callahan describes how, in
self-defense, schools translated business practices into an educational
philosophy that altered the objectives of public schools:

"Almost immediately after the country became acquainted with
scientific management procedures, pressure began to apply them to
the classroom. . . . As one superintendent writing in 1912 put it, 'the
results of a few well-planned tests would carry more weight with the
businessman and the parent than all the psychology in the world.'"
(Bliss, 1912, p. 12.)

". . . Wirt's innovation was to introduce an organizational scheme
which would offer children the benefit of . . . special studies and still
be economical. This would be done through a departmentalized system
in which the students moved from room to room. The plan was arranged so that all the rooms, either home rooms or special rooms, were
in constant use. . . . When the bell rang, the students would shift to
their next class. . . .

"Spaulding's application of Taylor's system resulted in a cost analysis. His contribution had been the introduction of the dollar as the criterion for judging the relative value of the various school subjects. . . . He didn't know, he said, whether music was more valuable than Greek, but Greek was more expensive and so from a financial standpoint it was less valuable. . . . (Robert Charles Harris') procedure was to determine the cost per pupil and divide this by the year-minutes of each teacher (a teacher with 5 weekly periods of 40 minutes each during the school year had 200 year-minutes) which gave him the cost per year-minute. . . . For example, he indicated what changes he would make in one of the high schools which was paying '329 percent above the average for Foreign Language.' 'Suppose the salary remains the same, $1,460. Let the teacher have five periods per day instead of 3.5. Let the size of the class be 25 instead of 12.8. Let the term be 40 weeks instead of 34. Then we shall have: salary, $1,460; number of pupils per teacher, 125; teaching time of teacher, 200 year-minutes. From these figures the cost-per-year-minutes is 5.84 cents as compared with 27.31 cents in the present case. The average for all the schools in Foreign Language is 6.37.' . . .

". . . *With this economic motivation to promote students, plus the practice of rating the efficiency of teachers on the basis of promotions, it is clear that two potent forces were at work which contributed to the practice of passing students regardless of educational considerations.* . . .

"Undoubtedly the 'efficiency' measures helped school administrators to defend themselves and to keep their jobs in a business-dominated, efficiency-conscious society, but the price the nation has paid has been high. Not only were our educational leaders devoting their time and energy to matters that are incidental to the real purpose of the schools, but our teachers were forced to spend countless hours on meaningless clerical workhours that should have been devoted to teaching and learning. And, unfortunately, much of this clerical work has survived down to the present time. This is so partly because administrators who were trained as bookkeepers in their graduate work in the twenties and thirties are still in key positions in our schools. It is also due to the adoption by teachers of some aspects of the business-managerial role in their classrooms. Just as administrators adopted this posture to please a business society and especially school boards dominated by businessmen, so teachers learned how to behave to please business-oriented administrators." (Callahan, 1962, pp. 100, 129, 159–60, 168, 178.)

Transactions between institutional value systems, such as the trans-formation described by Callahan, are inherent to complex organiza-tions, because organizations normally incorporate the values of several institutions. An organization like the school is, in effect, a compromise of a variety of institutions, including education, religion, business, politics, leisure institutions, and the military. The relative predominance of one set of values over another largely depends on the hierarchy of institutions in the society. Shifting institutional balances, and resulting conflicts, will be reflected in altered and inconsistent school practices —practices which develop independently of their "logical" functions. For example, as national interests have accentuated the academic pro-gram, now serving as a weapon in the cold war, new patterns of leisure have created a countervailing emphasis on extracurricular activities, all of which is responsible for the growing anxieties of parents about the increasing volume of homework assignments.

Callahan's analysis, then, shows the impact on the learning climate of practices developed logically for the convenience and efficiency of organizations.

MODELS OF ORGANIZATION. Callahan's analysis also suggests that the practices of an organization, no matter how rational in the sense of efficiency, are not always "rational" in another sense of the term, for they often are the accidental, unplanned products of outside pressures and internal problems. What role, then, *does* rational planning play in the determination of an organization's direction? Do its leaders actually "direct" it toward official goals? Are leaders actually in "command" of their organizations? Different answers to these questions are responsible for two opposing models of organization, identified by Gouldner as the rational model and the natural system model (Gouldner, 1959).

In the rational model, strongly apparent in Weber's work, organiza-tions are assumed to be goal-directed entities. Organizational goals determine the desired course of action and dominate the thinking of leaders, whose decisions are calculated to achieve those goals. Their rationality is, in turn, a function of the number of alternative courses of action considered and the amount of planning done.

In the natural systems model apparent in Michel's writing, on the other hand, direction is more dependent on commitments and con-straints than on official goals and planning. A commitment is an obliga-tion initiated by an organization; a constraint, one imposed by outside groups.[7] Schools sometimes commit themselves to unintended courses of action in the process of bargaining. Residents of the small town described by Vidich and Bensman (1960) at one time agreed to permit farmers in the surrounding region to control the school board in exchange for the rural area's support of a consolidated school to be built within the city limits. Over time, the consolidated school maintained a strong vocational agricultural program and other evidences of rural influence, long after rural domination had become useless to high school graduates.

Clark's (1959a) study of an adult education program examines the constraints responsible for that program's precarious development. Being marginal to the school system and facing a school board which favored the public schools in allocating funds, the program's administrators were forced to rely for monies on "enrollment economy" principles—i.e., as many students as possible were recruited to reduce the average cost per student. The program, consequently, became simplified and slanted toward crafts and hobbies in order to achieve popularity. The predominance of crafts and hobbies in adult education, then, evolved from constraints in the competitive enrollment economy rather than from rational planning toward some desirable outcome.

Clark (1960) also has documented a transformation in the official objectives of a junior college designed to provide technical training for high school graduates. Although vocational training officially was the school's primary purpose, the fact that the college was legally required to admit any resident who applied subjected it to the preferences of students, most of whom chose the college curriculum over the vocational program. In order to protect their reputations as college teachers, the faculty began to fail an inappropriately large proportion of students, diverting the college even further from its vocational goals.

To emphasize the prominence of commitments and constraints is not to deny the influence of official goals. Organizations do have goals which are integral to them and separate from the personal goals of their members. They can be considered as the *common* expectations applicable to all roles of the organization. As mutual and overlapping expectations, they apply to all members of the organization, and hence, they are part of the organization's structure. But the point is that organizational goals are only one source of commitment among many possible sources. Furthermore, different groups, even though sharing similar expectations, frequently attach different priorities to them. For example, teachers of both academic subjects and extracurricular activities can accept extracurricular goals while assigning them a different degree of importance. When consensus on the priority of goals throughout the organization is low, other types of commitments and constraints are more likely to predominate.

An integration of the two models, if accomplished, would provide a more coherent concept of organization. They can be compared on essentially three points: (1) the degree of consensus on stated objectives, (2) rational planning for the organization as a whole, and (3) the power of each segment of the organization to achieve its commitments. Rationality can be considered as the *limited case* where there is (a) complete consistency of stated objectives (as indicated by the degree of consensus on their relative importance), where (b) each central office and subunit within the organization has effective power and knowledge to achieve its commitments, and where there is (c) extensive organization-wide planning, involving consideration of several alternatives over a period of time. However, the natural concept represents the more general case. Complete consensus on objectives is unusual, and with less than full consensus the amount of effective planning that can be done is *inversely* related to the power of the subparts. Even with extensive planning toward several alternatives by a central office, over an extended period of time, an organization cannot achieve rationality if subunits are free to pursue their separate objectives autonomously. Realistically, in most large urban school systems, which are not especially noted for high consensus on objectives, some parts develop autonomy, making the limited case of rationality improbable.

Therefore, focusing on power relationships between subparts (i.e., the locus of decision making) promises to be a more fruitful approach to the study of educational organizations than analyzing the logic behind administrative decisions, a procedure more often preferred by educators.

EFFECTIVENESS. The alternatives available to an organization, and its capacities for adapting to change, are determined by the number of its commitments. Most schools in the nation traditionally have been comprehensive schools, or multifunction organizations, which typically offer a wide variety of programs and activities to heterogeneous student bodies. But because their objectives and other commitments are large in number, comprehensive schools are unlikely to have the capacity to fulfill all of them effectively. The fact that their activities are unequally rewarded by their communities encourages them to concentrate on some commitments more than others. For example, having winning teams or getting students into colleges are visible achievements which, regardless of the logical priority of some other educational objectives, some middle-class communities reward disproportionately. Hence, although they may be committed to a large number of goals, comprehensive schools in fact tend to informally specialize in a few to the neglect of others.

Some of the disadvantages of comprehensiveness can be overcome through systemwide specialization, i.e., by officially assigning each school in a system limited and distinctive commitments. Specialized schools are able to employ special personnel and resources without fear of being criticized for favoritism or for being "unbalanced." Duplication of services among schools in a system is reduced and the competence and incentive of each to fulfill limited commitments is correspondingly increased.

Some people oppose specialized schools on the grounds that they result in unequal educational opportunities; however, if specialization does increase a school's effectiveness, and if students are allowed to transfer freely between schools as their abilities and interests change, the charge is without much foundation. A more compelling argument is that diversified schools are more adaptable than specialized ones to changing social pressures and times. If public schools had not supported a broad range of objectives during the first part of this century, they would have had more difficulty assuming responsibility for new demands constantly being made of them, for more adult education and extracurricular programs, for example. Recognizing the restrictions that specialization imposes on the capacity for change, Clark says, "An image is a constraint, and the stronger the image, the stronger the constraint. . . . The college that strikes boldly for a highly distinctive character and a unique image is also making connections with the outside world that are not easily revoked. . . . When the times change, image and ingrained character resist change in the college. . . . Alumni and other outsiders remain identified with the old institution, and the old channels of referral and self-recruitment persist. To have a history of distinction is to accumulate resistance to change" (Clark, 1959b, pp. 165–66).

In a society characterized by both specialization and rapid changes, the question is whether a school can be more effective by limiting itself to a specialized objective or by diversifying its commitments in preparation for social change.

Boundary Definition and Maintenance Problems

The degree to which objectives are compromised by outside pressures depends on the organization's ability to defend its boundaries. Boundary definition—the demarcation of jurisdictional limits and the identification of members—and the maintenance of boundaries are necessary processes, because organizations depend on outsiders and must solicit their support without at the same time permitting them to interfere detrimentally with internal operations: The price paid by an organization for outside support is determined by its willingness and ability to defend its boundaries. Though legally under local lay control and traditionally subject to a community-school ideology favoring "democratic" participation of parents in school affairs, in fact a school is subject to the same fundamental principle as other organizations— outside control over the organization interrupts its direction, interferes with its coordination, and undermines its authority system.

Becker's (1952) study of school teachers describes their efforts to maintain authority in the face of challenges by outsiders. Fearing that parents will exercise their right to complain about school practices, teachers rely upon one another and upon the administration to reinforce their authority. Teachers are not supposed to question one another's teaching, especially in public, and they "stick together" informally. Most important, the principal is expected to support the teacher, to "back him up" against the weight of parents and students. His patronage is expected even when he personally disapproves a teacher's actions, so long as the teacher acted in good faith.

Although the concept, boundary, is implicit in discussions of school-community relations, the term has been used inconsistently in the literature. The geographical boundaries of public school districts identify one source of membership, but they do not establish the full limits of membership in the system. For example, are school board members outsiders? Are students? Is the P.T.A.? Is the American Legion exceeding its jurisdiction when it succeeds in determining textbook policy?

Boundaries are delineated by the jurisdictions of responsibility of members as opposed to nonmembers. They are based on two distinctions: (a) between insiders and outsiders, and (b) between cooperation and interference. Boundary problems develop when nonmembers interfere with activities that lie clearly within the organization's jurisdiction. But they also arise because distinctions concerning both membership and jurisdiction frequently are ambiguous, these ambiguities often producing challenges to membership rights and jurisdictional disputes.

Two basic types of conflict, then, can develop. First, where membership rights are not at issue, members may compete with nonmembers for jurisdiction over certain activities, e.g., parents compete with teachers for control over selection of textbooks. Second, where jurisdiction is not at issue (i.e., where a decision is clearly the school's perogative), conflict still may arise over who is authorized to represent the organization; e.g., can the P.T.A.'s public statements on school policy concerning vocational training ethically bind a school administration to that policy? These ambiguities are compounded when a particular party, such as an accrediting association, has a clear but limited jurisdiction within the organization over certain matters, but in all other respects is considered to be a nonmember without authority. Boundary disputes involve all facets. Some of these problems can be clarified by distinguishing between primary and secondary boundaries.

PRIMARY BOUNDARIES. Primary boundaries are fixed by official membership lists. They will be treated here categorically; that is, one is either a member or a nonmember as defined by certain possessions and rites of passage, such as swearing an oath, paying taxes, being on the payroll, signing an employment contract, or being listed on the membership roll. Schools utilize one of the most clear-cut of possible membership criteria, place of residence. However, even distinct school district lines are inadequate for placing some students, such as the many Puerto Rican children who "sleep around" among various relatives living in different parts of a city.

The consequential school boundaries are social, not geographical. However, district lines do have serious implications for social relations, as was illustrated in a study by Wilson (1959). Contemplating the fact that school districting tends to segregate youth of different social strata, and hence of different social aspiration, he asked, "Are the sons of manual workers more likely to adhere to middle-class values and have high educational aspirations if they attend a predominantly middle-class school?" Conversely, do the sons of professionals have more modest aspirations if they attend a predominantly working-class school? In thirteen high schools, located in each of three social class areas, a relationship was found between the fathers' occupation and the boys' grades; but pupils *of all classes* attending lower-class schools also exhibited lower educational aspiration than their counterparts in middle-class schools.[8] The performance of lower-class children in middle-class schools, on the other hand, increased.

Wilson's suggestion that geographical district lines modify schools' value systems only touches upon the full interplay between geographically defined boundary lines and social climates of schools. For example, one widely circulated, but largely untested, myth about comprehensive "neighborhood" schools is that they provide members of local communities with more incentive and opportunity to participate in and influence school affairs than would citywide or selected enrollment districts. Also, neighborhood schools presumably have more influence on their members than other types of districts. Yet, these assumptions are without much empirical support; it is even doubtful that most so-called neighborhood schools serve *neighborhoods*, in the sociological sense of that term. In view of the strong ideologies linking the neighborhood school with "democratic" education and growing countervailing pressures to desegregate neighborhood schools (also on the grounds of democratic principles), these appear to be fundamental issues in the nature of public education in the United States. Further analysis of the concept of secondary boundaries may prove to be fruitful for understanding them.

SECONDARY BOUNDARIES. Primary boundaries categorically separate members from nonmembers. However, in practice this elementary dichotomy does not take fully into account the more tenuous relations that many groups develop with schools. For example, are P.T.A. members, the school board, the state department of education, accrediting associations, and even students completely either nonmembers or members?

The problem of classifying marginal groups often has been handled by modifying *definitions* of social positions so that they will fit *a priori* conceptions of boundaries. For example, for some purposes part-time night school students are not considered to be "students," because they do not have complete membership in the school (not because their rights and obligations differ greatly from full-time students). The alternative is to consider them to be students who simply are further removed from the organization's boundaries than those attending full-time. The extent of membership needs to be determined independently from the definitions of positions.

What seems to be needed is an explicit set of criteria for extending boundary profiles beyond simple dichotomies between members and nonmembers without modifying the usual definitions. Some of these criteria are suggested in the commonsense notions of *containment* and *permeability*. Containment refers to how well an organization controls its official members. It includes (1) the *cohesiveness* of relationships among official members, and (2) the *pervasiveness* of control over official members. Permeability refers to how far groups not on the school's official membership list can penetrate into the organization's affairs. This concept includes both (3) the *extensiveness* of their participation, and consequently, (4) the degree of *external influence* they exercise.[9] These properties establish *secondary boundaries*—i.e., those, in addition to official membership, which identify the degree of membership and establish jurisdictions of control. They represent an organization's vulnerability to the influence of nonmembers and its ability to influence its own members. Each concept will be briefly described below.

The *cohesiveness* of an organization refers to the rate of both person-oriented and task-oriented interaction among members, as reflected in the number of mutual friendships among faculty and/or among students, and in the proportion of the student body regularly participating in extracurricular activities. The prototype of a cohesive school has (a) a fluid clique structure that includes most members and (b) extensive participation in group activities.

Pervasiveness refers to the scope of the activities of members which are controlled.[10] While all schools control the learning process, some, more than others, also regulate dress, language, and personal conduct. A school with well-established norms (rules or traditions) regulating numerous nonacademic spheres of teachers' and/or students' lives represents a pervasive system, while one which confines its regulations to academic or task-related activities is less pervasive. Principals are sometimes able to increase their control by recruiting tractable teachers (often less well-trained women) who are not likely to support the more militant members of the faculty in their efforts to resist the administration's normative controls.

The ability of organizations to defend their internal structure increases with pervasiveness. Regardless of dissent that may exist internally among members, a pervasive school can present a unanimous front, helpful in warding off criticism of outside groups; it is in a position to convey an impression of consensus on its actions (e.g., the children are too young to read Faulkner); and it can maintain enough control over its members to conceal some of its practices from public attention.

Extensiveness refers to the number of nonmember groups participating in the system. Some schools make extensive use of citizens' committees and serve the total community by making facilities, time, and staff available for nonschool-related activities (e.g., the boy scouts), while other schools have much less contact with outside groups and organizations. In an extensive school, then, rates of interaction between school members and outside groups are unusually high.

By *external influence* is meant the ability of a school to control other organizations relative to their control over it. Some schools are able to exert considerable influence over parents, local governments, and voluntary associations in the community, while perhaps more typically, other schools are dominated by these groups. An influential school, then, is able to control outside groups.

Profiles of secondary boundary characteristics can be used to classify nonmembers. For example, the national agency that accredits teacher education institutions (NCATE) would score low on extensiveness but high on influence in teachers colleges because it sets minimum standards and procedures. Thus, in this important sense, NCATE should be included within the secondary boundaries of schools of education.[11]

It should be noted that cohesiveness has been distinguished from extensiveness, and pervasiveness from influence, by whether or not members are interacting with nonmembers. For this discussion primary membership has been identified from official standards, which are independent of the secondary characteristics. However, it should be recognized that in conventional usage, the term "member" implicitly seems to presume certain secondary characteristics—i.e., high rates of interaction with other officials, relatively large numbers of their activities regulated by the administration, and more influence within the organization than most other persons. The conventional usage confuses the fact of official membership with a presumed degree of influence and participation. These two facets of the problem are being distinguished in the present discussion in order to portray boundaries as matters of degree. It seems desirable to visualize boundaries as a configuration of variables rather than as a mere dichotomy.

STRATEGIES OF BOUNDARY MAINTENANCE. The boundaries of schools are partially protected by the financial independence of districts and by other legal provisions, such as those guaranteeing separation of church and state. But the capacity of an organization to defend its boundaries also depends more specifically upon its power to control strategic boundary positions relating to outside groups. One investigator (Kerr, 1964) has enumerated several ways by which officials can control school boards, which perhaps represent the most crucial boundary positions in schools. The fact that in most states board members do not run for office on issues or represent specific constituents to whom they are accountable makes them vulnerable to the administration. Also, the fact that the public usually is split by class and ethnic interests reduces the influence of public sentiment, which might otherwise provide boards with more leverage against administrators. (Although here Kerr does not adequately recognize that cleavages and indifference in communities puts small cliques of citizens in a better position to gain disproportionate influence over school board members). Also, board members are dependent upon administrators for both technical information and for advice about policy. Since internal issues are the special preserve of administrators, board members are likely to feel uninformed about their responsibilities and about the technicalities of administration and teaching. In external issues with wider public appeal board members rely on administrators to define the issues and propose the alternatives, and because their own reputations depend on the success of the administration, they are unlikely to sabotage it in the absence of widespread public dissatisfaction. The visibility of outcomes of school board decisions and the risk of mistakes encourage members to conceal their actions from the public and to patronize the administration.

Vulnerable school boards, then, conspire with administrators against the public. Secrecy is a favorite strategy. Schools routinely withhold information from the public. Gross (1956) reported that all school board meetings were open to the public in only one-seventh of New England school districts, and 10 percent of the superintendents in the study reported that *none* of them were open. Three-fourths of the superintendents thought that newspaper editors should honor requests to withhold unfavorable information about the school from news stories. These and similar practices help to prevent public recognition of situations that might provoke outside interference and criticism.

As another defense, schools may try to confine threatening contacts with outsiders to situations they control. For example, before the local taxpayers association calls upon him to justify his school bond request, a superintendent may call a public meeting of his own. In one case a principal reportedly succeeded in having some meddlesome women, P.T.A. officers, replaced by men who had less free time than the women to devote to school affairs (Queen, 1965). Principals are universally expected to defend teachers' control over their classrooms in the face of parents' criticisms; whatever punishment the administration may impose upon a deviant teacher secretly, parents will not be permitted to believe they had anything to do with it. The complexity of many large systems also reduces parental influence by channeling complaining parents through an unfamiliar chain of command which extends from the classroom through a hierarchy of administrators, each of whom can disclaim responsibility for settling the problem. These "buck passing" procedures protect individuals in the system from time-consuming and awesome responsibilities which few busy administrators are willing to undertake, and at the same time they discourage outsiders.

Where interaction cannot be regulated by these bureaucratic devices, schools can use several informal strategies: implicit coercion, reciprocity, infiltration, and absorption. As an example of the first, some administrators have successfully coerced their districts into passing bond levies by threatening to close schools or to curtail the athletic program. They also can draw upon outside authorities for support, and superintendents are not above reminding their communities of the preferences of accrediting agencies if it will enhance the chances of a pet program.

School teachers also have cultivated a little-recognized, but effective coercive means of throttling potential parental intervention. Teachers' grading practices and the special recognition and privilege they give or withhold can influence a child's immediate social status among his peers and, ultimately, his later career and the social status of his family. Consequently, some parents live in mortal fear (whether well founded or not) that if they complain too much or too actively oppose school policies, teachers will covertly "take it out on the child," with more homework, more harassment, fewer honorary distinctions and appointments, or lower grades. This implicit threat undoubtedly keeps many parents away from teachers' classrooms. Although perhaps the threat is more imagined than real, since many schools seem to be as willing to bargain with troublemakers by devoting special attention, and perhaps favorable treatment, to their children in order to forestall criticism.

Reciprocity is a principle of bargaining whereby a favor performed by one party indebts another to return it. One's power depends upon obtaining a favorable balance of indebtedness, so that others owe him more than he owes any one of them (Blau, 1964). Using this principle a superintendent might "buy" the support of an influential construction company by arranging for it to secure school building contracts, or of a school board member by helping him to enter politics; the latter case eventually could provide a school with direct access to the community power structure.

A school may bargain away its authority over some activities in order to gain control of others. For example, it may defer to groups who seek to remove specific books from the library shelves in order to appease them with regard to more extensive controls over the school's library. Thus, it concedes a specific demand in exchange for its right to maintain general control over the books. In similar ways, schools sometimes implicitly bargain with specific groups for financial support, for example by teaching a distorted version of the Civil War in order to avoid alienating influential taxpayers.

As still another strategy, school administrators *infiltrate* influential community organizations where they sometimes develop enough influence to use these organizations' resources to support their school's projects. On the other hand, schools also have *absorbed* some activities in order to increase their scope of control. Sponsorship of dances, booster clubs, PTA's, the athletic program, vocational education, and advanced placement programs have helped to pacify outside pressures and at the same time to control these facets of student life and parental concern to a greater extent than would be the case if these activities were not school-sponsored. In the process, schools have extended their own boundaries. The absorption of some activities can also help to divert outsiders' attention from the school's intrinsic functions to its extrinsic ones. A booster club may interfere with the athletic program, but at the same time it is not concerned with the more critical aspects of curriculum planning and development.

Co-optation is a specific form of absorption in which an organization admits outsiders into its leadership circles in order to control them. In one community, a school which had been criticized by local businessmen for its commercial ventures successfully used the PTA as a front for the same activities while deriving the profits through that organization for its own use. One example of how a school co-opted parents is illustrated in Vidich and Bensman's (1960) study of a small town where a principal gained behind-the-scenes control of the PTA and curtailed the influence of parents while increasing his own. The PTA became a "front" organization and a pressure group for his proposals. By working informally through committees, his ideas were presented to the school board as those of the parent body. Then, the principal could not be blamed either for proposals that were defeated or for those of a controversial nature, while at the same time the PTA provided a sense of legitimacy and community support for his proposals.

Dahl reports a similar situation in New Haven, Connecticut where a principal enlisted the support of a PTA:

". . . He went to an important neighborhood leader, he said, and persuaded her that "the kids in the neighborhood needed help." Together they started a PTA. In order to involve the parents even more heavily, they then induced the PTA to endorse a hot lunch program; this required PTA members to raise funds and even to hire kitchen help. As participation in the PTA increased, the principal began to work for a new school to replace the old one. When obstacles were raised by the city administration, the principal called a meeting of PTA members and other neighborhood leaders and 'gave them a rousing speech asking for their help.' Within twenty-four hours they were on the phone and in other ways bringing pressure on the administration. The problem was solved." (Dahl, 1961, p. 156.)

DETERMINANTS OF BOUNDARIES. The influence of outsiders depends upon the procedures used to legally control and finance an organization. When both control and support are located in the same group, a school will be more vulnerable than when it has a degree of financial independence from its board of control. The effect of the source of support on the internal functions of a junior college is described in Maccoby's study of thirty *two-year* colleges:

"Two types of control hierarchies are easily distinguishable within these institutions. In one, the *local-autonomous*, the two-year college has its own tax district and an autonomous board of supervisors. In the other type, the *local-unified*, the college is a branch of the local public school system, responsible to the same board as are the secondary and elementary schools in the system, administered through the same superintendent of schools, and supported by the same tax district. . . . The local-autonomous colleges, because of their greater degree of independence, may have greater freedom to encourage competition of ideas, controversy, and non-conformity, and thus to support more strongly academic freedom practices. The local-unified institutions, in contrast, may be constrained by an administrative hierarchy whose members' primary concern and experience are with pre-college students—students whose education stresses themes of cohesion and unity. It may be more difficult to protect the local-unified college from community pressures that affect the pattern of education in elementary and secondary schools.

"The staffs of local-autonomous colleges are more likely to approve each practice (examined)[12] than are those of the local-unified colleges. Furthermore, the pattern of difference between the two types of schools remains the same within each teaching specialization and functional status group. Type of administrative control, however, has greater significance for some of these structurally defined groups than for others. Thus, the views of social science teachers in local-autonomous and local-unified colleges are similar (74 percent of each type approved seeking out controversial social issues; 44 percent of the former and

39 percent of the latter approved the expression of personal views), but administrators' views are quite different (78 percent in local-autonomous colleges approved seeking out controversial social issues compared to 56 percent in local-unified colleges; 42 percent in the former approved the expression of personal views compared to 32 percent in the latter).

"The data reported in this paper support the major thesis presented at the outset. On the two practices considered, both central to the concept of academic freedom, faculty and staff opinions were divided along principal structural lines of professional and institutional differentiation within higher education. The proffered interpretation points to professional roles and professional ties to the general and academic communities as intervening variables between the structure of higher education and academic opinion. However, the interpretation does not exclude the possibility that there are other intervening variables operative here, or even that the relationship between institutional structure and academic opinion may in part reflect their interconnection with factors other than those examined—for example, with differential recruitment.

"In effect, the thesis and interpretation apply to the academic world two axioms of sociological theory: that men's ideas and actions to a considerable extent are determined by the positions they occupy in a social system, *and* by the over-all form of the structure of that system." (Maccoby, 1960, pp. 890–892.)

This comparison of financial arrangements shows that these purely administrative decisions, having little apparent connection with class-work, nevertheless can affect the type of education going on in classrooms.

The control structure is equally important. Locally elected school boards provide citizens with easy access to schools. For, the myth of the "independent school district" notwithstanding, schools are not independent of local politics. In fact, school districts and other units of local government are very interdependent. They freely exchange facilities and services (such as playgrounds and library facilities and tax collection services), and schools are embroiled in political issues, such as is clearly implied in the controversies raging in Chicago and elsewhere over the school administration's policies on *de facto* segregation —policies backed by local politicians. Being elected, boards are subject to pressures from special interest groups; indeed, a substantial proportion of them represent such groups.[13]

State departments of education represent another, equally important, link in the control structure. They are major policy-making bodies, setting minimum standards and controlling such significant policies as the certification of teachers, the curriculum, and fiscal procedures. Because they are more remote and less involved in local politics than local school boards, state departments are more immune to purely local interest groups. By minimizing the influence of local groups (which some people equate with democratic control) and by protecting schools from purely provincial interest groups, state control can help local schools to preserve educational standards.

More recently, high rates of nationwide mobility and concentrations of wealth have promoted growth in federal aid to education, and with it more federal influence over local schools—which so far has been used to force schools to desegregate and to require loyalty oaths from students who receive federal assistance. Like state control, federal controls can offset regional inequities in educational opportunities while encouraging schools to respond to national needs rather than purely local ones.

The role of federal agencies in nationalizing education is being supplemented by a host of ancillary organizations (Wayland, 1964). The practices of private foundations, accrediting associations and testing organizations, programs in major teacher training institutions, and the policies of professional associations are all linked to a national system. Clark's discussion in Chapter 3 illustrates the complicity and alliances forming between scholars, the textbook industry and the federal government. The National Merit Scholarship program also, in supporting the federal interest in talented students, has encouraged teachers to produce scholarship winners, often to the neglect of terminal students (Campbell and Bunnell, 1963). Also, many middle-class schools gear their programs to prepare students for scholarship and college board examinations.

But, again, while evolving regional and nationwide standards of education have made schools more susceptible to national pressures, the often overlooked fact is that the same standards provide them with leverage to defend themselves from small, unrepresentative local or statewide cliques exercising provincial and often arbitrary power.

POTENTIALS OF SCHOOLS FOR ORGANIZATIONAL RESEARCH

The field of complex organization shares a shortcoming with the sociology of education: neither field has made substantial contributions to a *general* theory of organization. Although this is a grossly oversimplified statement, reliance on case studies limited to specific organizations has provided only slow headway toward a *general* theory of organizations; and studies of specific schools often have been so narrowly focused that they have not contributed widely to the parent field of sociology. A major handicap is the lack of a conceptual scheme to guide the projection of research findings on business, military, and other organizations to educational organizations, and through which research on educational organizations can feed back and contribute to the discipline of sociology. Until a general model classifying organizations is developed, it will be impossible to establish with any confidence the relevance of findings from other organizations for school settings, and the reverse.

THE SEARCH FOR UNIVERSAL PRINCIPLES OF ORGANIZATION. However, social scientists now are engaged in an exciting, if sometimes bewildering, search for principles of organization from which the basis of such a model might be formed. One approach to the problem is detailed in Caplow's (1964) essay on the subject. Treating human organizations as a separate and partially unique class of natural events which are neither culture-bound nor time-bound, he asserts a series of general "principles" of organization that presumably are universally applicable to all types of organizations.

Assuming the universality of his principles, Caplow does not entertain the possibility that they are more relevant to some types of organizations than to others. Aside from the fact that most of the principles have not been systematically tested, and are at times so abstract that they approach tautology, the approach is disconcerting because there are necessarily fewer universal principles than there are principles which apply under more limited conditions to specific *types* of organizations. The fact that a principle is limited to a specific organizational type does not make it any less a principle. At this stage of organizational theory it seems more fruitful to identify the principles which apply to specific types of organizations. This approach will require a relevant, and perhaps necessarily complex, typology of organizations.

THE UTILITY OF TYPOLOGIES. At least two strategies for developing a useful typology are available. One is to employ factor analytic, or profile analysis, techniques, for building an empirical taxonomy from a large catalogue of variables on the basis of descriptive correlation coefficients (Haas, 1965). A complementary but alternative approach begins with a *few* variables—the significance of which has been demonstrated by previous theory and research—that can serve as a basis for systematically evolving a typology from accumulating evidence. Although it risks overlooking some variables of potential significance, this procedure nevertheless safeguards against building a typology that is not systematically integrated with theory. Certainly at this stage there is ample opportunity to pursue both strategies.

If a valid typology were established, several purposes would be served. First, it would provide a basis for qualifying principles according to their scope of application; a principle could be limited in application to only one type of organization or, at the other extreme, it could be completely universal. Second, it would serve as a tool for integrating and interpreting the voluminous literature now accumulating on a wide range of organization. Third, it would facilitate the transfer of findings between samples of organizations serving different practical functions, but having theoretical similarities (such as elementary schools and colleges, or high schools and hospitals). Finally, by illuminating the gaps in the literature and by providing prior systematic knowledge about which variables are of importance, a typology of organizations will establish guidelines to future research.

AVAILABLE TYPOLOGIES. Sociologists already have become dissatisfied with the prevailing commonsense classifications based on simple distinctions between educational, business, and religious organizations. These simple classifications are inadequate because, depending on their size and complexity, their sources of support, their control structure, and other structural characteristics, there appears to be as much similarity as difference between churches, volunteer associations, hospitals, and other organizations. And there is as much difference as similarity among organizations in similar institutional settings; consider the potential number of differences in allocation problems, recruiting procedures, etc., between a consolidated parochial school and a metropolitan high school, or the differences between a retail department store and an automoible factory.

Recognizing the shortcomings of classifications based on conventional definitions, Blau and Scott (1962, pp. 45–58), have proposed a four-way classification based on the "primary beneficiary" of an organization: (1) the rank-and-file participants benefit most in *mutual-benefit associations;* (2) owners or managers benefit most in *business concerns;* (3) clients or "outsiders" who have regular contact benefit most in *service organizations;* and (4) the public-at-large benefits most in *commonweal organizations.* Conflict between professional and administrative norms is most characteristic of service organizations, where organizational principles sometimes impair the professional's ability to render a service to his clients.

Although useful for some purposes, classifications based on a single characteristic obviously miss many important characteristics. For instance, are private universities business concerns or service organizations?

Etzioni's (1961) typology, based on two types of distinctions, is somewhat more complex. First, in it three kinds of sanctions which an organization may employ to induce members to participate are recognized— coercive (the use of force), remunerative (the use of monetary and similar rewards as inducements), and normative (reliance on ethical and moral involvement of the members). The second basis of the typology consists of a distinction between three types of involvement of members: (1) *alienative,* or the fact that they are negative toward the organization; (2) *calculative,* or the fact that they are neutral and participate because of contractual bargains, and (3) *moral,* or the positive involvement of members in the values and activities of the organization. Etzioni then proposes three major types of organizations, depending upon the "congruence" between the preceding two dimensions: (1) *order*-type organizations have a simultaneously alienative-coercive pattern, as exemplified by prisons and forced labor camps; (2) *economic*-type organizations have a remunerative-calculative pattern, and are exemplified by factories and business; (3) *culture*-type organizations have a moral-normative pattern, and are exemplified by universities, schools, clubs, and fraternities.

Schools are classified in this typology as predominantly normative, culture-type organizations, with coercion in varying degrees as a secondary pattern. In the same class Etzioni puts general hospitals, ideological political organizations, social unions, voluntary associations, etc. If this classification is accurate, then research findings on these other culture-type organizations would be applicable to schools, and research on predominantly coercive organizations or utilitarian ones would not.

Although illuminating what are undoubtedly important variables, the typology can be misleading insofar as schools are concerned. In normative organizations, moral commitments of the membership presumably are high; yet there is little evidence that most teachers are deeply involved in their teaching careers. Only two in five persons trained to teach are in the classroom at any one time. Only 16 percent of the women and 29 percent of the men in a study of first-year school teachers expected to stay in classroom teaching until retirement (Mason, Dressel, and Bain, 1959). Indeed, this intermittent career pattern and the strong influence that business has had on public schools places them closer to the utilitarian classification. Normally students also share this utilitarian view, as reflected in their view of education as a means to a better job, for example. As Etzioni recognizes, the rates of alienation among students are higher than normal for normative organizations (at least one in three drops out). Indeed, with respect to the compulsory attendance laws necessary to keep substantial numbers of students in school and the more than occasional use of corporal punishment in some schools, they perhaps are closer to belonging in the coercive category than in either the normative or utilitarian ones.

Differences between these types are at best matters of degree; most organizations fall within the middle ranges of the typology where there is little difference among them. It is hardly reasonable to ignore the relevance of research on utilitarian organizations for schools because the findings are only slightly less applicable.

In final analysis, the typology is spoiled because most organizations use several forms of compliance and pursue diverse goals simultaneously, and because the vast majority of organizations will be concentrated among a few of the types (there are probably relatively few predominantly order-type organizations, for example).

Perhaps the underlying problem is that, despite the promise of newer typologies for dispensing with traditional institutional categories, their key terms—goal, commitment, prime beneficiary—in fact are derived from the customary institutional perspective. If more useful classifications are to be developed, distinctions based on broad institutional differences must be abandoned and substituted with the structural variables inherent to organizations *per se*.

A TYPOLOGY OF ELEMENTARY PROPERTIES OF ORGANIZATIONS. During the course of this chapter, several structural properties have been identified, properties which are of potential significance for explaining how educational organizations function. To the extent that these properties are relevant to *most* complex organizations, in combination they can form the nucleus of a more extensive typology which eventually can become relevant to organizations of diverse purposes. In this sense, they can be considered *elementary properties.*

Carlson's typology, based on the organizations' and the clients' respective control over participation, can serve as a point of departure for building a more elaborate typology from elementary properties. His analysis, however, needs to be elaborated to include variations in levels of professionalization and the organization's relation to the dominant institutions. Sources of control and finance also need to be incorporated within it. To illustrate, at one extreme, where both control and finance are the responsibility of one outside group, the organization is easily accessible to outsiders; the autonomy of its members is at a minimum. As another alternative, control can be distributed among laymen as well as among professional and administrative personnel, with financing controlled by a single outside group, such as is sometimes the case in single-industry communities having only one major source of tax revenue; in this case, coalitions between the financial source and other lay groups and administrators are likely to compromise the otherwise relatively favorable position of professionals stemming from the fact that outside control is distributed rather than concentrated. Third, control can be concentrated in the hands of a dominant group (a school board or a faculty) with financing distributed over a broad base. In this case the controlling group is likely to have a great deal of autonomy, even though some financial supporters may be reluctant to support the program. Finally, both control and financing can be distributed among a number of independent groups and power blocs, as is typical of the more esteemed privately endowed colleges and some of the largest public school systems; group autonomy and conflict will characterize such a system. It seems likely that these configurations of control and financing, in turn, are associated with the functional autonomy of subparts within the system and with profiles of power distributions within the hierarchy.

Secondary boundary profiles also can be incorporated as another dimension of the typology. An organization "high" on all four secondary boundary characteristics—cohesiveness, pervasiveness, extensiveness, and influence—would be a powerful one. However, perhaps the typical school is cohesive, pervasive, and extensive without being influential; it seems unlikely, on the other hand, that a school could have influence without being pervasive. Among pervasive schools, it might be useful to distinguish the cohesive from the less cohesive, for perhaps they have different types of control structures. Similarly, among more extensive schools, those with high influence can be distinguished from those with low influence; each would have very different implications for the meaning of local control.

Structures of control and boundary profiles are probably associated with internal organizational characteristics. For example, the status of professional employees may differ in publicly and in privately controlled organizations; and for a given level of professional expertise and bureaucratic complexity, the authority of outsiders will differ in each class of organization. The way public and private organizations are controlled also may influence their social prestige and upset the status security of their subunits. In some, the social prestige of subunits is comparable to their autonomy, while in others these statuses are inconsistent, either because a department has more internal autonomy than its outside prestige warrants, or the reverse.

Adding still another layer of concepts to the typology, the complexity of structure can be compared with the level of professional expertise of subordinates (and their supply relative to the demand for their services). The more complex the organization, the more authority administrators will have and the less control laymen can exert. The more professional expertise that subordinates demonstrate, on the other hand, the greater their authority will be relative to that of both administrators and laymen. It is expected that organizational conflict will increase as both professional expertise and organizational complexity increase; that in organizations of similar complexity, conflict will increase with professional expertise. Conversely, in organizations of similar levels of professional expertise, conflict will increase as bureaucratic complexity increases. Professional authority will be modified as well by differing *configurations* of complexity (e.g., combinations of high centralization and standardization compared to low centralization and high standardization). The extent of conflict with laymen is likely to be higher in public organizations because of strong community resistance to professional control.

ELEMENTARY PROPERTIES AND CHANGE. Organizational profiles contrived from combinations of these elementary properties will be of assistance with several key problems, especially the problem of organizational change. Whether or not outside influence can be resisted depends upon the pattern of elementary properties within the organization. For example, if an organization can select its members, it can keep out unwanted influences. But even if it cannot, a well-organized membership can resist outside pressures with the aid of certain tactics; the proportion of members active in professional organizations and unions should therefore be of significance. But while they are in a position to resist changes being advocated by laymen, professional groups are prone to accept and disseminate changes advocated by their colleagues. So it is difficult to anticipate the total *volume* of change.

The ratio of local to nonlocal control also will alter the rate and direction of change. With federal assistance and provocation many schools have changed their math and science programs and teaching techniques extensively during the past few years. In fact, a school which is impervious to local influences may be among the first to succumb to national ones. Educators in public and private schools un-doubtedly differ in their willingness and capacity to defend their boun-daries effectively from local and national thrusts. With the aid of stringent controls over admitting new members and independent sources of income, well-endowed private schools are in a more favorable position to resist local assaults, and the strategies of defense that are useful to them are not necessarily the most effective for public organizations of equal wealth.

The significance that source of support can have for organizational change was alluded to in Carlson's analysis. Dwelling on the fact that schools are protected and need not attend to all of the ordinary needs of an organization, he asserts that "domesticated" organizations adapt to change more slowly than wild ones. On the other hand, Callahan's thesis appears to be almost the opposite—that public schools are so domesticated and responsive to the dominant social trends that, far from lagging behind, they have been oversensitive to the wishes of reigning groups as each has successively gained national influence. Whenever the *dominant* figures happen to advocate updating the cur-riculum or other modern trends, the anomoly is complete.

However, the anomoly is more apparent than real. The two writers are not talking about the differences in *rates* of change, actually, but about different sources of pressure toward change. The difference be-tween "domesticated" and "nondomesticated" organizations is not their sensitivity to change as such, but the different sources of pressure to change to which each is subject. Carlson sees few pressures for change originating from the *internal* organization itself. But the very feature which makes a school domesticated—guaranteed clientele and other resources—makes it susceptible to *outside* forces. Domesticated organ-izations, therefore, quickly adapt to pressures from the outside to modify their *objectives*, while jealously guarding existing *internal pro-cedures* which outsiders have not attempted to control. What from one point of view permits domesticated organizations to withstand required internal changes, from another point of view makes them susceptible to outside pressures for changes.

Summary

To recapitulate, the following is a list of the elementary properties of organizations that were isolated and illustrated in this discussion, properties which, it is proposed, could form the basis of a universal typology of organizations:

A. Characteristics of the coordination system.
   Number of subparts
   Discrepancy between objectives and structure (structural lag)
   Level of professional expertise of subordinates and their supply relative to demand
   Proportion of activity and personnel devoted to maintaining the system (administration)
   Degree of standardization throughout the system (emphasis on rules and common procedures)
B. Characteristics of the power and authority systems.
   Number of levels of authority
   Power distribution profiles
   Functional autonomy of subparts
      Dependency on a central office and on other organizations in the system.
      Consistency in levels of autonomy, authority, and prestige
   Number of informal power cliques
   Drive toward professionalization among subordinates
C. Characteristics of the recruiting process.
   Selectivity in admitting new members
   Members' control over their own participation
   Rates of turnover for locals and cosmopolitans
D. Direction.
   Number of commitments
   Consensus on commitments (consistency)
   Abstractness of commitments
   Discrepancy between commitments and external constraints (goal displacement)
E. Characteristics of the boundary system.
   Source of legal control—private (religious or secular), public
   Sources of finance—local, state, and federal support
   Penetration of nonmembers into the organization—extensiveness and influence
   Organization's control over official members—cohesiveness and pervasiveness

Systematic comparisons of these properties with one another should gradually produce an empirically based, valid system for classifying organizations. For preliminary analyses, each of the preceding characteristics can be dichotomized into either "high" vs. "low" or "yes" vs. "no" categories. A school's character, then, would be defined by a profile based on the ratio of "high" or "yes" responses to the "lows" or "no's." Once schools have been differentiated among themselves by use of such profiles, hopefully the typology can be extended to noneducational systems. Within the guidelines of such a typology sociological studies of educational organizations can benefit from the growing theory and research on a wide variety of organizations. And this field, in turn, can contribute more systematically to the development of a theory of complex organizations.

Ronald G. Corwin is Associate Professor of Sociology at the Ohio State University, currently on leave with the Bureau of Research of the U.S. Office of Education. He received his Ph.D. in Sociology at the University of Minnesota and has held an appointment there, in the College of Education, and has also taught at Teachers College, Columbia University. He is author of *A Sociology of Education: Emerging Patterns of Class, Status and Power in Public Schools* (Appleton-Century-Crofts, 1965).

NOTES

1. These characteristics, however, are not necessarily directly associated with one another; some complex organizations may be relatively unspecialized and highly centralized, whereas in others the reverse is true.

2. It is useful to distinguish between a degree of power which permits complete *control* and relatively minor *influence* (Kahn and Boulding, 1964).

3. In some organizations these conflicts have been forestalled by adjustments in the traditional authority structure. For example, Goss (1961) observed a hospital in which administrators and physicians had divided administrative and professional authority. Administrators could only advise on medical questions, whereas physicians retained final authority over these matters; on the other hand, administrators retained final authority over scheduling and purchasing and similar administrative functions.

4. Carlson's studies of recruitment parallel the industrial studies of Gouldner (1954) and Guest (1962), and are related to McGee's study of institutional inbreeding in universities (1960).

5. *Structural* lag occurs when organizations fail to adapt their *procedures* to new commitments produced by changing conditions. This discussion, on the other hand, will focus on the relationship between an organization's *commitments* and external social changes; goal displacement is the process by which an organization substitutes outmoded commitments for new ones.

6. The degree of goal displacement can be measured by the difference between the priority of public expectations acknowledged by schools and the

priority actually given by schools to each expectation in distributing their resources.

7. A commitment requires evidence that the organization has little alternative but to fulfill its obligations. For example, a contract to pay teachers is a legal commitment; doubling the size of the athletic department and reducing the size of the language department are nonlegal commitments which also reduce alternatives and perpetuate a certain line of action. But, a stated goal does not become a commitment until some type of obligation has been incurred.

8. However, such evidence does not warrant the conclusion that schools of homogeneously lower-class composition are necessarily more detrimental to students than mixed schools (Havighurst, 1963). In the first place, there is probably a selective factor; children of lower-class families living in predominantly middle-class neighborhoods are likely to have initially higher educational aspirations. More important, the evidence may be a simple reflection of a self-fulfilling prophecy due to schools' neglect of problems in lower-class schools (relative to middle-class schools). Random samples of existing lower-class schools do not provide a fair test of what *could* be done for lower-class schools if special programs, such as the "Higher Horizons" program in New York City, were provided. With eduactional programs distinctively *designed* for lower-class students, it is possible that homogeneously lower-class schools would be more effective for the "undermotivated" lower-class students than are mixed schools.

9. A useful conceptual discussion of the term boundary is contained in Etzioni's analysis of complex organizations (Etzioni, 1961, pp. 20–21, 257). This discussion pursues some of his suggestions. Dr. Kent P. Schwirian collaborated in early discussions of this topic.

10. A high degree of cohesiveness and pervasiveness in combination define what Goffman (1961) refers to as a "total institution." Schools tend to become total institutions when they apply moral criteria for hiring teachers, and when they regulate students' conduct on the way to and from school.

11. Operationally, a boundary might be identified as that point at which the attempts of a group to influence the practices of an organization bring successful resistance from members. If a textbook advocated by the American Legion encounters less resistance than one introduced by the principal, then the American Legion is not totally an "outside" group.

12. That is, classroom discussions of controversial social science issues led by social science instructors, and the expression of an instructor's personal conclusions about topics which require the questioning of traditional values.

13. In emphasizing the absence of *visible* constituencies, Kerr's analysis of board membership, summarized previously, grossly underestimates this connection that some board members have with the informal power struc-

ture. One fourth of Massachusetts board members said that they represent a certain group in the community, and an additional 9 percent listed desire for political experience as a reason for seeking election (Gross, 1958, p. 73).

WORKS CITED

Anderson, James George (1964), *An Empirical Study of Bureaucratic Rules In the Junior High School*. Unpublished Ph.D. dissertation, John Hopkins University.

Anderson, Theodore R., and Seymour Warkow (1961), "Organizational Size and Functional Complexity," *Am. Social. Rev.*, **26**: 23–27.

Argyris, Chris (1957), *Personality and Organization*, Harper and Row, New York.

Argyris, Chris (1956), *Diagnosing Human Relations in Organizations: A Case Study of a Hospital*, Labor and Management Center, Yale University.

Argyris, Chris (1954), Human Relations in a Bank, *Harvard Bus. Rev.*, **32**: 63–72.

Barker, Roger G., *et al.* (1962), *Big School—Small School: Studies of the Effects of High School Size Upon the Behavior and Expectations of Students*, Midwest Psychological Field Station, University of Kansas.

Barnard, Chester I. (1938), *The Functions of the Executive*, Harvard University Press, Cambridge, Mass.

Barton, Allen H. (1961), *Organizational Measurement and Its Bearing on the Study of College Environments*. College Entrance Examination Board.

Becker, Howard S. (1952), Social-Class Variations in the Teacher-Pupil Relationship. *J. Educ. Sociol.*, **25**: 451–463.

Bendix, Reinhard (1962), *Max Weber: An Intellectual Portrait*. Anchor Books, Doubleday and Co., Garden City, New York.

Blau, Peter, and W. Richard Scott (1962), *Formal Organization*, Chandler Publishing Co., New York.

Blau, Peter M. (1964), *Exchange and Power in Social Life*, John Wiley and Sons, New York.

Blau, Peter M. (1956), *Bureaucracy in Modern Society*, Random House, New York.

Bliss, Don (1912), The Standard Test Applied. *Am. Sch. Bd. J.*, **XLIV**: 12.

Bonjean, Charles M., and Reece McGee (1965), "Scholastic Dishonesty Among Undergraduates in Differing Systems of Social Control," *Sociol. Educ.*, **33**: 127–137.

Callahan, Raymond E. (1962), *Education and the Cult of Efficiency*, University of Chicago Press, Chicago.

Campbell, Roald F., and Robert A. Bunnell (1963), *Nationalizing Influences on Secondary Education*, Midwest Administration Center, University of Chicago.

Campbell, Ronald F., and Russell T. Gregg (1957) (eds.), *Administrative Behavior in Education*, National Conference of Professors of Educational Administration.

Caplow, Theodore (1964), *Principles of Organization*, Harcourt, Brace, and World, New York.

Carlson, Richard O. (1964), "Environmental Constraints and Organizational Consequences: The Public School and Its Clients," in Daniel E. Griffiths (ed.), *Behavioral Science and Educational Administration Yearbook, Part II*, National Society for the Study of Education, Chap. XII.

Carlson, Richard O. (1962), *Executive Succession and Organizational Change: Place-Bound and Career-Bound Superintendents of Schools*, Midwest Administration Center, University of Chicago.

Cicourel, Aaron V., and John I. Kitsuse (1963), *The Educational Decision-Makers*, The Bobbs-Merrill Co., Indianapolis.

Clark, Burton R. (1960), *The Open Door College: A Case Study*, McGraw-Hill Book Company, New York.

Clark Burton R. (1959a), *Adult Education in Transition*, University of California Press, Berkeley.

Clark, Burton R. (1959b), "College Image and Student Selection," in *Selection and Educational Differentiation*, Center for the Study of Higher Education, University of California.

Corwin, Ronald G. (1965a), *A Sociology of Education: Emerging Patterns of Class, Status and Power in the Public Schools*, Appleton-Century-Crofts, New York.

Corwin, Ronald G. (1965b), "Militant Professionalism, Initiative and Compliance in Public Education," *Sociol. Educ.*, **38**:310–331.

Dahl, Robert A. (1961), *Who Governs? Democracy and Power in an American City*, Yale University Press, New Haven.

Dimock, Marshall E. (1952), "Expanding Jurisdictions: A Case Study in Bureaucratic Conflicts," in R. K. Merton, A. P. Gray, B. Hockey, H. C. Selvin (eds.), *Reader in Bureaucracy*, The Fress Press, New York.

Drucker, Peter F. (1953), "The Employee Society," *Am. J. Sociol.*, **58**:358–363.

Etzioni, Amitai (1961), *A Comparative Analysis of Complex Organizations*, The Free Press, New York.

Fichter, Joseph H. (1958), *Parochial School: A Sociological Study*, University of Notre Dame Press, Notre Dame, Ind.

Gerth, H. H., and C. Wright Mills (1958) (trans. and eds.), *From Max Weber: Essays in Sociology*, Oxford University Press, New York.

Goffman, Erving (1961), "The Characteristics of Total Institutions," in A. Etzioni (ed.), *Complex Organizations: A Sociological Reader*, Holt, Rinehart, and Winston, New York.

Gordon, C. Wayne, and Leta McKinney Adler (1963), *Dimensions of Teacher Leadership in Classroom Social Systems*, University of California, Berkeley.

Goslin, David (1963), *The Search for Ability*, Russell Sage Foundation, New York.

Goss, Mary E. (1961), "Influence and Authority Among Physicians in an Out-Patient Clinic," *Am. Sociol. Rev.*, **26**:39–50.

Gouldner, Alvin W. (1959), "Organizational Analysis," in Robert K. Merton et al. (eds.), *Sociology Today*, Basic Books, New York.

Gouldner, Alvin W. (1954), *Patterns of Industrial Bureaucracy*, The Free Press, New York.

Griffiths, Daniel E. (1956), *Human Relations in School Administration*, Appleton-Century-Crofts, New York.

Gross, Neal (1963), "Organizational Lag in American Universities," *Harvard Educ. Rev.*, **33**:58–73.

Gross, Neal (1958), *Who Runs Our Schools?* John Wiley and Sons, New York.

Gross, Neal (1956), *The Schools and the Press*, New England School Development Association.

Guest, Robert H. (1962), "Managerial Succession in Complex Organizations," *Am. J. Sociol.*, **LXVIII**:47–56.

Haas, J. Eugene, Richard H. Hall, and Norman J. Johnson (1965), "Toward an Empirically Derived Taxonomy of Organizations," in *Proceedings Research Conference on Behavior in Organizations.*

Halpin, Andrew W., and Don B. Croft (1962), *The Organizational Climate of Schools,* Cooperative Research Report, U.S. Office of Education, Washington, D.C.

Havighurst, Robert (1963), "Urban Development and the Educational System," in A. Harry Passow (ed.), *Education in Depressed Areas,* Bureau of Publications, Teachers College, Columbia University, New York.

Homans, George C. (1964), "Bringing Men Back In," *Amer. Sociol Rev.,* **29**: 809–818.

Kahn, Robert, and Elise Boulding (eds.) (1964), *Power and Conflict in Organizations,* Basic Books, New York.

Katz, Fred E. (1964), "The School as a Complex Organization," *Harv. Educ. Rev.,* **34**:428–455.

Kerr, Norman D. (1964), "The School Board as an Agency of Legitimation," *Sociol. Educ.,* **38**:34–59.

Kimbrough, Ralph B. (1964), *Political Power and Educational Decision-Making,* Rand McNally and Co., Skokie, Ill.

Laski, Harold (1960), "The Limitations of the Expert," in George B. DeHauser (ed.), *The Intellectuals,* The Free Press, New York.

Latane, Henry A. (1963), "The Rationality Model in Organizational Decision-Making," in Harold J. Leavitt (ed.), *The Social Science of Organizations,* Prentice-Hall, Englewood Cliffs, N.J.

Likert, Rensis (1961), *New Patterns of Management,* McGraw-Hill Book Company, New York.

Maccoby, Herbert (1960), "Controversy, Neutrality, and High Education," *Am. Sociol. Rev.,* **25**:884–893.

March, James G., and Herbert A. Simon (1958), *Organizations,* John Wiley and Sons, New York.

Mason, Ward S., Robert J. Dressel, and Robert K. Bain (1959), "Sex Role and Career Orientations of Beginning Teachers," *Harvard Educ. Rev.,* **29**:370–383.

McGee, Reece (1960), "The Function of Institutional Inbreeding," *Am. J. Sociol.,* **LXV**:483–488.

Midwest Administration Center (1962), "Bureaucracy and Teachers' Sense of Power" *Administrator's Notebook,* **11** (November).

Midwest Administration Center (1955), "Who Should Make What Decisions?" *Administrator's Notebook,* **3** (April).

Miles, Matthew B. (1964), "Educational Innovation: Resources, Strategies, and Unanswered Questions," *Am. Behav. Scient.,* **7**:8–25.

Miller, Norman (1958), "Social Class Differences Among American College Students." Unpublished Ph.D. dissertation, Columbia University.

Miller, Van, and Willard B. Spaulding (1952), *The Public Administration of American Schools,* World Publishing Co., Cleveland.

Moore, Wilbert (1951), *Industrial Relations and the Social Order,* The MacMillan Company, New York.

Mort, P. R., and F. G. Cornell (1941), *American Schools in Transition,* Bureau of Publications, Teachers College, Columbia University, New York.

Neff, Herbert B. (1964), "School Size and Scholarship," *The Ohio Sch. Bds. J.,* **8**:18.

Page, Charles Hunt (1946), "Bureaucracy's Other Face," *Soc. Forces,* **25**:88–94.

Peabody, Robert L. (1964), *Organizational Authority,* Atherton Press, New York.

Presthus, Robert (1962), *The Organizational Society,* Alfred A. Knopf, New York.

Queen, Bernard (1965), "Boundary Maintenance and the Public Schools," unpublished research paper.

Schultz, T. W. (1961), "Investment in Education," in A. H. Halsey, J. Floud, and C. A. Anderson (eds.), *Education, Economy, and Society,* The Free Press, New York.

Scott, William A. (1965), *Values and Organizations,* Rand McNally and Co., Skokie, Ill.

Sills, David L. (1957), *The Volunteers,* The Free Press, New York.

Solomon, Benjamin (1961), "A Profession Taken for Granted," *Sch. Rev.,* **69**: 286–299.

Stern, G. G. (1963), "The Intellectual Climate of College Environments," *Harvard Educ. Rev.,* **33**:21–24.

Sykes, Gresham (1956), "The Corruption of Authority and Rehabilitation," *Soc. Forces,* **34**:257–262.

Tannenbaum, Arnold S. (1961), "Control and Effectiveness in a Voluntary Organization," *Amer. J. Sociol.,* **LXVII**:33–46.

Taylor, Frederick W. (1911), *The Principles of Scientific Management,* Harper & Row, New York.

Terrien, F. C., and D. C. Mills (1955), "The Effect of Changing Size Upon the Internal Structure of an Organization," *Am. Sociol. Rev.,* **20**:11–13.

Udy, Stanley W., Jr. (1959), "Bureaucracy and Rationality in Weber's Theory," *Am. Sociol. Rev.,* **24**:791–795.

Vidich, Arthur, and Joseph Bensman (1960), *Small Town in Mass Society,* Doubleday and Co., Garden City, New York.

Wayland, Sloan R. (1964), "Structural Features of American Education as Basic Factors in Innovation," in Matthew B. Miles (ed.), *Innovation in Education,* Teachers College, Columbia University, New York.

Wilson, Alan B. (1959), "Residential Segregation of Social Classes and Aspirations of High School Boys," *Am. Sociol. Rev.,* **24**:836–845.

Wilson, James Q. (1966), "Innovation in Organization: Notes Toward a Theory," in James D. Thompson (ed.), *Approaches to Organizational Design,* University of Pittsburgh Press, Pittsburgh.

6 Education and the Sociology of Work

Joel E. Gerstl

Temple University

PERSPECTIVES OF THE SOCIOLOGY OF WORK AND OCCUPATIONS

The essence of occupational analysis is to probe in depth into the worlds of work of particular occupational groups. Its relevance for the sociology of education, accordingly, lies in dealing with the men and women who work as educators and the manner in which they shape and are shaped by their occupation. But a comprehensive view initially requires attention to cultural, historical, and social contexts. Before focusing upon the drama of work, the stage must be set.

A basic point of departure involves recognition of the cultural context within which occupational activities are pursued, for, work is so highly valued in contemporary American society, it is difficult to acknowledge that it has not always and everywhere been similarly esteemed. Our elites are anything but a leisure class; this circumstance is highly novel. In fact, the tradition of Western civilization involves an inheritance of a variety of orientations: for the ancient Greeks all work was servile; for the medieval world it was a necessary fate resulting from Adam's fall; the Calvinist ethic held work to be a means of self-discipline and a sign of the achievement of grace; and modern themes —whether grounded in religious or political philosophy—emphasize work as essentially creative (Tilgher, 1930; De Grazia, 1962; Fogarty, 1964).

The most important general implication of the cultural value placed upon work in our own society, as shown in studies of the retired, the unemployed, and through fantasy questions about alternatives to employment, is that work is motivated by more than mere economic necessity. It is a social bond. Those accustomed to spending some third of their day at work, in its absence, are not clear that they are among the living (Wilensky, 1964).

Variations of orientations within similar cultural contexts also occur. The Greek philosophers and slaves might have agreed that work was not pleasant, but it is no more likely that the medieval serf, craftsman, crusader, and monk agreed about the meaning and worth of their everyday activities than do contemporary cosmonauts, school teachers, and coal miners. Like job satisfaction, commitment to particular occupations is highly related to the status of the occupation. Although there are differences between professions (Blauner, 1960), a high degree of commitment to the area of specialization is a general characteristic of all professions. Accordingly, if the aim is to place an occupation in its cultural context, both the high value placed upon the pursuit of work in general and the unique nature of commitment in the professions must be considered. A related issue, especially important with respect to educational occupations, is the different meaning and evaluation of work for men and for women in our society.

Historical perspectives—which might be construed as part of the cultural context focusing upon questions of change—have been sadly neglected in occupational studies (as in most sociological analysis). Attention to changes over time, like comparisons between occupations or between societies, could serve to broaden the level of explanation. The peculiarities of historical antecedents may frequently illuminate anomolies of the present world of work. But it must not be assumed that homage to antecedents is invariably relevant to current understanding. Historical materials to which aspirants to an occupation are frequently exposed—and history of education courses are prime examples—may serve mainly ritualistic functions. Occupations, like families, "seek an heroic geneology to strengthen their claims to license and mandate" (Hughes, 1959, p. 453). Tracing education from Protagoras or Confucius through Abelard to Dewey can, at best, provide a sweeping perspective.

The added depth of interpretation of the world of work afforded by an appropriate sense of history is demonstrated in American sociology by the writings of such persons as Mills (1951) and Riesman (1950). Systematic use of historical materials in the study of occupations is, however, best exemplified by the tradition of British sociology. Carr-Saunders and Wilson's study of the development of professions (1933) remains a classic in the field. More recently, Lockwood's *Black-Coated Worker* (1958) and Tropp's *The School Teachers* (1957) demonstrate the rich yield resulting from a combination of historical and sociological frameworks. In studies such as these, the described evolution of the particular occupations under investigation is revealing, but tracing patterns of development requires recognition of political, social, and economic transformations within the context of which occupational changes took place—and which occupational changes helped to bring about.

At the most macroscopic level, there are the basic processes that are altering the nature of contemporary society: urbanization, bureaucratization, mass communications, and the acceleration of technological innovation. This is the context within which a comprehensive occupational analysis needs to be cast. Industrial and occupational trends— the changing nature and distribution of the work force—reflect these sweeping societal transformations. Mention of some of the major patterns serves to indicate the crucial relevance of these materials, above all in the recognition that particular trends in one occupation may (or may not) be part of more general trends. For example, the very term "manpower" is today somewhat misleading to the extent that womanpower has become an increasingly significant component of the work force. The most pervasive transformation in the industrial structure in the past half century has clearly been that from farm to nonfarm employment; within the latter sector, changes have been equally dramatic, concentrations shifting from goods-producing industries to service-producing ones. The service-producing sector has come to employ a majority of the work force. Correspondingly, in terms of occupational structure, the United States has become the only country in the world with more white-collar than blue-collar workers, professional and clerical-sales groups having doubled their proportions in a half century (cf. Wolfbein, 1964).

WORK SETTING. The cultural, historical, social, and demographic dimensions thus far referred to serve but a locational function: they provide the milieu for occupational analysis. More immediately akin to the occupational world is the specific setting of employment. An initial consideration is of organizational context (or its absence, as is the case for the declining breed of independent practitioners). Beyond the general trend of an increasing proportion of all occupational roles being pursued in organizations, it is necessary to recognize the array of settings of employment for any one occupation.

The setting of employment specifies the structure within which occupational roles are played (cf. Chap. IV, *Supra*). Initially, it aids in delineating the contours of an occupation and suggests the degree of homogeneity or heterogeneity behind occupational labels. Thus, for example, the extent to which teaching represents a unitary profession is immediately brought into question when the distinction between primary or secondary and university settings is introduced.

An organization incorporates a system of positions, which comprise the rungs its members might hope to climb. What is more important for understanding occupational behavior, organizations, as authority systems with formal hierarchies, will designate who is responsible to whom. The rules of an organization—whether a factory, an army, a school, or a governmental bureau—will structure the behavior of occupational groups involved in it.

As has been thoroughly documented in the literature on organizations, the complexities of organizational life cannot be accounted for by attention to formal aspects alone. Indeed, organizational goals sometimes may be enhanced by deviations from rules. The subtleties of informal work-group and colleague relationships within formal systems may be more informative than the formal structures themselves.

In addition, exterior work-linked organizational allegiances frequently influence occupational behavior, perhaps more than the workplace itself does. For industrial workers, the issue is that of dual loyalty toward employers and unions. Elsewhere in the occupational hierarchy, similar conflicts may be found in terms of the norms and controls of employers as opposed to those of professional groups, between local and cosmopolitan orientations (see, for example, Kornhauser, 1962). Accordingly, attention to processes of professionalization is as essential to occupational analysis as is that to unionization for the interpretation of the industrial scene.

Although the notion of employment setting focuses upon the organizational and occupational structures within which work roles are played, the roles themselves also require scrutiny. In simplest terms, they involve the activities performed by the holder of an occupational position.

CAREERS. Although attention to structures and organizational influences are important elements of occupational analysis, the one concept most integral to the sociology of work is that of careers. Its use in the field has not, however, been entirely consistent. The narrower connotation refers to predictable steps within bureaucratic hierarchies as suggested by Wilensky's reference (1960) to careers as well-ordered work lives within managerial levels of organizations, gripping only a minority of the labor force. At the other extreme, it has been indicated that although, "Careers in our society are thought of very much in terms of jobs, for these are the characteristic and crucial connections of the individual with the institutional structure . . . the career is by no means exhausted in a series of business and professional achievements" (Hughes, 1958, p. 64). Or, "Career, in the most generic sense, refers to the fate of a man running his life-cycle in a particular society at a particular time" (Hughes, 1959, p. 455).

Both of these usages are appropriate for the particular types of issues they deal with, but a great deal of occupational analysis is better served by a blend incorporating components of each, restricted to occupational paths, *but* not merely to clear bureaucratic steps. Thus careers may be defined as the succession of positions in the occupational life cycle, including movement into and out of the work world.

The first phase of the career cycle is that of recruitment. It is an area of investigation with strong practical implications in light of shortages encountered in various occupations, but is also intriguing from a broader, sociological point of view: given the large number of occupations in a complex industrial society, how are they filled? For the individual, each phase of his career is characterized by the making of decisions. The complex process of occupational choice (see, for example, Ginzberg, 1951) is likely to be the most momentous of these, yet much remains unknown about it. Recent work has focused upon the influence of values associated with various occupations (Rosenberg, 1957). The understanding of occupational choice must, of course, take into account sources of constraint upon individuals, for example through controls upon entry imposed by occupations. More is known about the caliber and origins of recruits in various fields than about how occupational roles come to be filled. Again, the implications of these findings are both practical in terms of standards of performance, and revealing of more pervasive processes, such as mobility trends—the extent to which "careers are open to talent" (cf. Gerstl and Perrucci, 1965).

The second phase in an occupational career (which may not in all cases be separate from either recruitment or further advancement) is one of transition. Whether through formal instruction, apprenticeship, or initial experience, it involves learning how to play occupational roles. The manifest purpose of occupational training is to pass on particular skills; but much more is transmitted during the process. New recruits have to be socialized to acquire the appropriate meanings and values of occupational cultures. It is curious that although sociologists have long been fascinated by the generic process of socialization—the manner in which a child learns to be a social being and to play his various social roles—adult socialization into the occupational world has only recently become a topic of interest. To date research has concentrated most heavily upon medical schools (Merton et al., 1957; Becker et al., 1961). Studies such as these have shown the subtleties of learning appropriate occupational behavior from classmates, clients, and associated personnel as well as from faculty. Further comparative work is needed in this area, not only to trace the intriguing processes of transmission, but also to discover the elements of occupational cultures that are passed on. Occupational cultures contain bodies of knowledge, ideologies, and myths as well as norms and technologies. Much remains to be learned of the interplay of these elements.

Both of the initial phases of careers subsume numbers of separate steps—as the occupational decision becomes more firmly crystallized, or as the trainee advances from novice to journeyman. It is, however, in the final, mature phase of occupational life that developmental stages assume most significance. Once one becomes an accepted bona fide member of an occupation, what lies ahead? What are the career contingencies?

The analysis of career patterns tends frequently to focus upon movement, of either a vertical or horizontal type. But the connotation of development implicit in the term "career" does not mean that movement is equally characteristic of all occupations. Neither need job changes be related to each other in a coherent manner, nor when a general pattern does seem to exist, do all steps invariably lead upward.

At one extreme are the unrelated shifts from one job to another, mainly at the same status level, common among unskilled workers. Lifetime commitment, on the other hand, is the general pattern among professionals. "So strong is this tendency that the ex-lawyer or ex-physician is likely to be regarded rather like an unfrocked priest, as a person who has proved unworthy of great responsibilities" (Caplow, 1954, p. 106). But clearly, the ex-teacher or the engineer turned salesmanager are not so regarded. The degree of career stability varies considerably even within the professional category (Reiss, 1955).

Accordingly, in addition to questions concerning stability and rates of mobility, it is necessary to consider the unique career contingencies that confront various occupational groups. If there is a hierarchical ladder, how many rungs does it have and what are the requirements for the various levels? How common is it for members of an occupation to reach various heights? What are the consequences of horizontal moves for getting ahead? Are there norms concerning the appropriate amount of movement between jobs? Might a change to a different position at a similar hierarchical level under some conditions be considered more rewarding than a higher rank? To what extent does advancement require a change of activity—perhaps even abandonment of previous occupational identity (e.g., from teaching to administration)? Is such a change still part of one career pattern?

Most important of all are the typical career patterns that characterize occupational groups seen in the context of *their* values and ideologies. Gross indicators of success, such as income, reveal a great deal about career curves in the very plotting of age by income graphs, showing when peaks are reached. But although a reasonable income is obviously a universal aim, levels of aspiration and appropriate points of comparison differ from one occupation to another. Indeed, honorific or intrinsic rewards may sometimes be the most highly coveted. Thus the evaluation of attainment, like that of the career patterns pursued, needs to be made in terms of structural and ideological contingencies of occupational groups.

WORK AND SOCIETY. Although careers, as we have defined them, constitute the pivotal materials of occupational studies, they do not exhaust the concerns of occupational analysis. Even when the career is cast within its cultural and historical milieu and the structure of its organizational contexts, a major area still remains to be explored if the reciprocal influences of work and society are to be explained. Indeed, the links between work and other social roles, the connections between changes in occupational and other statuses, touch upon the most theoretically fruitful areas of investigation. They require firm grounding in research about the world of work itself, but not without recognition of the permeation of their social institutions.

The most general question involved is the extent to which the work role influences general orientations and nonwork activities. To what extent are occupational groups status groups with distinctive life styles? Alternatively, the impact of forces such as legal mechanisms or community norms upon the performance of the occupational role are also fundamental.

The foregoing account of perspectives in the sociology of work and occupations does not pretend to be a comprehensive overview of what is known in the field. This purpose can only be pursued in textbooks or collections designed for such an aim (see Caplow, 1954; Gross, 1958; Nosow and Form, 1962). The attempt has been merely to indicate the nature of the perspectives involved—some angles of vision felt to be essential for occupational analysis, for understanding work as a social activity.

In the next section some of the sociological dimensions of education as an occupation will be treated in more detail. It is not intended to take into account all the perspectives that have been referred to, nor to summarize the gamut of social factors impinging upon the process of education (for a comprehensive review of the latter, see Charters, 1963). Rather, by confining the discussion to a limited number of issues, the aim is not only to concentrate upon those felt to be unique to the field of education, but also to consider their potentials for the understanding of occupational life as an aspect of social life.

EDUCATION: AN OCCUPATIONAL ANALYSIS

Locating the Occupation

"Education" is a generic term. Even if confined to school settings, it subsumes both teaching and administration at all levels of the educational hierarchy: primary and secondary schools, universities and colleges, and professional schools. Each of these includes a variety of separate occupational constellations.[1] Whatever other distinctions might be introduced, the occupational worlds of college teachers and school teachers have little in common in terms of the characteristics of incumbents, their careers and their roles. The discussion in this chapter will focus on school teachers.

Two basic demographic characteristics of the contemporary American teaching profession serve to explain many of its unique problems. In a society committed to mass education, it is not surprising that teaching is the largest profession. Yet the magnitude of this occupational category is overwhelming: there are currently over one and a half million persons engaged in primary and secondary teaching (*Statistical Abstracts*, 1964), representing about one in every forty-five employed adults. The singular magnitude of the teaching profession is revealed most dramatically in its current recruiting of a third of all college graduates (Davis, 1963).

Equally crucial is that most fundamental of all human dichotomies: sex. The social repercussions of the differences between men and women hardly need to be documented (*Vivent les différences!*). The implications of sex for occupational behavior are not patent, however, and nowhere more relevant than in the American teaching profession. Here, women have constituted a majority for the past century and currently are more highly represented than they are in any other country (Lieberman, 1956; Hans, 1953). Although a fourth of all teachers are men—the sex ratio being nearly equal in secondary schools, with all but a seventh of elementary teachers female (NEA, 1964)—the occupational image and predominant stereotype has been a feminine one. Men in teaching have hardly even been thought of as a minority group. Recent increases in the proportion of men beginning teaching careers (Mason, 1961), and the publicity given to Mr. Novak rather than Miss Brooks, cannot negate but may serve to attenuate the view of teaching as "woman's work."

The need for an increasing number of teachers engendered by the growth of mass education, combined with the feeling that such work was appropriate for the fair sex, account for the high proportion of women in teaching. The limited deference accorded to female occupations, and the sheer numerical preponderance of teachers—resulting in a high degree of visibility and patterns of recruitment which were not highly discriminating of sex, training, or origins—are among the most important factors explaining the social standing of the occupation.

In spite of golden age theories that suggest things must have been better in the past, there is little evidence that teachers were more highly esteemed previously. The appropriate comparison can only be made in terms of public education, teachers of elites being a special case. The less-than-reputable status of teachers in the early days of state education is obvious in the use of various societal castoffs to fill this role (those who can, do; those who cannot, teach.) Thus, Frederick the Great employed invalid soldiers, and Peter the Great's schools were staffed with drunken drop-outs from seminaries. Early grammar schools in many countries derived from charitable relief institutions "manned" by women, cripples, and those incapable of physical labor (Hall, Hans, and Lauwerys, 1953).

Given these origins, the position of teachers in society would appear to have improved considerably. Historical factors need to be taken into account in explaining the present status situation of the occupation —for example, the early precedents for recruiting women, or the tradition of limited training standards. On the other hand, disreputable origins in themselves, even if generally known (which they are not), are unlikely bases for current prestige judgments. Barber-surgeon ancestry hardly colors our views of doctors. The present status of teaching must be seen mainly in terms of contemporary determinants and criteria of comparison.

The prime touchstone of occupational respectability is increasingly that of "professional" standing. The concept—appropriately or not based upon the traditional models of law and medicine—is, at best, elusive in its descriptive connotation. But it clearly indicates a desirable level of prestige. Like many other occupations unsure of measuring up to the criteria of professionalism, education has been very much concerned with its relative standing. Of course, it ranks lower than most educators—reflecting the egocentrism common within occupational groups—feel it should.

Readings of occupational prestige which have been taken in the United States over the past forty years (both by disinterested sociologists and by members of other occupations worried about their own status) have shown a remarkable stability through time (Hodge, Siegel, and Rossi, 1964). Teachers have consistently been placed below most professional categories, although, interestingly, they now rank above cultural and communication professions—i.e., artist, musician, author, journalist.

Between 1947 and 1963, although not arriving in the league of the established professions, the prestige rating of teachers did improve (from a rank of 34 out of 90 to one of 27.5; ibid., p. 290). Other occupational upgrading that took place in this time period, most dramatically that of the nuclear physicist, has been attributed to the increased publicity such work received. Similar considerations would apply to teachers, whose improvement was comparable to the average increases among scientific professions and greater than that of other professions.

The consistent location of teachers below other professions, however, is the major factor that needs to be explained. Comparisons between countries have also revealed remarkable consistency in the relative standing of occupations—including that of teachers. Because these similarities persist despite cultural differences (for example, in the value placed upon education) the universal features of industrial occupational systems have been emphasized in interpreting the findings (Inkeles and Rossi, 1956). Yet the many hidden assumptions in such studies raise serious questions about the sources of the similarities. Furthermore, studies focusing upon narrower segments of the occupational hierarchy show less consensus and suggest the importance of cultural differences in values (Gerstl and Cohen, 1964).

Accordingly, the relative standing of an occupation in the social structure needs to be assessed in terms of the criteria of evaluation. Most important of all is the recognition of the multidimensional bases of prestige judgments. Cultural values, the occupational structure itself, and the characteristics of incumbents are the basic determinants. Each of these subsumes numerous components, which are not consistently invoked in evaluating occupations.

Values are most important in defining the functional importance of the specific activity performed by the members of an occupation, as well as that of the worth of work as such and of public service as contrasted with extrinsic rewards. They also explain judgments concerning the desirability of a variety of work situation attributes, for example, office versus manual work, dealing with people versus ideas, and being autonomous.

The possibility of autonomy is a function of the occupational structure, which delineates the power and influence of occupational groups —dimensions that tend to be inextricably bound up with prestige evaluations. The occupational structure determines the degree of control incumbents have over their status situation, most obviously in the financial rewards they are able to command, more broadly in their bargaining position, including the determination of their scarcity value by criteria of entry such as educational requirements. Control of behavior on the job vis-à-vis superiors and clients (or pupils) is also contingent upon the occupational structure. Indeed, it has been suggested that this element correlates almost perfectly with rank order prestige ratings (Caplow, 1954).

Shaped by cultural values and occupational structure, the visible referents of evaluation are the incumbents themselves, thought of— some more accurately than others—in terms of stereotypes and social characteristics. The latter include their numbers, sex, social origins, and amount of talent or skill (the last named, although judged by typical performance, can, except for esoteric occupations, be indicated by amount of training or IQ).

Both enhancing and diminishing factors contribute towards the social standing of an occupation. In terms of contemporary American values, education—whether conceived instrumentally as a means for other ends, or as intrinsically worthwhile—ranks among the highest (see, for example, Williams, 1956; Barrett, 1961). Moreover, teaching is thought of as providing a public service. Yet only limited deference is accorded to the purveyors of education. The amount of attention given to educational problems in these post-sputnik years has influenced attitudes concerning the importance of education and slightly altered evaluations of teachers. It may be partly because the recently growing concern with educational issues has not been uncritical, because education has not quite been deified, that its practitioners have been regarded as less than holy men or less than vestal virgins.

The characteristics of teachers and their occupational structure afford more immediate explanations of their social standing. First are the phenomena previously referred to of a female occupational image and numerical abundance. Furthermore, the social origins of teachers are more lowly than are those of members of most other professions (Mason, 1961), as is their amount of professional training and level of intelligence (Lieberman, 1956).

The occupational structure of teaching also has a mainly negative valence upon status, especially in contrast with that of other professions. Education associations are weak, the financial rewards of teaching are low, and autonomy is limited. Not only is the teacher an employee subject to the authority of direct supervisors and school boards, but those whose behavior she controls are mere children.

If the status situation appears overly grim, it must be emphasized that other—more esteemed—professions are the frame of reference. It is because teachers compare unfavorably on a variety of criteria that their standing is incommensurate with the value placed upon education, and below that of most professions. Clearly, teaching is more highly thought of than the vast array of types of work that complete the occupational hierarchy. Teachers may feel that they suffer from *relative* deprivation, but if the pursuit of teaching was not found essentially attractive, recruitment difficulties would be much more extreme than at present.

Career Stages

RECRUITMENT. Discussions of occupational recruitment tend mainly to be descriptive of the characteristics of incumbents. Although such information is in itself revealing, its significance lies in the implications of patterns of recruitment for role performance, career orientations, and the development of the profession. Why does teaching draw upon particular sectors of the population and what are the consequences?

A most salient factor influencing the process of recruitment is the visibility of teachers as possible role-models for their pupils. Children see the teacher at work as they see no other; Daddy's job may be talked about, but with rare exceptions (including teacher-fathers) it remains mysterious. Apparently, familiarity with the teacher's classroom performance does not breed contempt, for students assign higher prestige to teachers than do adults (Hutchings, 1963). The teacher's visibility in large part accounts for decisions about becoming teachers being made at an earlier age than are commitments to other professions, for example, law and medicine (Kendall and Merton, 1958). Half of beginning teachers made their occupational choice before entering college, and all but a fourth by their junior year (Mason, 1961). That women choose teaching careers at an earlier age than men do is also partly due to the visibility of women in elementary education. In addition, the cultural restrictions defining teaching as one of the few feminine professions buttress this tendency.

The numerical needs of the teaching profession, as we have indicated, have been among the prime factors explaining the early and continuing pattern of female dominance. The very fact of female dominance is *the* crucial characteristic of those recruited into teaching, establishing a pattern of self-fulfilling prophecy, the presence of women attracting more women.

Numerical needs also account for the amount of upward mobility into teaching. Although rates of direct occupational inheritance (sons and daughters of teachers) are comparable to those found in other professions, and there is considerable recruitment from professional strata (*ibid.*) these sources alone could not supply the number of teachers needed. Thus, three-fifths of beginning teachers have advanced beyond the occupational status of their fathers (*ibid*). College students planning to do graduate work in education represent lower socioeconomic backgrounds than do students in almost every other graduate field (Davis, 1964). Although teachers are more likely to be of middle-class origin than is the population at large, they are less frequently recruited from white-collar families than are members of the established professions. Interestingly, men and women teachers tend to be drawn from different class backgrounds, the majority of women being from white-collar homes and men more often from working-class origins (Mason, 1961). Accordingly, teaching tends to involve status continuity for women and upward mobility for men.

Furthermore, "teaching 'selects' different kinds of people from each social stratum. Persons from upper and upper middle-class backgrounds *who are also upwardly mobile* [in aspiration] are less likely to enter teaching (and more likely to enter upper-class occupations such as medicine and law) than persons from working-class backgrounds who are upwardly mobile. Teaching, for the latter, is a step upward; for the former, it is not" (Colombotos, 1962, p. 66). The alternative mobility orientations corresponding to social origins are reflected in career plans. Working-class men express more ambitious career aspirations within education than middle-class men: in one study over a third of the former and only a fifth of the latter are reported as hoping to advance from classroom teaching to administrative posts. But higher proportions say they realistically *expect* to stay in classroom teaching than would like to stay, the disparity being greater among those of working-class origins than among middle-class teachers (Colombotos, forthcoming).

Evidence concerning the consequences of social origins upon the actual classroom performance of teachers remains inconclusive. But, ". . . if teachers are drawn largely from social classes which offer very limited opportunities for intellectual and cultural development, classes which do not even place a high valuation on such development, it would be surprising indeed for this to have no effect on the over-all quality of educational services" (Lieberman, 1956, p. 467). The issue requires attention to the relative impact of social origins and subsequent socialization.

A characteristic of teachers, the consequences of which are more pervasive and unalterable than origins is that of the quality of recruits. Again, the numerical needs of the profession, together with the nature of entry requirements, are major determinants. Despite defensive statements on the part of educators that teachers compare favorably with other occupational groups in intellectual ability, there is considerable evidence that they do not. Whether in terms of intelligence test scores (Wolfle, 1954) or an academic performance index [based upon cumulative grade point average and the quality of the school attended (Davis, 1964)] those in education rank below most other fields. For example, both men and women students in education include a smaller proportion from the top fifth in academic performance than in *any* other academic subject (save minor health fields), men of high caliber being especially underrepresented (*ibid.*). Even if the average level of teachers' abilities is adequate for many purposes, it can have only negative effects upon the state of education. The low standing of education departments is reflective of the quality of their students. The inability to attract good students will, in turn, contribute to a vicious cycle of reinforced intellectual mediocrity.

Although such factors as the visibility of an occupation and its entrance requirements will strongly influence patterns of recruitment, they refer to the dimension of feasibility—the mechanisms of entry; they need to be supplemented by consideration of an occupation's intrinsic appeal. To the extent that types of work represent distinct clusters of values and styles of life, they will draw those whose personal expectations are consistent with those the occupation seems to afford, given the possibility of entry. Although the values of incumbents will eventually be influenced by work experience itself, particular types will be attracted. In light of the economic rewards of teaching and the nature of the task performed, it is not at all surprising that students in education de-emphasize the value of money and are highly interested in people rather than things. More revealing is that they are not highly concerned with the opportunity to be original and creative, think of themselves as conventional in their opinions and values, and are more conservative than liberal in political ideology (*ibid.*).

TRAINING AND SOCIALIZATION. The nature of the teaching profession, then, is in part a function of the types of people recruited—in terms of such characteristics as their sex, intellectual caliber, social-class values, and occupational aspirations. But these "raw materials" are malleable and not by themselves determinant. Women *might* be more appropriate vehicles for certain educational aims than men, as might individuals of working-class origins be better suited to some settings than would their middle-class colleagues. Similarly, there is no *a priori* reason to assume that merely average college students could not perform effectively in a classroom. The process of molding recruits into teachers is likely to explain more about the end product than are the raw materials, assuming that they do not remain raw.

Professional socialization involves the learning not only of skills, but also attitudes and values. Although a great deal of attention has been paid to the education—and increasingly to the miseducation—of American teachers, little is known about the more subtle aspects of the socialization process. There can be little question that occupational orientations are both overtly and covertly inculcated during the period of educational training. Even if the details remain unexplored, inferences can be drawn from the contexts in which training occurs.

The most general characteristic of teacher training, both in settings and content, is its heterogeneity, reflecting the impact of numerical needs. Perhaps "education which is usually cited for its failures, has had too much success: it has grown too large too fast on too slippery a foundation" (Koerner, 1965, p. 23).

Contrary to popular images, beginning teachers have been found to attend universities as frequently as teachers' colleges (about a third of teachers from each) and as many as a fourth obtained their undergraduate education at liberal arts colleges (Mason, 1961).[2] In spite of some state certification requirements of course work beyond the bachelor's degree, the background of the vast majority of teachers is an undergraduate period of four years. This is the extent of socialization which takes place before independent teaching is begun. Whatever the contrasts between individual colleges or the similarities between educators cross-cutting institutional divides, the separate cultures of teachers' colleges, universities, and liberal arts colleges will likely produce unique breeds.

Such contrasts may, however, be more apparent than real, as suggested by Roberts' recent study of the development of attitudes toward teaching at three colleges:

". . . The underlying proposition of the study was that the development of such attitudes will depend as much on the nature of the college attended and the training offered as on the personal predispositions derived by trainees from their social backgrounds. Three basic sets of independent variables were examined: policies and curricula of the colleges, the social environment within the colleges, and social background of trainees.

" 'Oldcity' and 'Newcity' were non-residential teachers colleges located within the city and under the control of the local board of education. Oldcity's curriculum was a relatively conventional blend of general education and specialized education courses related by tradition to schooling in the inner city. Newcity, a new experimental college designed to present a new approach to teacher education for the urban environment, emphasized interdepartmental work and social science courses designed to give students understanding of their social environment. The third college, 'State College,' which was residential and located outside the city, was in the process of changing from a teachers college to a state university . . .

". . . We learned that in the course of their development teachers colleges in general, and the three we studied in particular, had become increasingly like liberal arts colleges and universities in the range of subject matter taught and in the low level of coordination between different subject areas. Consequently, it appeared likely that overspecialization in the various subject areas could lead to a subject-matter bias in all three colleges which might lead the trainees increasingly to prefer to teach in fast-learning situations in general . . .

"It is apparent that teachers colleges can be meaningfully categorized in terms of their approach to teacher education. Differences in official policies are reflected in differences in curricula and faculty. Specifically, a distinction can be made between a more professional approach and a more vocational approach to teacher education, where the more professional approach is seen as leading college and faculty to put a greater emphasis on attitude change in the trainee.

"These differences, however, may be less important in influencing trainees' attitudes than is the academic orientation that appears to be present in the learning situation of these colleges. Factors in the history of the teachers colleges and the ambiguity surrounding the best approach to teacher education seem to have encouraged high specialization in subject matter areas. The consequence of this was an emphasis on the importance of mastering individual subject matter that led trainees to place less value on other professional challenges such as those of the slower learning situations found in urban problem areas. The three colleges did lead trainees to become more flexible in other, more general professional attitudes that are relevant to the teaching needs of urban problem areas. Consequently, a distinction seems to exist between the teachers college's ability to encourage general flexible attitudes and the effect of factors in the learning situations that channel such attitudes in directions unsuited to the needs of urban teaching.

"Against this general trend, the college with the professional approach to teacher education appeared to be somewhat more successful than the other two colleges in encouraging trainees to value the kinds of teaching attitudes suited to the needs of these areas. Newcity encouraged its trainees to have favorable perceptions of the attitudes of their faculty and college and it encouraged them to see the value of their training in other than narrowly vocational terms. Trainees who valued their training in non-vocational terms were more likely than others to have a higher opinion of the prestige of their future profession and were more likely to be favorable to the challenges of teaching in urban problem areas. This suggests that both the formal and the informal aspects of their college environment must be taken into account when the development of trainees' professional attitudes is studied.

"Especially important was the finding that the social background attributes did not have important influences on the development of trainees' professional attitudes. Neither independently of the college settings nor in interaction with it was social background found to produce consistent effects on trainees' attitudes. Compared with the effects of differences in the approach that the three colleges adopted to teacher education and with the effects of length of stay, its influence seemed negligible. Of course, the relative social class and residence homogeneity of these particular samples of students probably reduced the effects of social background over what has been found in other studies with more heterogeneous samples. The findings strongly suggest, however, that social backgrounds do not seriously limit the potentialities of education which the teachers' colleges have. Other, more individual influences, such as contacts with persons already teaching, may be the most important determinants, outside of the colleges' efforts, of trainees' professional attitudes." (Roberts, 1964, pp. 1–2, 4, 9–11.)

The foregoing excerpt indicates, most importantly, the manner in which attitudes as well as training are taught in professional schools. Although there are differences between schools, there are surprising similarities between them, and between teachers colleges and liberal arts colleges. The content of educational training has consequences upon resulting professional attitudes, even if some of the consequences are unanticipated. Yet, strangely enough, the situation would appear to be that, "No one is quite sure, or ever has been, just what the proper business of education is . . . . The professional courses required of elementary and secondary teachers . . . are not constructed around programs of proven worth. Rather, they represent a half century's haphazard accretions for which no very specific rationale, either theoretical or empirical exists" (Koerner, 1965, pp. 24, 50). More strongly, this critique continues, "Most education courses are vague, insipid, time-consuming adumbrations of the obvious, and probably irrelevant to academic teaching" (ibid., p. 56).

The quality of education that prospective teachers receive, as indicated by such critics of those who teach teachers or by the textbooks used, is serious enough an obstacle to effective socialization. The questionable relevance of what they are taught to the practice of teaching is even more serious. Although it may be true that the even more narrow curricula in medical or engineering schools also contain a quota of the seemingly irrelevant, nowhere is the gap between "theory" and the eventual occupational task as great as in education. There is little agreement concerning the weighting which should be given to "content" or liberal arts courses as opposed to courses in education— exposure to the latter varying from a sixth to almost half of the curriculum (ibid.). Frequently, neither the content nor methods courses have much to do with preparing teachers for their job. The liberal arts courses may provide broad background, but Restoration comedy and fourth grade English are hardly the same subjects. Methods courses also tend to be abstract, dealing with "a study of ends rather than means, 'objectives' of teaching rather than teaching itself . . . . Medical training would be more like teacher training if two-thirds of the time were devoted to rephrasing and discussing the Hippocratic Oath . . . . What future teachers need, and cannot now find, is the course which attempts to explore the profound aspects of the deceptively simple material they are going to teach . . ." (Mayer, 1963, pp. 472–473).

Failures in the socialization of teachers are reflected in the low entry and retention rates of the field (see below). Those who survive and become teachers are less than enthusiastic about their training. Koerner (1965) reports 70 per cent of the education graduates responding to his poll having unfavorable attitudes toward their courses in education, while almost all evaluated their other academic work favorably. Other studies have shown half the education students of one university less than satisfied with their education courses, with only half of a national sample of beginning teachers in academic subjects giving their education courses credit for merely being "helpful" to their work (ibid).

If course work in education is found wanting, practice teaching is almost universally regarded as viable. But it is not without deficiencies either, above all in the supervision involved. At best, supervision of practice teaching is uneven (Conant, 1963; Lieberman, 1962). It cannot bear the brunt of socializing teachers, especially if it remains divorced from educational course work.

In sum, would-be teachers receive indoctrination of a variety of types; their training is also variable, reflecting inconsistent educational philosophies, and reinforced by the vicissitudes of state certification requirements. Recent trends in colleges of education in recruiting social scientists from various disciplines professionally concerned with unraveling problems in the field of education augur change of the prevailing patterns.

CAREER PATTERNS. Careers in teaching are simultaneously static and unstable. As in most professions, the element of stability is reflected to the extent that the novice and the person on the verge of retirement pursue the same work. In spite of the teacher being part of a bureaucratic hierarchy, movement into administration cannot be considered a normal part of a career in education, for there is little room at the top. Increments accrue with seniority, or with advanced training, but teachers occupy but one rung on the official educational ladder. The typical career of the school teacher thus involves repeated classroom confrontation, with but little change in duties or responsibilities.

Discontinuities in teaching careers are paramount when attention shifts to broader occupational patterns. It is initially reflected in the leakage represented by one-fourth of those trained in education not taking teaching jobs the year after their graduation (NEA, 1959). The separate career contingencies of men and women are already evident before first jobs are begun. For while male education graduates defect more than men in other fields, women in education are more faithful to their chosen area of study than are women in most other subjects (Wolfle, 1954).

The most dramatic indicator of the instability of teaching careers is that half of beginning teachers expect to leave their posts, at least temporarily, within five years of their initial appointments (Mason, 1958).

The effect of sex role upon career orientation is crucial (Mason, Dressel, and Bain, 1959). For women in contemporary American society, teaching obviously is not viewed as an alternative to marriage and child-rearing. Neither is it regarded merely as a stopgap until a husband is snagged, for only 12 per cent of beginning teachers expect to become homemakers and not return to teaching later. The modal pattern, for almost three-fifths of women beginning teachers is to anticipate leaving their work for a period of homemaking, but returning later. In spite of the dual allegiance of women—to their families and to their jobs—they represent a more stable element in the teaching profession than men do. Three-fourths of beginning women teachers expect to continue teaching until retirement, or to return after a period devoted to familial obligations (*ibid.*).

Only three out of ten male beginning teachers plan to continue teaching until retirement; a fifth expect to leave education for another occupation, and half hope eventually to move from classroom teaching into some other area of education.

"Thus, most men do not see teaching as a terminal occupation or career, but as a stepping stone to some other position, either in or out of education. It is virtually impossible for all of the men who expressed the ambition to enter non-teaching educational positions (mostly administrative and supervisory positions) to achieve this goal. Those who do not succeed in making this move may remain as teachers, but others may leave for other occupations when they find their path of mobility blocked. . . . (That) the proportion of men among the total teaching population is much smaller than the proportion of men among the beginning teachers may indicate a heavy exodus of men to either non-teaching or non-educational posts or both." (Mason, Dressel, and Bain, 1959, pp. 374–375.)

Although the gross career pattern of teachers is characterized by instability—in-and-out for women, and up-or-out for men (Clark, 1964)—the element of stability which we referred to applies most directly to the minority who do in fact spend their working lives in the classroom. There is also an aspect of stability for the woman who leaves and returns, to the extent that she returns to the same task and organizational rung.

Beneath the stability, however, there is also movement, much of it horizontal. Geographical mobility has traditionally been common among teachers. Currently, half of beginning teachers are new to the community of their teaching appointment, but the pattern of movement from small rural districts to larger urban ones now appears defunct (Mason, 1961).

Another type of movement is between grade levels. While going to a higher grade is a promotion for pupils, it likely involves a horizontal move—or perhaps an informal promotion—for teachers, its major reward being more interesting, or at least different, subject matter. Even the shift from elementary to secondary teaching is not clearly vertical given single-salary schedules, albeit the high school teacher is accorded greater prestige.

Intrinsic rewards of the teaching situation, rather than promotions or salary increases, also account for horizontal mobility within large school districts. Becker's (1952) description of the manipulation of the transfer system in Chicago shows how the majority of teachers attempt to move from their initial assignments in slum schools to "nice" neighborhoods where discipline is less of a problem. Although Becker's analysis is based on only sixty interviews, it reveals the process involved. That the pattern is a common one is seen in the present problem most big city school systems face in attempting to get experienced teachers to work in slum schools. The importance that teachers place upon horizontal mobility is indicated by the strike threat of the Chicago Teachers Union in May 1965 against the school board's proposal restricting the possibility of teachers transferring to schools of their choice after a minimum period of service. On the national level, the creation of a Teachers Corps, "to give a year to places of the greatest need," speaks to the same problem, allowing teachers to give the services so badly needed in city slums and areas of rural poverty, without jeopardizing the possibility of their moving on to other settings.

The Teacher's Roles

It may well be that the *feel* for what teaching involves—"What teaching does to teachers . . . by furnishing them those roles which habit ties to the inner frame of personality and use makes one with the self" (Waller, 1932, p. 381)—can only be captured through personal experi-

ence, or occasionally by insightful works of fiction (for example, Kaufman, 1964). But the experience of one person will reveal only a small
number of the roles involved in occupational behavior.

The concept of *role* provides the link between social structures and
the actors within them. Roles refer to uniformities of behavior in social
positions—what a person does in playing his many parts—in light of
various expectations. Alternative expectations apply to the same person
in different statuses (e.g., teacher, wife, mother), but also to the complement of relationships in one status—the *role-set*. Thus,

"the status of public school teacher has its distinctive role-set, relating
the teacher to his pupils, to colleagues, the school principal and
superintendent, the Board of Education, and, on frequent occasions,
to local patriotic organizations, to professional organizations of teachers, Parent-Teacher Associations, and the like." (Merton, 1957, p. 369.)

The stage upon which the central teaching roles are played is obviously the classroom, in dialogue (or monologue) with pupils. Even
when analysis focuses upon this setting, it is clear that diverse roles are
involved and intimately connected with pressures from other components of the role-set, as indicated by Naegele:

"Generally speaking, a teacher is expected to achieve several states
of affairs which, however, vary both in specificness and the 'audience' to
whom they apply. He must balance a concern with specific accomplishments with some concern for a state of well-being: he has to keep a
relatively 'happy' class which 'learns.' But a class is more than a collection of individuals. The teacher always has to manage children in
groups. His act towards individuals must somehow be interpreted
either as expressions of general rules or of a particular circumstance.
In the latter case he must draw the further line between legitimate
special treatment and favouritism. He must teach the relegation of
private needs as well as their occasional relevance. He must cope with
the present exigencies of the classroom as one kind of social system, as
well as the necessity to transform others into adults, both on the
delimited plane of various skills and knowledge and the more general
plane of more pervasive dispositions or capacities. Clearly his work is
further facilitated and impeded by a series of others—including
superiors, parents, colleagues, and experts—singly or organized into
groups.

"Within this system the role of the teacher is differentiated in several
respects; degree of specialization and amount of administrative re-

sponsibility stand out as the most prominent lines of distinction. Our work was for the most part in the elementary schools. There the role of the teacher is more commensurate with that of the mother, though the structure of social arrangements as part of which the role is played is considerably different. The teacher's role becomes of course increasingly 'specific' and concerned with various academic or athletic accomplishments as well as with the issues of occupational choice. It is then judged by others on the basis of 'how much he knows' and 'how well he can teach it.' In the lower grades the complementary capacity for 'understanding,' 'warmth,' 'keeping order without making children afraid' is the more immediate base of assessment. In that case, assessment of the teacher (by others, and himself) proceeds by reference to general standards which bind, rather than divide, otherwise heterogeneous sectors of the population. Again, though, various disparities arise. Parents differ in their assignment of relative priorities for the different elements of the teacher's role. These differences, one must propose, are not haphazard or just individual. Similarly the ten elementary schools, located in neighborhoods that varied in their age composition, economic status, or degree of ethnic homogeneity, generated between them differences of 'atmosphere' that in turn affected co-operative arrangements with 'outsiders.'

". . . Teachers are not anonymous. They are representatives of the values of society in a fairly concrete sense. They facilitate or impede processes of mobility and experiences of success and failure in a much more public manner than a psychiatrist. They are, as it were, civil servants, yet have advertent or inadvertent access to the privacy of others. They can assess other adults through sustained acquaintance with children, who are, after all, always both representatives (of their parents) and individuals in their own right. The situation of teaching and the social definitions of education as such thus generate a balance of conflicting pressures toward and away from penetrating access to the full history of pupils by teachers.

"The teacher, then, not only acts *in* public and *with* many, he also shares as an outsider a child who as part of a kinship system is at the same time cared for by parents. His time is filled with implementing the requirements of a curriculum and limiting the number of distractions that could easily come at him from many quarters. Yet at the same time, counselling has achieved prestige, and being known for one's insight can be counted an asset. Parents, in turn, want their child understood, though not necessarily soberly assessed. . . ." (Naegele, 1956, pp. 53–55.)

Although Naegele mentioned that the teaching role tends to be specific in contrast to that of the mother, the number of divergent obligations referred to indicate that it is more diffuse than other professional roles (see Parsons, 1951). For ". . . the business of socializing children—of motivating, inspiring and encouraging them, of transmitting values to them, awakening in them a respect for facts and a sense of critical appreciation—all this is unspecific" (Wilson, 1962, p. 22).

The most immediate consequence of diffuse role obligations is an ambiguity resulting from, ". . . the absence of clear lines of demarcation whereby the role-player knows he has 'done his job.' Because the teacher's work—like all socializing tasks—is unending, he must continually ask himself whether he has fully discharged his obligations" (*ibid.*, p. 27). Since diverse duties are likely to include incompatible ones, they may result not only in ambiguity, but role-conflict as well. For the teacher, the greatest conflict in the classroom arises from being, ". . . both the affective agent and the disciplinary agent; he is the advocate of a pupil, but also in considerable measure the objective assessor. He must win approval and respect, but he must also maintain standards" (*ibid.*, p. 27).

The ambiguity or possible role conflict stemming from the diffuse nature of the socializing function is unlikely to be a major source of strain in itself. A much greater disparity is that between the authority roles of the teacher in the classroom as contrasted to the constraints of being an employee in a public bureaucracy.

Whatever the teaching ideology inculcated in the course of professional training—to teach the whole child or the subject, to be permissive or rigid—role relationships with children receive most attention. Furthermore, these are the ones likely to be remembered from one's own schooldays. The greatest fact of life of teaching is, accordingy, likely to strike as a culture shock: the recognition that the teacher is an employee. The demands of pedagogy must be placed against (and often subservient to) those of bureaucracy—the world of Delany cards, attendance sheets, supply requisitions, toilet passes, and fire drill regulations. The point is not the tyranny of paperwork (which, although probably greater in teaching than in any other profession, is elsewhere also felt to be excessive), but of organizational rules and constraints, of limited autonomy, epitomized in the extreme by punching time clocks.

Essentially, the conflict is between professional and organizational roles. It is a problem generic to professionals employed in organizations and is capable of various solutions. Frequently, for example, some members of a profession will be guided mainly by local (organizational) norms, and others by cosmopolitan (professional) ones (Kornhauser, 1962; cf. Corwin, 1965). The teacher's situation is unique in that although the two orientations may conflict, the viability of each is limited. "The teacher may have a role conception stressing his professional training, but he finds that this is not rewarded in the system where he works, neither is violation of this role punished. It seems largely ignored by the administration" (Washburne, 1957, p. 394). Alternative patterns of accommodation which characterize professional roles must be considered in terms of their organizational contexts (cf. Presthus, 1962; Wilensky, 1964). Thus, local orientations of a careerist or upwardly mobile type are inhibited by limited promotion possibilities and missionary or service ideals will also wither through lack of support and in the face of bureaucratic obstacles. Neither are professional orientations which had been stressed in the course of teacher training bolstered by strong professional ties.

The most common response to the situation is likely to be an ambivalent compromise between organizational pressures and professional standards. Alternatively, yielding to administrative dictates would involve an alienated view of teaching as a mere job. While the high rate of teacher turnover cannot be ascribed to role conflict alone, leaving the field clearly represents an obvious—if extreme—solution to the role dilemma.

Apart from the drop-outs, however, the extent of commitment to the teaching profession is considerable. Over four-fifths of all teachers would choose teaching as a career if they had it to do over again (NEA, 1963)—a proportion comparable to that found among scientists and established professions (Blauner, 1960). But the meaning of this commitment is difficult to establish, as are the implication of professionalism as applied to teaching. For example, in spite of aspects of our society that lead one to expect greater professionalism among men (feminine mystique notwithstanding, work roles for women are secondary to family roles), it has been found that women teachers are more professional than men in terms of the importance placed upon technical competence, autonomy, and service (Colombotos, 1963). Based upon these findings, it has been suggested that,

"The orientations required of women in the teaching role may be an extension of the orientations required by the dominant roles as mothers and housewives, despite obvious conflicts between these roles in terms of time and energy. . . . It is important to emphasize that these findings are restricted to professional *orientations*. It is possible that in terms of certain behavioral indicators—such as advanced training and participation in professional organizations—men teachers are more professional than women teachers. This is indeed the case, and it is consistent with other accounts that see women as barriers to the professionalization of teaching." (*Ibid.*, pp. 37–38.)

Another anomolous aspect of the teacher's divergent role obligations stems from the public nature of the work. Not only is the teacher a subordinate in the school hierarchy where employed, but in addition to being subject to the dictates of school boards, she is held accountable to the whims of community groups. In addition to community groups being part of the teacher's role-set *qua* teacher, community standards are invoked more broadly. In both respects, the situation of the teacher is more extreme than that of any other profession.

The susceptibility to community pressures is partly explained by the "clients" of teachers being children who belong to others. It is also influenced by the diffuse nature of what is involved in teaching—allowing the layman to believe he knows better. However, the more limited influence of the community upon teachers' authority in a highly urbanized country such as England (Baron and Tropp, 1961) suggests the organization of community life in America provides a large part of the explanation.

In spite of gross patterns of urbanization in America, much of the material dealing with the teacher's community role, for example in emphasizing the position as one of a "stranger," mainly derives from the small town situation of the 1930's. Charters provides a useful summary:

"Today, we can see that these writers had in mind a community of a special type—the culturally homogeneous small town or village relatively untouched by urbanization and industrialization. The city and the suburb were ignored in the educational sociologists' descriptions of the modes of social relations between teacher and community. Thus, their implicit model was . . . the sacred (or folk) community which is economically undifferentiated, socially homogeneous, tradition-bound, and the relationships among its members are highly personal. . . .

"THE DESCRIPTIVE MODEL.[3] The outstanding features of the teacher's relations in the sacred community are (1) the unusual degree to which relationships are lacking altogether, and (2) the highly constrained nature of those relationships which are present. . . . Contractual provisions typically preclude marriage, at least by females, so the teacher cannot enter the social fabric of the community as a householder, a neighbor, a parent, etc. Strict codes of conduct enforced by the community with respect to recreation, entertainment, and courtship prevent the unmarried, young teacher from entering into the role relationships normally associated with his age-sex. . . . Highly visible in the small town, he is always 'the teacher.' He can only escape his identity by withdrawing completely from the town, and even this is prohibited except during summer vacations. . . .

"The occupational identity is a trying one. The teacher is a public servant, and his life is public property. His time is demanded for Sunday school teaching, for charity bazaars, for sponsorship of youth activities, and for other innocuous enterprises well removed from the realms of decision and power. At the same time, he loses freedom of choice as to where he takes residence, where he buys his clothes and groceries, where and how he entertains himself, etc. Codes of conduct cover a wide range of deportment, both public and private, from matters of personal adornment to smoking, drinking, and card-playing. In the activities he is expected to undertake as well as in those he is obliged to forego the teacher stands as a symbol of the sacred values of the community. . . .

"Most public of all is the teacher's performance in the classroom. Close surveillance is exercised by board members and citizens to insure not merely that he succeeds in his teaching but that his means of attaining success conform to the local image of proper teaching, to insure not only that he teaches what he is expected to teach but that he teaches nothing that is unexpected or 'controversial.'

"As the educational sociologists viewed it, the prime function of the restrictive role into which the teacher is cast is to preserve intact the sacred values of the culturally homogeneous community and to defend the status quo of the prevailing social order. . . . Teachers are selected for their positions and dismissed from their positions not on the grounds of their technical merit as teachers but on the degree of threat they pose to the sanctity of the local value system. . . . Constant vigilance is demanded to certify that persons from whom the children would learn alien ways of life do not get in or stay in the local schools.

". . . As a group . . . [teachers] command no bargaining power and are vulnerable to arbitrary acts of employment officials. . . . Informal mechanisms of social control—the lifted eyebrow, the unexplained coolness of acquaintances, the circulation of rumor and gossip, all arts in which the community members are well versed—frequently suffice to correct the teacher in his transgressions. Further, the teachers selected for service in the provincial community normally are unmotivated to conduct themselves in any way other than that prescribed by community expectations. . . .

". . . The teacher is a pawn, a passive agent, of community forces and exercises only the narrow band of discretion in the classroom. No points of discontinuity exist between the classroom and the environing community. As the community, so the teaching. If the dominant community values are those of the business ethic or those of religious fundamentalism, they are immediately reflected in the content and method of teaching. . . ." (Charters, 1963, pp. 765–767.)

Community constraints of so rigid a nature are less conceivable today, especially in urban settings, but increasingly in small towns as well. The decline of such sacred values is suggested by the findings of a recent study (Mason, 1961) that although rural communities continue to be more demanding of conformity by teachers, the difference from urban areas is not extreme. Yet even if special codes for teachers are no longer as rigid, they still persist. Three-fifths of those beginning teaching careers felt there were more extensive restrictions placed upon their personal lives than upon other professional groups (*ibid.*, p. 91).

If the teacher is now more often allowed to keep her occupational and community roles distinct, there is no comparable major trend of declining influences upon the teaching role itself. Community forces remain very much a part of the teacher's role-set (Ramsøy, 1963). Both the nature of community power and that of the organization of the teaching profession must be taken into account in order to delineate the processes involved. The unequal balance of power is most vividly illustrated in the ineffective response of teachers to extremist censorship pressures (see Nelson and Roberts, 1963). It would appear that the political role is one played least well by teachers, albeit conflict is mitigated by such mechanisms as the differential concern with the behavior of teachers by parents and by those without children in school. "Were all those involved in the role-set of the teacher *equally* concerned . . . the plight of the teacher would be considerably more sorrowful than it presently is" (Merton, 1957, p. 373).

POTENTIALS OF EDUCATION AND THE SOCIOLOGY OF WORK

The major tradition of the sociology of work almost suggests a concupiscent interest, with such prosaic callings as teaching taking a back seat to prostitution. The tradition dates back to the research developed at the University of Chicago in the 1920's and 1930's, involving an ethnographic attempt to depict the curious subcultures that thrive in an urban setting. Initially, the theoretical guidelines for this work were those of urban disorganization (cf. Stein, 1960), focusing upon occupations felt to epitomize the unique social relationships that characterize urban life—for example, hotel employees, taxi-dance hall girls, the professional thief, and the nonoccupation of the hobo (Hayner, 1936; Cressey, 1932; Sutherland, 1937; Anderson, 1923). Although the majority of the occupational vignettes of the Chicago school dealt with disreputable, marginal, and underworld groups, less exotic types—the school ma'am, the saleslady, and the realtor (Donovan, 1928 and 1929; Hughes, 1928)—were also studied.

Increasingly, as urban life became the typical pattern of American society, and perhaps as provincial midwestern sociologists of rural origins themselves became accustomed to urban existence, the emphasis upon pathological groups waned. The occupational literature came to include a gamut of points on the status hierarchy, reflecting the influence of Everett C. Hughes, who directed and inspired a major portion of the work done in this area:

"Our aim is to penetrate more deeply into the personal and social drama of work, to understand the social and social-psychological arrangements and devices by which men make their work tolerable, or even glorious to themselves and others. . . . Specifically we need to rid ourselves of any concepts which keep us from seeing that the essential problems of men at work are the same whether they do their work in some famous laboratory or in the messiest vat room of a pickle factory. Until we can find a point of view and concepts which will enable us to make comparisons between the junk peddler and the professor without intent to debunk the one and patronize the other, we cannot do our best work in the field." (Hughes, 1958, p. 48.)

Clearly then, the prime contribution of occupational analyses of education (or of any occupational study) for the sociology of work is to provide additional "case studies" helping to penetrate into "the personal and social drama of work," and to develop conceptual frameworks. Simultaneously, use of existing frameworks for the dissection of a particular occupation reveals the viability of existing schemes of analysis as well as needed refinements and revisions. More specifically, particular types of problems are highlighted by attention to the teaching profession. Although there is yet much to learn about teachers in their occupational roles, we already possess considerable information.

To what extent is it made more understandable by what is known about other occupations? Alternatively, what aspects of the educational realm that appear unique shed light upon related attributes in other occupational worlds?

Although comparisons up and down the entire occupational spectrum may yield insights, as Hughes suggests, they are unlikely to further sociological explanation unless grounded in relevant theoretical contexts. Probably *the* basic issue in the sociology of work—of even greater significance today than in Durkheim's classic statement (1933)—is the nature of work as a social bond and the integrative function of occupational groups. Differing levels of commitment to various occupations and differences in the commitment of segments within any one occupation are among the primary factors involved. Attention to teaching in this context not only demonstrates the fruitfulness resulting from the use of a theoretical focus, but also reveals the interconnections between seemingly discrete dimensions.

The appropriate genus for the occupational species "teacher" is the professions. As we have indicated, although teaching like other professions elicits a high degree of psychological commitment from practitioners, it is at the same time subject to drop-out rates unusual among professionals, and thus reveals low structural commitment. Indeed, the rates of teacher turnover inhibit the process of professionalization. Similarly, the different meaning of occupational commitment—in terms of both attitudes and affiliations—among men and women in our society also would appear to be a barrier to professionalization. But here we are confronted with an almost unexplored area of occupational analysis: the comparative meaning of work for men and women. For example, as we have noted, in spite of women's family obligations, their professional orientations towards teaching have been found to be stronger than are those of their male colleagues. Would this be the case in other professions? To what extent is this phenomenon a function of the unique compatibility of teaching and maternal roles? In this compatibility largely grounded in historical circumstance, and hence problematic in a rapidly changing and professionalizing occupation, so that perhaps in another generation, the mother wanting to re-enter teaching after having launched her children will have to return in a subprofessional capacity? The compatibility of teaching and maternal roles also reflects the extreme pressures on American men to "get ahead"—pressures which detract men but not women from professional orientations. What are the implications of the contrasting professional and mobility orientations of upper-middle- and working-class recruits?

In order to satisfactorily deal with questions such as these, more needs to be known about the elusive professional touchstone. In terms of the model represented by the "established" or "learned" professions, teaching tends to fall short. Its knowledge base has less mystery than theology or medicine, less rigor than the sciences, and less aesthetic content than the arts. Although teaching has elements of mystery, science and art, its foundation is broad, and not readily identifiable as the exclusive license of one community of experts. Professional autonomy is limited both by school hierarchies and community constraints. Obligations, when articulated, are less often formulated by peers than by outside forces. Commitments tend to be contingent. Yet teaching has more in common with the professions than not.

It may well be that greater attention to the process of professionalization would be more instructive than is the dissection of the traditional professional model. For, even the established professions are in process (cf. Bucher and Strauss, 1961). While the growing numbers of aspiring professions—and teaching is unquestionably among them—aim to emulate the established model, not all of its components are equally relevant for all occupations, nor even for the parent from which they derived, given changing social circumstances. Indeed, the emulation frequently yields little more than absurd parody.

Were the new technological professions themselves not so concerned with the traditional model, they might serve aspirant groups as an appropriate prototype. For the same forces that explain the development of so many new professions in the past century and the increasing size of professions both old and new—the patterns of specialization, urbanization, and bureaucratization—need to be taken into account in order to understand what forms professions in contemporary life have taken.

There is nothing anomalous in the teacher being both a professional and an employee of a large bureaucracy. Most professionals today are employees in this age of the organization man, in which,

"Blood brother to the business trainee off to join DuPont is the seminary student who will end up in the church hierarchy, the doctor headed for the corporate clinic, the physics Ph.D. in a government laboratory, the intellectual of the foundation-sponsored team project, the engineering graduate in the huge drafting room at Lockheed, the young apprentice in a Wall Street factory." (Whyte, 1956, p. 3.)

What remains unclear is the extent to which patterns of conflict and accommodation between professional and organizational allegiances are similar in these various settings.

Patterns of professionalization in the teaching field help reveal one of the most important processes in a complex industrial society. To the extent that "professional" is but a status symbol, there is a clamber on the part of all sorts of occupations for the label. But even applying the most stringent definitions—of attitudes of professionalism or of professional occupational structure—reveals an increasing number of occupational groups in the process of professionalization. Both similarities to and differences from previous pathways are instructive. It may be that accommodations developed in teaching are suggestive of future trends, both of professional standards and organizational responses.

If, as is likely, the axis of professionalization is the key to understanding the teaching occupation, and educational processes in general, it needs to be penetrated at many points. Beginning with recruitment, there is the very difficult question of quantity and quality: need more mean less? Is professional upgrading possible in light of the ever-expanding unwieldy growth of the educational establishment? Are the types of people attracted to teaching susceptible to, or capable of, professional orientations?

Whatever the raw materials, as we have indicated, their molding in large part explains the end products. Yet information about the socialization of teachers is meager. Their training is frequently criticized, but little is known about their indoctrination. Occupational norms are inculcated in teachers' colleges, but what are they? Are the professional norms that the professor of education has adopted to guide his own conduct appropriate for potential school teachers?

Proceeding to the teacher at work, the professional dimension is again crucial, whether considered in relation to organizational contexts, problems of role conflict, the links between work and other social roles, occupational communities of teachers, or their life styles. In all these areas some beginnings have been made, but a great deal remains to be ascertained. In spite of the roots of occupational sociology in issues of community disorganization, the community setting has received little attention recently. When considered, there has been an obsolete emphasis upon traditional types of communities, ignoring that, ". . . today New York is more like America than Sinclair Lewis' Main Street was. Urban problems are increasingly the . . . priority issue—especially in education" (Hechinger, 1966). Given the decline of traditional forms of community in American society, occupational analysis might point to the degree of continuity or discontinuity involved in the progression from small town to suburban life. It may also be the case that nongeographic occupational communities have assumed a new significance. Although information about teaching careers is considerable, there are also sizable gaps. How, for example, do career plans compare with actual careers? What becomes of the drop-out from teaching? More important, who are the drop-outs and what are their reasons? What are the long-range results of career patterns characterized by both stability and instability?

Multitudes of theoretical, empirical, and policy questions abound in the occupational analysis of teaching. The three types of questions, which have usually been considered separately, need to be linked if we are to attain fruitful results. An extreme comment about the results of artificial boundaries is that,

"Most . . . money goes to projects designed not so much to solve problems of the public schools (e.g., better vocational training) as to answer the questions which now head the agenda of the discipline in which the applicant has made, or hopes to make, a reputation (e.g., studies in occupational sociology). Sometimes the concerns of the academicians prove relevant to the schools, but often not." (Jencks, 1965.)

However desirable immediate practical results may be, they are not the sole criteria for research worthy of being undertaken. Even if practical solutions are the ultimate aim, the history of science demonstrates that they frequently come about in unexpected ways. Accordingly, the ultimate test of significant research lies in dealing with basic questions, whether or not clearly suggesting solutions to social problems. In this connection, the cross-fertilization of the sociology of education and the sociology of work can be of great benefit. The perspectives of the latter place many issues of the teacher's world into focus through such general processes as professionalization and the basic recruitment-socialization-career stages of occupational life. In turn, viewing one occupation in depth contributes toward the understanding of occupational institutions and processes.

Joel E. Gerstl is Associate Professor of Sociology at Temple University. He received his Ph.D. in Sociology at the University of Minnesota and has taught there as well as at the University of Michigan and Purdue University. He has also been a lecturer at the University of South Wales and Monmouthshire (Cardiff) and at Cambridge University. Most of his research and writing has been in the sociology of occupations and professions. His British investigation, *Engineers: the anatomy of a profession,* (with S. P. Hutton) was published by Tavistock in November, 1966.

NOTES

1. The array is vividly illustrated by the very titles of recent studies of college teachers. Wilson's classic, *The Academic Man* (1942), has been supplemented by *The Academic Mind, The Academic Marketplace, The Academic Woman,* and *The Academic Man in the Catholic College* (Lazarsfeld and Thielens, 1958; Caplow and McGee, 1958; Bernard, 1964, Donovan, 1964).

2. Men and women come in equal proportions from universities, but men more often from teachers' colleges and women from liberal arts colleges. Rural origins are strongly associated with attending teachers' colleges, but the traditional links between elementary teaching with teachers' colleges and secondary teaching with liberal arts colleges appear defunct (*ibid*).

3. The portrait of the teacher in the sacred community . . . is a composite from a number of sources, the most comprehensive of which are Beale (1936), Brookover (1955), L. A. Cook and Cook (1950), Dahlke (1958), Grambs (1952), Greenhoe (1941), Havighurst and Neugarten (1957), Lieberman (1955), and Waller (1932).

WORKS CITED

Anderson, Nels (1923), *The Hobo,* University of Chicago Press, Chicago.

Baron, George, and Asher Tropp (1961), "Teachers in England and America," in A. H. Halsey et al. (eds.), *Education, Economy and Society,* The Free Press, New York.

Barrett, Donald N. (ed.) (1961), *Values in America,* University of Notre Dame Press, Notre Dame, Ind.

Beale, H. K. (1936), *Are American Teachers Free,* Scribner's, New York.

Becker, Howard S., et al. (1961), *Boys in White,* University of Chicago Press, Chicago.

Becker, Howard S. (1952), "The Career of the Chicago Public Schoolteacher," *Am. J. Sociol.,* **LVII** (March), 470–477.

Bernard, Jessie (1964), *Academic Women,* The Pennsylvania State University Press, University Park, Pa.

Blauner, Robert (1960), "Work Satisfactions and Industrial Trends in Modern Society," in W. Galenson and S. M. Lipset (eds.), *Labor and Trade Unionism,* John Wiley and Sons, New York.

Brookover, W. B. (1955), *A Sociology of Education,* American Book Company, New York.

Bucher, Rue, and Anselm Strauss (1961), "Professions in Process," *Am. J. Sociol.,* **LXVI** (January), 325–334.

Caplow, Theodore, and Reece J. McGee (1958), *The Academic Marketplace,* Basic Books, New York.

Caplow, Theodore (1954), *The Sociology of Work,* University of Minnesota Press, Minneapolis.

Carr-Saunders, A. M., and P. A. Wilson (1933), *The Professions,* Clarendon Press, New York.

Charters, W. W. (1963), "The Social Background of Teaching," in N. L. Gage (ed.), *Handbook of Research on Teaching,* Rand McNally & Co., Skokie, Ill.

Charters, W. W., and N. L. Gage (eds.) (1963), *Readings in the Social Psychology of Education,* Allyn & Bacon, Boston.

Colombotos, John L. (1963), "Sex Role and Professionalism: A Study of High School Teachers," *The School Review,* **71** (Spring), 27–40.

Colombotos, John L. (1962), *Sources of Professionalism: A Study of High School Teachers,* U.S. Office of Education, Washington, D.C.

Colombotos, John L. "Class Background and Career Mobility," forthcoming.

Conant, James B. (1963), *The Education of American Teachers,* McGraw-Hill Book Company, New York.

Cook, L. G., Lloyd Allen Cook, and Elaine Forsyth Cook (1950), *A Sociological Approach to Education,* McGraw-Hill Book Company, New York.

Corwin, Ronald G. (1965), "Militant Professionalism, Initiative and Compliance in Public Education," *Sociol. Educ.,* **38** (Summer), 310–331.

Cressey, Paul G. (1932), *The Taxi-Dance Hall,* University of Chicago Press, Chicago.

Dahlke, Helmut Otto (1958), *Values in Culture and Classroom,* Harper & Row, New York.

Davis, Hazel, et al. (1963), "Economic, Legal & Social Status of Teachers," *Review of Educational Research,* **33** (October), 398–414.

Davis, James A. (1964), *Great Aspirations,* Aldine Publishing Co., Chicago, Ill.

Donovan, Frances R. (1928), *The School Ma'am,* Frederick A. Stokes, New York.

Donovan, Frances R. (1929), *The Saleslady,* University of Chicago Press, Chicago.

Donovan, John D. (1964), *The Academic Man in the Catholic College,* Sheed and Ward, New York.

Durkheim, Emile (1933), *The Division of Labor in Society,* The Macmillan Company, New York.

Fogarty, Michael Patrick (1963), *The Rules of Work,* Geoffrey Chapman, Ltd., London.

Gerstl, Joel, and Lois K. Cohen (1964), "Dissensus, Situs and Egocentrism in Occupational Ranking," *British Journal of Sociology,* **XV** (September), 254–261.

Gerstl, Joel, and Robert Perrucci (1965), "Educational Channels and Elite Mobility: A Comparative Analysis," *Sociol. Educ.,* **38** (Spring), 224–232.

Ginzberg, Eli, et al. (1951), *Occupational Choice: An Approach to a General Theory,* Columbia University Press, New York.

Grambs, Jean D. (1952), "The Sociology of the 'Born Teacher,'" *J. Educ. Sociol.,* **25**:532–541.

deGrazia, Sebastian (1962), *Of Time, Work and Leisure,* The Twentieth Century Fund, New York.

Greenhoe, Florence (1941), *Community Contacts and Participation of Teachers,* American Council on Public Affairs, Washington, D.C.

Gross, Edward (1958), *Work and Society*, Crowell, New York.

Hall, R. K., N. Hans, and J. A. Lauwerys (eds.) (1953), *The Yearbook of Education*, World Publishing Company, Cleveland.

Hans, Nicholas (1953), "The Status of Women Teachers in Europe," in R. K. Hall, et al. (eds.), *Yearbook of Education 1953*, World Publishing Company, Cleveland.

Hayner, Norman (1936), *Hotel Life*, University of North Carolina Press, Chapel Hill.

Havighurst, R. J., and Bernice L. Neugarten (1957), *Society and Education*, Allyn & Bacon, Boston.

Hechinger, Fred M. (1966), "New Guard Leads National Effort Toward Reforms," *New York Times* (January 12), p. 50.

Hodge, Robert, Paul Siegel, and Peter Rossi (1964), "Occupational Prestige in the U.S. 1925–63," *Am. J. Sociol.*, LXX (November), 286–302.

Hughes, Everett C. (1928), "Personality Types and the Division of Labor," *Am. J. Sociol.*, XXXIII (March), 754–768.

Hughes, Everett C. (1958), *Men and Their Work*, The Free Press, Glencoe.

Hughes, Everett C. (1959), "The Study of Occupations," in R. K. Merton, Broom, and Cottrell (eds.), *Sociology Today*, Basic Books, New York.

Hutchings, D. W. (1963), *Technology and the Sixth Form Boy*, Oxford University Department of Education.

Inkeles, Alex, and Peter H. Rossi (1956), "National Comparisons of Occupational Prestige," *Am. J. Sociol.*, LVI (January), 329–339.

Jencks, Christopher (1965), "Education: What Next," *The New Republic* (October 16), 21.

Kaufman, Bel (1964), *Up the Down Staircase*, Prentice-Hall, Englewood Cliffs, N.J.

Kendall, Patricia L., and Robert K. Merton (1958), "Medical Education as a Social Process," in E. Gartley Jaco (ed.), *Patients, Physicians and Illness*, The Free Press, Glencoe, Ill.

Koerner, James D. (1965), *The Miseducation of American Teachers*, Penguin Books, Baltimore, Md.

Kornhauser, William (1962), *Scientists in Industry*, University of California Press, Berkeley.

Lazarsfeld, Paul F., and Wagner Thielens (1958), *The Academic Mind*, The Free Press, New York.

Lieberman, Myron (1956), *Education as a Profession*, Prentice-Hall, Englewood Cliffs, N.J.

Lieberman, Myron (1962), *The Future of Public Education*, Phoenix Books, Chicago.

Lockwood, David (1958), *The Black Coated Worker*, Allen & Unwin, London.

Mason, Ward Sherman (1958), *The Beginning Teacher: A Survey of New Teachers in the Public Schools*, U.S. Department of Health, Education, and Welfare, Office of Education, Washington, D.C.

Mason, Ward Sherman (1961), *The Beginning Teacher: Status and Career Orientations*, U.S. Department of Health, Education, and Welfare, Office of Education, Washington, D.C.

Mason, Ward, Robert J. Dressel, and Robert K. Bain (1959), "Sex Role and the Career Orientations of Beginning Teachers, *Harvard Educational Review*, 29:4 (Fall), 370–383.

Mayer, Martin (1963), *The Schools,* Doubleday, Anchor Books, Garden City, New York.

Merton, Robert K. (1957), *Social Theory and Social Structure,* The Free Press, New York.

Merton, Robert K., *et al.* (1957), *The Student-physician,* Harvard University Press, Cambridge, Mass.

Mills, C. W. (1951), *White Collar: The American Middle Classes,* Oxford University Press, New York.

Naegele, Kasper D. (1956), "Clergymen, Teachers and Psychiatrists: A Study in Roles and Socialization," *Canadian Journal of Economics and Political Science,* 22:46–52.

NEA (1963), *The American Public-School Teacher 1960–61,* NEA Research Monograph.

NEA (1964), "Census of All Teachers," *NEA Research Bulletin* (October).

NEA (1957), "The Status of the American Public School Teacher."

Nelson, Jack and Gene Roberts, Jr. (1963), *The Censors and the Schools,* Little Brown and Co., Boston.

Nosow, Sigmund, and William H. Form (1962), *Man, Work and Society: A Reader in the Sociology of Occupations,* Basic Books, New York.

Parson, Talcott (1951), *The Social System,* The Free Press, New York.

Presthus, Robert (1962), *The Organizational Society,* Random House, New York.

Ramsøy, Natalie Rogoff (1963), "Public Education in America: A Research Program," *Sociol. Educ.,* 37:1–8.

Reiss, Albert J. (1955), "Occupational Mobility of Professional Workers," *Am. J. Sociol.,* 20 (December), 693–700.

Riesman, David, Reuel Denny, and Nathan Glazer (1950), *The Lonely Crowd: A Study of the Changing American Character,* Yale University Press, New Haven.

Roberts, Bryan R. (1964), "The Effects of College Experience and Social Background on Professional Orientations of Prospective Teachers," Working Paper No. 38, Center for Organizational Studies, University of Chicago (September).

Rosenberg, Morris (1957), *Occupations and Values,* The Free Press, New York.

Statistical Abstracts of the United States (1964), U.S. Bureau of the Census, U.S. Government Printing Office, Washington, D.C.

Stein, Maurice R. (1960), *The Eclipse of Community,* Princeton University Press, Princeton, N.J.

Sutherland, Edwin G. (1937), *The Professional Thief,* University of Chicago Press, Chicago.

Tilgher, Adriano (1930), *Work: What It Has Meant to Men Through the Ages,* Harcourt, Brace & World, New York.

Tropp, Asher (1957), *The School Teachers,* Heinemann, London.

Waller, Willard Walter (1932), *The Sociology of Teaching,* John Wiley and Sons, New York.

Washburne, C. (1957), "The Teacher in the Authority System," *J. Educ. Sociol.,* 30:390–394.

Whyte, William H., Jr. (1956), *The Organization Man,* Simon and Schuster, New York.

Wilensky, Harold L. (1960), "Work, Careers, and Social Integration," *International Social Science Journal,* 12 (Fall), 543–560.

Wilensky, Harold L. (1964), "Varieties of Work Experience," in Henry Borow (ed.), *Man in a World of Work,* Houghton Mifflin, Boston.

Williams, Robin (1956), *American Society,* Alfred A. Knopf, New York.

Wilson, Bryan R. (1962), "The Teacher's Role—A Sociological Analysis," *British Journal of Sociology,* **XIII** (March), 15–32.

Wilson, Logan (1942), *The Academic Man,* Oxford University Press, New York.

Wolfbein, Seymour L. (1964), "Labor Trends, Manpower and Automation," in Henry Borow (ed.), *Man in a World of Work,* Houghton Mifflin, Boston.

Wolfle, Dael L. (1954), *America's Resources of Specialized Talent,* Harper and Row, New York.

PART TWO   COMMENTARIES

7 The New Zealand Case

John Forster
Victoria University
Wellington, New Zealand

As the essays in this volume have made clear education is inextricably interwoven into the institutional context of a society. Only in the most abstract sense can it be wrenched from this context and examined in isolation. But as those concerned with economic and social development have become aware in the last few decades, education is as much a manipulable part of society as the bank interest rate. In an increasing diversity of countries education has come to be seen as one of the keys to progress, on the premise that the skill and knowledge of the labor force is as important to economic development as mineral resources. These two views of education as, on the one hand, an integral part of the institutional arrangement of the society and, on the other, an element of the social order subject to governmental manipulation are not necessarily incompatible. The encouragement of education of various kinds is not something that can be done blindly; what may be suitable in one context may be disastrous in another. For example, the sudden proliferation of institutions of higher learning in England may indeed be a wise move, but at this point in time it would hardly be wise in Ghana or Samoa. Thus to use education as an aid to growth one must first be aware of its implications.

Understanding the nexus of ideas, circumstances, and past experiences which give particular societies their distinctive character is one of the most intricate problems facing the social sciences. From time to time social scientists have used "ethos," "culture," "national character," and a variety of other concepts in their attempts to specify the qualitative differences. Each has its strengths and its weaknesses but none has grasped the essence of distinctiveness. As a result we have ceased to try, and come to rely instead on quantifiable distinctions which lend themselves to statistical manipulation. Perhaps this is as much as we may hope to achieve, but if that is the case there must always be a place for the descriptive sociologist or anthropologist or historian who strives to identify the particular essence of social systems.

The subtle nature of these qualitative factors strikes one forcibly when comparison is made between education in New Zealand and the United States. Both countries are populated by English-speaking peoples, both base their institutional arrangements upon English models, both have high standards of living, and both have urban and literate populations. A large number of the observations in the essays of this volume are as applicable to New Zealand as to the United States, as for example, those on the origins of teachers or the social status of teaching as an occupation. What I shall try to indicate in these brief comments is that there is a subtle shading of the "meaning" of education which can only be understood through an appreciation of the total institutional nexus.

I have ignored in the following pages the issues raised by particular aspects of the New Zealand educational scene, those, for example, of Maori education, private schools, and Catholic schools. Each of these, particularly the first and the last, have been the subject of much discussion over the years. However the Government Commission on Education decided in 1962 that it could not recommend any changes in the present organisation of private schools and suggested the situation of these be left as it presently stands, which is basically the same situation as that described by Sirjamaki for the United States.

The matter of Maori schools is a long and involved issue in itself. The basic issue in simplest terms is how best to provide for the educational needs of a small proportion of the Maori population of New Zealand. The vast majority of them are taught in the normal public school system where they are in no way differentiated from the rest of the population. There is a fairly large number of Maori teachers in the employ of the department of education but they too are not distinguished from teachers in general. Thus any class may or may not have Maori pupils or a Maori teacher.

However in some of the more isolated rural areas where there are heavy concentrations of Maoris, and where levels of attainment are not high, special provisions have been made over the years to develop "Maori schools" with specialized curricula and services. The role of Maori schools is too complex to be discussed in these few pages but it represents an excellent case of institutional adaptation to meet a particular national condition.

The major characteristics of New Zealand are its small size (the population is slightly more than 2.7 million) and its remoteness (1200 miles from its nearest neighbor, Australia). At variance with the American experience is the homogeneity of New Zealand. As an area of British settlement the population is composed of settlers from Ireland and the United Kingdom, and a small but increasing proportion of Maoris. In such circumstances many of the strains of adaptation in education brought about in the United States with the enormous flow of immigrants were avoided. With such conditions it comes as no surprise to learn that the country is highly centralized in its governmental operations, including education. To this must be added the fact that for most of its one hundred years of European history, New Zealand has had a colonial economy producing agricultural commodities for the British market. Although its economy rests upon agriculture, New Zealand is a newly settled area without a backlog of antiquated agricultural techniques. Thus farming is relatively efficient and employs a small proportion of the labor force. (In 1963 the distribution of the labor force was as follows: primary industry 14.5 percent, manufacturing 26.2 percent, administration and professional 15.2 percent, commerce 17.6 percent; the remainder was made up of public services, personal services, transportation and communication.) Because of inadequate mineral resources industry is not highly developed, with the result that the country has a concentration of labor in service and clerical occupations. Partly through government policy, and partly because of its isolation New Zealand has not suffered from unemployment as have other countries. (Unemployment has remained at less than 1 percent for many years.) In fact one of the major platforms of any New Zealand government, and one of the proudest boasts of the country at large, is full employment, a truth which carries a great many implications for education. Finally in this brief characterization of New Zealand the point must be made that the country was effectively settled in the middle of the last century, two hundred years later than New England. By this time England was in the throes of industrial upheaval and a growing awareness of the need for social legislation in all forms. While the basis of the early English colonies in the Americas was religious and political freedom, for a later generation of Englishmen in New Zealand the issue was social conscience. It is this which gives depth to the New Zealander's feeling for such matters as full employment or universal education.

From this it is obvious that Perrucci's comments (p. 110–152) on the opportunity structure and the rewards of education are especially relevant in the New Zealand case. The absence of a highly diversified economy and the low margins of differentiation in the economic structure serve to minimize the returns derived from education. This condition is furthered by full employment which creates high wages for relatively young people. Thus although education is compulsory to age 15 and virtually free through university, the percent of those who leave at the minimum age is high. Further, the percentage of eligible candidates entering the university is much lower than comparable figures for the United States. Some of this difference however is accounted for by the fact that the functions of the New Zealand universities are more restricted than those in the United States. Teacher training for example is a nonuniversity affair, as is the training of nurses, artists, and others. At the same time the universities have not fully elaborated their services into fields of business management, mortuary science, or journalism.

There is therefore less need for a young person to pursue education to enter the economy at a satisfactory level and less pressure from the community for him to do so. In sum although education is free and compulsory to age 15 there is less need to maximize educational opportunity. Government policy has placed greater stress on providing a general education for all than on providing advanced and specialized higher education—a policy suited to the conditions which have prevailed in the country for the past half century or more.

It is in this context of work and opportunity that teaching must be seen. Traditionally teaching has provided a means of mobility in New Zealand just as it has in the United States. Migration to teacher training colleges from rural areas and lower socioeconomic groups has been the pattern. In the last few years as higher education has expanded, the teachers colleges appear to be drawing on a somewhat different section of the population, but as yet it is too soon to know exactly what the differences are and whether the change is permanent.

However, teachers make up a very significant proportion of the labor force. In 1963 one in every 20 members of the labor force was engaged in some form of educational enterprise, and 1 in 38 was actually teaching in a primary or secondary school (cf. Gerstl, 1 in 45 in the United States, p. 231). In marked contrast to the United States the percentage of males and females in teaching and educational services is identical (males: 17,775, females: 17,618 in 1963), although women predominate in primary school teaching and men in high school teaching. While the intake of women to teacher training greatly exceeds that of men, the drop out of women from the profession is a significant loss, particularly as only a small percent are brought back to the profession at a later date. The training of primary teachers is based on a three-year course in a college distinct from the university. High school teachers on the other hand are required to complete a university degree in a specialized field, after which they are required to spend an additional year in a teaching training college.

One major variant of the American educational pattern is to be found in organization and in administration. Viewed as a formal pattern of control the New Zealand administration of education does not appear to differ significantly from that of the United States. There is a central government department of education, below it are regional boards, and beneath them, school committees and parent-teachers associations. In the case of primary schools there has been a tendency over the years for authority to become concentrated in the hands of the government department. This has entailed a consequent loss of influence for the regional boards and most clearly for the local school committees and parent-teacher associations. While this is regretted by some, it has one interesting by-product. Teachers in New Zealand have a high degree of security and protection from community pressure. They are subjected to few of the pressures or personal restrictions mentioned by Gerstl. Whether this is desirable depends upon the point of view which one adopts—clearly its value to the teacher cannot be overstated; whether the loss of local control is more important is open to debate. The point, however, shows the need to pursue the question of administration and bureaucratic organization beyond the level of formal analysis into the realm of administrative practice of informal authority. For high school teachers the degree of security is little different, but in this case it is due to a rather neat balance of power between local governing boards and the central department of education. If this balance shifts it is likely to follow the pattern of the primary school rather than tend toward local influence.

A further aspect of administration which is worthy of investigation has been the subject of much comment in New Zealand and elsewhere —but has not been systematically studied. With any large scale organization there is a tendency to rationalize the organizational activities. In teaching—which, in the final analysis, is a highly personal relation —there is a need to be constantly alert for innovation. Teachers need to experiment, to explore, and to innovate, and administration needs to be receptive to the results. A formal and rationalized administrative approach is not inherently permissive of this. How innovation can best be achieved is open to question, but clearly this is an area in which sociologists might be very useful if they were to bring to education the knowledge they have gained from studies in industrial sociology, particularly those studies which have focused on the role of scientists and other innovators in large corporations.

During the 1960's greatest attention has been directed to higher education in New Zealand. As with other branches of the country's education the universities have their origins in a mixture of English and Scottish traditions. However, unlike the elementary and secondary schools, or for that matter unlike universities in the United States, the universities of New Zealand have not had their character radically transformed by the New Zealand setting. The reasons for this are numerous. Already mentioned is the relative absence of need for higher education in the existing economy, and the relatively slight advantages to be gained from university training. These two factors have led to a renowned characteristic of New Zealand education, namely, that the system exists for the export of talent. Both students wishing to pursue higher education and practicing scholars have left New Zealand continually for many years.

This "brain drain" has not only been a result of economic factors but has complex roots in the character of the universities and in decisions which have been made regarding their policies. The separation of functions from the universities is only now being seriously reconsidered.

During the 1920's there was established in New Zealand by the government a Department of Scientific and Industrial Research which has as its major function the conduct of research in all fields of science, but with a bias towards those areas useful to agriculture. This research activity, separated from the universities, resulted in duplication of both function and research. The Department of Scientific and Industrial Research also took from the universities many potential scientists who devoted their time to "pure" research rather than to the traditional combination of research and teaching of university life.

In the same period, and in much the same way, separate institutions of agriculture were established in New Zealand. After more than forty years these organizations have almost become fully integrated constituent parts of the universities, similar to the land grant colleges of the United States. However, for most of their existence they have had only an indirect relationship to the universities, and again the duplication of functions and the nonrecognition of agriculture as an academic enterprise served as a barrier to the involvement of the universities in the full life of the community.

More pertinently for present purposes is the position of the Teachers Training Colleges referred to above. As long ago as 1869 trainees in the training colleges were encouraged to attend lectures in the universities at the same time as they followed their training courses. The division created between the colleges and the universities was for the college to provide the practical and pedagogical training while the universities provided academic education. This division of labor persisted into the 1920's when the training colleges gradually took over responsibility for the entire training of future teachers and the relationship with the universities ceased to have any formal or informal meaning. This separation which had always existed but which became more precise forty years ago has continued to the present, in spite of continued suggestions that cooperation be increased and an equitable division of labor developed.

These three examples demonstrate the separation of the universities from many of the more directly practical functions which universities have come to serve in other countries. What has been described as the "ivory tower" quality of New Zealand universities is thus a result in part of governmental policy, for in each case the institutions established in the 1920's were responsible to government departments rather than to universities. The universities have responded to community needs to some extent by the establishment of special schools of art, public administration, and so on, but these have been further removed from more publically apparent development in agriculture or education. It is this diversity of functions and duplication of activities which has become a matter of public interest in recent years. The creation of two new universities and the possibility of more, together with the consolation of the agricultural colleges, and a sharp increase in the numbers of university students have combined to make many more people aware of the role and the potential contribution of higher education. The next decade is likely to show an increased tendency to consolidate and expand the functions of universities in a manner more in line with university development in other countries.

All observations of the New Zealand scene must be tempered by an appreciation of potential change. In the last few years government commissions have inquired into education in general, higher education specifically, and into the condition of the economy. Each commission has been impressed by the changes which lie in the immediate future.

As the report of the Commission on Education in New Zealand of 1962 observed:

". . . the Commission has particularly noted the following five points:
"(1) The general agreement among economists that 'both manufac-

turing and service industries must expand considerably if production is to rise more rapidly than population and yield rising living standards in New Zealand in the future.' "

"(2) The possibility—to put it no more strongly—that the future development of this country may have to be undertaken in an atmosphere of less favorable terms of overseas trade.

"(3) . . . Above all we shall have to pay more attention to the education of our labour force, both by providing a broad, general education of high quality in our schools and by doing much more than we have, in universities, technical colleges, and in public and private enterprises, in developing skills of all kinds and the arts of management.

"(4) The need for a degree of economic flexibility, allowing the labour force to transfer, where necessary, to more essential and more profitable employment. Only in this way can New Zealand benefit fully from technological progress. The development of adaptability through education is, therefore, important both for the economy and for the individual, who might otherwise be confronted with unemployment through technological change.

"(5) The significant contribution education can make in helping to raise levels of skill and knowledge in under-developed areas.

"These, then, are the real urgencies that move the Commission to its strong conviction that the schools must in the next decades place intellectual needs high, but not, it is to be hoped, thereby losing valuable gains in other directions, or narrowing the concept of the intellectual to a dry and bookish remnant of the mind. It is not just skill and scholarship that this country will need, but men and women of open minds and wide sympathies, resourceful and enterprising, confident and trustworthy—the workers, the parents, and citizens upon whom the State depends. The schools have a great deal to contribute to the development of such citizens."

The development of a more diversified economy and the creation of new industries and new markets will require changes in the traditional patterns of education. Although New Zealand does not yet exploit education as a key to social change and economic progress, the signs are clear that this viewpoint is likely to become part of the political scene. Increased awareness of education in Australia and England has already influenced New Zealand thinking. Questions of cultural deprivation and the inadequate use of human potential are already matters of discussions. Concern is expressed in many quarters over the ineffective employment of trained women and the need for continuing education is commonly recognized.

In the next few years many shifts are likely to occur in New Zealand education in response to both internal and external changes. As these alterations come about the relationship between sociology and education in New Zealand will become more apparent. Hansen (15) has pointed out that the generalizing interests of sociology and the particular interests of education are frequently at cross purposes. At the same time, as these notes may show, the two interests are closely intertwined. "Problems" are inevitably local. The function which sociology may usefully offer is to place particular issues in a larger social context and create a greater awareness of the nexus of condition—economic, political, historical and ideological—within which a particular system of education exists.

John Forster is Senior Lecturer in Sociology at Victoria University, New Zealand. He holds a Ph.D. from UCLA in Anthropology and Sociology and taught at the University of Minnesota for several years. Most of his research has been concerned with social change in the Pacific, currently focusing upon educational and technical skills required for economic growth. He is co-editor of *The Maori in the Sixties*, to be published by Blackwood and Pauls in 1967.

WORKS CITED

Beaglehole, J. C. (1937), *The University of New Zealand: An Historical Study*, New Zealand Council of Educational Research.

Report of the Commission on Education in New Zealand (1962), New Zealand Government Printer.

Parkyn, G. (1959), *Success and Failure at the University*, New Zealand Council of Educational Research.

UNESCO (1960), Compulsory Education in New Zealand.

Watson, J. E. (1965), *Horizons of Unknown Power*, New Zealand Council of Educational Research.

Watson, J. E. (1964), *Intermediate Schooling in New Zealand*, New Zealand Council of Educational Research.

8 The Australian Case

Raymond S. Adams
University of Queensland

Chaste and innocent, educational practice in Australia has been protected paternalistically from the overtures of would-be researchers. Frustrated, they have sought satisfaction vicariously in the romantic tales of their more favored American brethren. Inevitably (as is the way with sublimation), reality becomes confused with fantasy, and the differences between the glamorous but available American model and the homely, reclusive Australian one remain unclear. The problem of seeking clarity is the problem that is considered here. The task is to try to discern ways in which the essays in this book are germane to Australian scholarship.

If visiting commentators can be believed, education in Australia has its own very distinctive character.[1] Each of the six states (which together are just larger than the continental U.S.A.) is virtually autonomous. For geographical and historical reasons each has chosen to retain an extremely centralized form of administration. Within the state school systems, teachers are appointed by the central authority, are inspected and assessed by its officers, and are allocated to positions at the discretion of the central administration. In addition, syllabuses for all primary and secondary grade levels are prescribed by the authority and public examinations, controlled de facto by the central authority, set the official seal of approval (or disapproval) on the graduating pupils. The casual observer might also be impressed by a number of superficial characteristics of the system, for example, the widespread use of school uniforms, the tendency to regiment pupils, the "parades" (as in Queensland) that preface the school day, the lack of extensive choice of secondary school subjects, and the restricted role permitted parents (mainly fund-raising). At the risk of gross oversimplification,

274

the systems seem characterized by paternalistic authoritarianism on the part of the administration, traditional conservatism on the part of the schools themselves, conformist acceptance by the teachers, and unquestioning acquiescence by the pupils. Outside the state system the great private schools, themselves encrusted by tradition, provide ideal archetypes which the less well endowed state schools strive vainly to emulate. Despite this somewhat austere state of affairs, the products of the system appear to be well adjusted to their society. Delinquency rates are low, responsibility among young people is high, and even university students, though occasionally berated for lack of initiative, are excessively diligent and quite responsive.

Education as a subject of disciplined study falls mainly to the lot of University departments of education, whose main preoccupations have been with teacher training. Consequently much Australian writing and public commentary on education is more concerned with building a better educational world than with becoming aware of the realities of the present one. Within the framework of academic courses, educational philosophy and educational psychology provide a staple diet which is occasionally augmented by exotic morsels of comparative education, educational measurement, guidance, educational sociology, and the like.

To a certain extent then, Australian students of education when invited by Hansen in the first essay to consider the philosophical consequences of sociological approaches to behavioral analysis will draw near with confidence. Gradually, however, that confidence may be undermined because Hansen assumes an awareness of, and concern for, the issue of normative theory versus empirical theory that so far has not been characteristic of Australasian contemplation. Nonetheless the challenge to confront the normative-empirical problem cannot be ignored. Whether the resulting discussion will lead to the same conclusions as Hansen puts forward is an open question, but undoubtedly much thought will be provoked by his treatments of science and pragmatism versus practicality and scientism; the hiatus between education and sociology; the rapproachement of normativism and empiricism, and the "verification" of philosophical premises in the social sciences.

To some extent Hansen's outline of the academic status struggle of both education and sociology in the U.S.A. visits similarly unfamiliar territory. While antipathy towards neonate sociology exists in Australia, education has been enshrined at university level for some time. Consequently, the lines of the status battle are differently drawn. The prejudices that are expressed in Australia are less selective; their focus is principally on the upstart social sciences in general.

The existence of such cultural differences provides a challenge both to Hansen's discussions and to Australian practices. For example, does Hansen's brief historical analysis of the stages of development of American sociology provide an anticipatory model for Australia? (One advantage of backwardness is that the trail to modernity blazed by others permits those following to travel faster.) Has Hansen arrived at some "universal truths"? At first sight it would seem as if he has. He does seem to succeed in straddling the boundaries of culture when he provides a basic approach to the delineation of both educational sociology and the sociology of education, when he relates reform and improvement to social fact, and when he provides a script for the role of the sociologist qua reformer and the reformer qua sociologist. Australian sociologists would do well to subject his positions to test. Australian educationists would also profit from the exercise. Their predilection for reformative zeal has led them to make many assertions that rest on slender grounds. Nowhere is this more apparent than in their treatment of the school as an organization.

If Robbie Burns' laconic aphorism "A man's a man for a'that" had been instead "a school's a school for a'that," little elaboration would have been necessary in order to recount the general Australian approach to the school as an organization. The traditions of inspectorial assessment have produced a mystique in which the intuitive interpretation of "school tone," "school 'atmosphere'," and "school 'character'" play prominent and unchallenged roles. Corwin's essay then is particularly timely. His analysis of the structural properties of the school organization not only will command respect for its own systematic and thoughtful approach but bids fair to upset some of our most cherished and mindless preconceptions.

For instance, what Australian, accustomed to the maintenance orientation of his centralized administration systems could pass lightly over the conclusion that with the appointment as school superintendents of two insiders in a row rather than candidates from outside the system: ". . . a school system would experience on the average about twenty years of leadership which operated in a manner designed to maintain the system as is. . . . During such a period adaptation and development would be lacking."

The major contribution of Corwin's essay lies in its attempt to provide a comprehensive and ordered framework within which many facets of school function and structure might be conceptualized. By implication it also warns the amateur prognostician of education that the facts of school life are about to catch up with him. Data are imminent and it will soon no longer be adequate merely to have pure intentions and an eloquent delivery.

Two of the reasons why Corwin's essay is apposite are reviewed below. Firstly, the study of educational administration is burgeoning in Australia. Its development is conditional on the systematic analysis of the educational institution. Corwin provides one example how this might be undertaken. The essence of his approach is discernible in his definition of an organization. An organization comprises "(1) stable patterns of interaction; (2) among coalition of groups having a collective identity (e.g., name and location(s)); (3) accomplishing given tasks; and (4) coordinated by a structure of power and authority." This attempt at injecting precision into a usually disorganized domain is also an exercise in courage, because by avoiding reference to organizational goals, Corwin violates one of the most sacred rituals of educational normativism. If this represents a deliberate attempt on Corwin's part to relegate the ill-defined, nebulous, and confusing concept to limbo pending a more precise statement and operational definition, then he has made a major contribution to scholarship.

Secondly, a more sophisticated approach to educational theory is gradually emerging in Australasia. It stems from an increasing determination to discover the behavioral nature of the educational beast. For example, observational researches into school and classroom settings as behavioral and learning contexts are being undertaken at the University of Queensland. Corwin's contribution then provides a counter model for these other emergent theories. Hopefully, Corwin will not leave his readers too long wondering at the basis for the theoretical framework he has adopted. His model has compelling face validity, but why, for instance, did he settle on such concepts as "roles," "control," "status system," "rules and procedures," "division of labor," and "offices"?

Perrucci's essay on education, social class, and mobility distinguishes itself from the preceding two because it does not attempt to provide a basis for systematizing the field of study. Rather it presents a comprehensive integrated review of a great amount of research. Perrucci accepts the social-class concept without question—indeed to some readers it may also seem that he reifies it. In Australia and even more in New Zealand, where class lines are yet crudely drawn and where the social spectrum is constricted at both ends[2] his meticulous argument will be regarded with some caution. Rather than appreciating the broad sweep of Perrucci's canvas the Australian scholar might be more apt to accept selected segments germane to his taste.

However, there is a different use to which Perrucci's work might be put. By synthesizing so many research findings he has given us a glimpse of the ultimate in empirical sociological analysis. It is a vision both fascinating and frightening—fascinating because it demands intellectual agility from the reader, frightening because it makes more credible a mechanistic interpretation of behavioral man. Approaching his task with systematic thoroughness Perrucci reverses the economic research model. Rather than beginning with a comprehensive set of rigorous conditions which are subsequently and successively relaxed until the gap between the ideal and actual is bridged, Perrucci starts from the simplistic position of accepting only one or two gross findings on social class. Thereafter, step by step, he proceeds to complicate his model, injecting new finding after new finding, and qualification after qualification. As a result he arrives at a whole series of *de facto* conditional clauses developed in the following way: if A then Z, but if $A = a_1 + a_2$ then $a_1 = z_1$ and $a_2 = z_2$, but if $a_1 = x_1 + x_2$ then $z_1 = x_1 + x_2$ etc. The net result is the prospect of identifying multivariate factors of social-class background that will permit prediction to multivariate educational factors. For example, after focusing on "the capacity of various social structures to provide channels for transmitting mobility oriented values and aspirations," Perrucci pursues findings that have sought to discover how this occurs. His quest leads him to the "structural context of mobility" and the variety of characteristics of different family and school social networks in relation to aspiration for and expectation of, success.

The work is a mine of useful information on social-class and mobility research as it is related to education. To an Australian scholar who would see the American social scene as an "ideal type" or as the most advanced "end" (or its opposite) of a cultural continuum the study has crystal ball qualities. To another who would consider social-class data as somewhat culture-bound it can serve as a sounding board for argument. To yet another interested in research methodology it may serve as an example of fine synthetic scholarship.

Gerstl in his essay, "Education and the Sociology of Work," is also not concerned with providing a complete conceptual framework although he does present his analysis in such a way that the outlines of his own model can be discerned. Australian readers would most likely find the greatest appeal of Gerstl's work to be at the substantive level. He marshalls many facts to garnish his descriptive interpretation. Unfortunately, however, face-value evidence in Australia and New Zealand suggests that Gerstl's "points of fact" in the U.S.A. would not gibe with "fact" in this corner of the educational world. Such a state of affairs should disappoint only those who would seek to transpose American research findings with uncritical mindlessness. To others, who would rather utilize sociological data derived in outside cultures as a provocation to their own thought and theories, there is much that would appeal in this chapter. In the brief commentary that follows an attempt has been made to utilize several of the points made by Gerstl as launching pads for one or two Australasian-based thoughts.

Gerstl makes several deductions about the professional status and career appeal of teaching based on the fact that "the occupational image and predominant stereotype (in the U.S.A.) has been a feminine one." He supports his argument by reflecting on the fact that but one-fourth of all precollege teachers, and but one-seventh of all primary school teachers, are men. In Australia Gerstl's basic thesis would not apply. Apart from infant and domestic science classes which invariably have women teachers, men predominate in all other branches of the profession. Given too, in Australia, a greater degree of egalitarianism, a lesser degree of social-class awareness and a less intense aspiration for affluence, the role of any occupation as a vehicle of status definition is probably less salient. Again, Australia has come to internalize some social welfare beliefs, and teaching, as a social service, is well in tune with the idealist orientation of some prevailing social opinion. Potential recruits to the profession may not be unaware of its ideological acceptability. The career patterns of teachers are also likely to be subjected to influences other than those perceived by Gerstl. For instance, in Queensland women teachers, once married, lose their right to permanent employment. Consequently far fewer follow the teaching-marriage-then-teaching-again pattern Gerstl discerns in America.

Nevertheless, Gerstl's description of aspects of the teaching profession in the U.S.A., its personnel, their attributes as members of a particular vocation, and so forth, will prompt many a thought among Australians interested in the teaching profession. None, I venture, could, for example, read either of the following quotations with equanimity—neither could they deny them:

"No one is quite sure, or ever has been, just what the proper business of education is . . . professional courses . . . are not constructed around programs of proven worth. Rather, they represent a half century's haphazard accretions for which no very specific rationale, either theoretical or empirical, exists." (Koerner, 1965, pp. 24, 50.)

"Medical training would be more like teacher training if two thirds of the time were devoted to rephrasing and discussing the Hippocratic oath." (Mayer, 1963, pp. 472–473.)

The relevance of these two quotations to contemporary Australian education implies that if Australian education has been resistent to change, it is nonetheless in need of it. Whether it is ready for it is another point.

One of the superficial judgments an observer of American society might permit himself is that Americans seem to venerate change. In contradiction to Britain where things ancient are valued for their age, in the U.S.A., novelty is justification in its own right. While this does not always hold so for education, innovations are customarily made within such a climate of social opinion. Understandably, then, in America change and the various attributes of change generate their own enthusiasm among social scientists. In Australia where education has enshrined much of the tradition-directedness of turn-of-the-century Britain, changes are seldom regarded in the same light. Innovation, when it occurs, is not the result of osmosis from one teacher or school to another but the outcome of (1) deliberate and systematic planning, (2) some limited experimentation, (3) and subsequent organization, all of which stem from the centralized education authority. As a consequence, a given change spreads throughout the system with remarkable speed but almost inevitably its advent is delayed, and when it is ultimately implemented, considerable hostility (mostly latent) is generated among the teachers.

On face value it would seem as if the highly centralized systems of educational administration create their own organizational climates. Consequently, writings on change derived from the American educational culture are often viewed in Australia with a measure of skepticism. However, McGee's essay, although it relies heavily on American theorizing, does not seem dependent on current American educational administration practice. Like the earlier essays in the book, this one provides a systematic and orderly basis for the examination of a particular sociological phenomenon (in this case, social change).

Seeking resolution of the basic problem of how to approach social change and education, McGee produces a multiple-factor diagnosis of the nature of social change that would appear viable in the materialistically oriented Australian society. However, applying McGee's concepts of education as an *agent* or *condition* or an *effect* of change in an analysis of Australian education would very likely reveal many differences from the American scene. To illustrate, in Australia, Sputnik I

was no affront to national pride. The man in the Australian street sees
little reason to be concerned over education. He would not willingly
change a system that, after all, made him what he is. Herein lies the
clue to education's task. Education is to produce good Australians who
are honest, forthright, responsible, moral, and who, in respecting authority, show an appropriate reverence both for their English antecedents and their independent Australian heritage. Vocational training
is subservient to these higher purposes. Education consequently is not
an agent of change. More often, in defense of established values, it is
resistant to change. The character development orientation of Australian education has also permitted education to ignore technological
developments in society itself. Language laboratories, teaching ma-
chines, television, etc., play but a small part.

The problem of the cross-cultural viability of sociological insights is
perhaps best illustrated in Sirjamaki's contribution. The term "institution" is a culture-bound concept and while its definition in abstract
terms (e.g., Sumner's "a concept plus a structure") provides a satisfactory conceptual starting point, elaboration inevitably demands
reference to a specific culture. To this extent Sirjamaki's chapter was
predestined to focus on the American scene and to the same extent it
was predestined to hold less immediate attraction for the Australian
reader.

American social science often (and no doubt, unintentionally) gives
the impression that the world begins at the eastern seaboard and ends
at the western one, that there is but one kind of human nature worthy
of all men to be believed-American, and that social phenomena manifested in the U.S.A. represent genera rather than species. When sociology does this it constricts its own generalizing power. However,
Sirjamaki had a legitimate reason for his single-minded approach and
perhaps in the last analysis his essay will appeal to the Australian
educational sociologist because of its culture-bound nature. For, by its
example, it may both invite and challenge scholars in other parts of the
world to supplement and complement its data, thus providing a broader
basis for interpretation.

When the essays in this book are placed alongside other writings on
educational sociology, certain distinctive features are discernible. The
work does not pretend to be inclusive. Rather than bouncing happily
and haphazardly from topic to topic, after the fashion of most books
in the field, it confines its attention determinedly to six significant areas.
Within these areas it draws on much current research and produces
comprehensive reviews, thus again distinguishing itself from current

literature. More importantly this book attempts a task that is inevitably skirted in conventional texts as they pursue their dilettante ways—the task of providing structured and systematic bases for conceptualizing some subfields within the sociology of education. In a subject that has long been heir to the untidy conceptualizing habits of its parent, education, the book both indicates that reform is possible and indicates how it can be achieved.

The individual reader in Australia will react to the book according to his own idiosyncratic needs. However, to those who have hoped for some systematization of the extensive subject matter of the sociology of education, or who have wished for a more rigorous approach to the utilization of research data, the work of these sociologists will immediately commend itself. In part, Australians will still have to assume the cross-cultural utility of American work. However, the assumption will be made less unwillingly because the authors have not relied on reporting social characteristics without reference to conceptual and theoretical rationalizations. The outcome of this scholarly approach is that the book itself provides readers with the means for examining and ultimately evaluating its own cross-cultural viability.

Raymond S. Adams is Senior Lecturer in Education at the University of Queensland in Australia. His Ph.D. is from the University of Otago (New Zealand), where he has also taught. He has been employed by the New Zealand Education Department as an itinerant advisor to teachers, and has been a visiting research professor at the Social Psychology Laboratory of the University of Missouri. His research has included video-tape recording analysis of classroom interaction.

NOTES

1. See Butts (1961), Kandel (1955, 1961), and Jackson (1962).
2. One American scholar with an unconscious touch of Irish whimsy described New Zealand as a one-class society—all middle!

WORKS CITED

Butts, R. F. (1961), *Assumptions Underlying Australian Education,* Australian Council for Educational Research.
Kandel, I. L. (1955), *The New Era in Education: A Comparative Study,* Houghton Mifflin, Boston.

Kandel, I. L. (1961), *Types of Administration with Particular Reference to the Educational Systems of New Zealand and Australia*, Australian Council for Educational Research.

Koerner, James D. (1965), *The Miseducation of American Teachers*, Penguin Books, Baltimore, Md.

Mayer, Martin (1963), *The Schools*, Doubleday, Anchor Books, Garden City, N.Y.

Jackson, R. W. B. (1962), *Emergent Needs in Australian Education*, Australian Council for Educational Research.

9 The English Case

Asher Tropp

London School of Economics and
Political Science, University
of London

The several essays in this book have exhibited different approaches
to the sociological analysis of education and different aspects of the
task of the sociologist. Here will be presented a personal view of the
"field" as it appears to a British sociologist.

THE SOCIOLOGY OF EDUCATION

There appear to be three distinct levels at which the sociological
analysis of education can usefully proceed. The first is that of the
educational system *as a whole*, its changing relationship to other
systems (polity, economy, family, religious, military), the way in which
it reflects, reinforces, or modifies the "value system" (or "systems") of
society, the bases it provides for the organized action of various groups
associated with it and the way in which other groups can exert pressure
upon it. Here the sociologist can both draw upon macro-sociological
theories (e.g., functionalism, conflict theories) for valuable and test-
able hypotheses and also hope to contribute to a sharpening and
clarification of these theories. His basic data will often be similar to
that used by historians and students of comparative education, but his
approach will be more clearly and consistently sociological in the kinds
of questions that are addressed to the "documents," the concepts that
are used, and the structure of his explanations. Although the analysis
of educational systems in this way is important in itself, it can also be of
use to the educational planner and administrator. By analyzing the past

284

and present forces impinging on educational systems, assessing the possibilities of success of various educational reforms, warning of obstacles to change, and analyzing the experience of other nations, the sociologist can point to the types of choices that must be made and the likely consequences of these choices for other areas of social life.

The second level of analysis is that of the educational system as an "input-output" system and the school as a complex organization. Pupils come into the school system already socialized, motivated, and instructed by family and community. They spend, for the most part, only a minority of their time exposed to school influence and, even inside the school, pupil peer-group culture can be a powerful force of counter-socialization. Teachers, on their part, have their own social and cultural backgrounds, training, peer groups, human and professional needs and interests. The structure of the school itself as a complex organization affects the educational process. Here again there can be a fruitful interplay between developing bodies of sociological middle-range theory such as the sociology of occupations and the sociology of complex organizations and the analysis of these middle-range educational problems. Again the range of research techniques developed by sociologists, from participant observation to multivariate analysis, is essential in testing hypotheses. The policy implications of this level of work are obvious. Decisions have to be made, for example, on the ways of selecting and training teachers, on the selection and guidance of pupils, or on the planned organization of educational systems and schools. Sociological research and generalizations are not, in themselves, sufficient for policy formulation but they are clearly necessary.

The third level of analysis is the examination of the classroom, teacher-pupil interaction, and the learning process. Unless we know what kinds of teachers can communicate various forms of knowledge, skills and values to pupils of different social and cultural backgrounds, it is difficult to see how a satisfactory educational policy is possible. Research in these areas has presented many problems both in theory and in empirical research techniques but the past few years have seen a renewed attack on the problems of classroom climates, teacher-pupil interaction, appropriate size and composition of classes, teaching techniques, and so on.

The three levels at which I have discussed the sociology of education are, of course, only analytically distinct. Variations in teacher-pupil interaction are affected by the pattern of recruitment of teachers and pupils, their motives, ideologies, and aspirations. These, in turn, are affected by the value systems and power structures of the larger society and by the educational structure and curriculum. This is not to say that in order to study anything we must study everything, but simply that progress in the understanding of education as a social institution and social process depends upon work proceeding concurrently at all stages. Again, well-planned comparative studies which aim to test hypotheses on a cross-cultural basis are likely to produce a more rapid and sounder advance.

SOCIOLOGY IN BRITAIN

Until recently the number of professional sociologists in Great Britain was minute, and the great expansion in the subject with the proliferation of new teaching departments and research units is still too recent to have produced a significant narrowing of the gap between Britain and the U.S.A. However, it is possible to argue that, in spite of the paucity of personnel and research funds, sociologists in Britain have had a greater influence upon educational thought and educational policy than those of any other country. Sociological research techniques have been employed by recent government commissions and committees. Sociologists are often included as members of these official bodies, and the results of sociological research are freely utilized in the formulation of policies. Much of the research may appear to be simple and descriptive, but, for the most part, this is not due to ignorance of recent methodological innovations in the U.S.A. and elsewhere but to a predilection for the apparent and immediate rather than the subtleties of social existence.

The mainstream of British sociology has always been empirical, descriptive, and policy oriented. Indeed Nathan Glazer (an American sociologist) has argued forcibly that "we may say with some confidence that the major lines of empirical, first hand investigation of social problems, and even of statistical reporting based on first-hand inquiry, were developed in England." The tradition runs from the political arithmeticians of the seventeenth century (William Petty, John Graunt, Gregory King) through the social statisticians and social surveyors of the first part of the nineteenth century (John Sinclair, Francis Eden, James Kay-Shuttleworth) to the great urban survey of Charles Booth at the end of the century. Between the two World Wars the tradition was somewhat in abeyance but, with minor fluctuations, interest in sociology has grown steadily since 1945. In the last five years, this interest has increased enormously into an almost nation-wide concern with sociological investigation. The success of a weekly journal like *New Society*, the vast expansion of teaching departments, the setting up of a Social Science Research Council, and the increased use by government departments of sociologists as research workers and advisors are some signs of this increased interest.

The primary aim of much British sociological research is still the same as in the nineteenth century—adequate description. This attempt at accurate description of social events and social institutions is generally motivated by a feeling that something is not altogether right in the arrangements of society and should be investigated and publicized. It is generally assumed that if the "facts" about poverty, old age, hospitals, prisons, schools are exposed, then social policy will be reformed. Such investigations then are based on certain premises. The first is that the social world is fundamentally simple. The causes of social problems are assumed to arise from either poverty or ignorance. Many British sociologists tend to become impatient with involved explanations, prolonged conceptual clarification, or research that appears irrelevant to social policy. Secondly, while the sociologist is expected to use value judgments to decide what problems he thinks are important, he will assume that his values are widely shared—that others will become as indignant as he is at poverty, disease, cruelty, or inequality and that social reform will follow closely upon social investigation. Thus there is less tendency for British sociology to model itself upon the supposedly "value-free" natural sciences but a great danger of value premises being concealed and both ethically and sociologically naive.

SOCIOLOGY OF EDUCATION IN BRITAIN

The sociology of education in Britain can be said to have begun in the first half of the nineteenth century with empirical investigations of educational facilities by Royal Commissions, Select Committees, Her Majesty's Inspectors of Schools, and private social investigators. Lack of education was regarded as part of the complex of ill health, poverty, malnutrition, and overcrowding in which lower classes were enmeshed and from which only social policy and self-help could provide a way out. As the system of public instruction developed in England, it moved slowly from a policy of providing a working-class education for working-class children which would fit them for manual employment to a broad conception of an "educational ladder" up which the intelligent and motivated working-class child could climb to a middle-class job and style of life. By the 1930's this pattern was clearly institutionalized both in educational ideology and in the educational structure. It was the contribution of the first generation of professional educational sociologists to point out the inequalities of opportunity and the consequent waste of ability that remained inherent in the system.

In 1944, under the wartime coalition government, a new act was passed which had, as one effect, the opening up of all places in most of the grammar schools to competition. With the exception of the socially important private and "public" school sector, selection for grammar school places was to be based solely on ability and in almost all areas this was ability judged by "objective" intelligence and attainment tests. The attention of educational sociologists shifted to showing that the seemingly objective tests contained implicit class biases, that "early leaving" (drop out) from grammar school was due both to differential motivation on the part of pupils and to a failure of the grammar school to adapt its "culture" and organization to the needs of students from working-class families. It was calculated that although over two-thirds of the "intelligent" children in the country were of working-class origin, only one-quarter of university students came from the working class. Research moved into a new phase of the investigation of the economic, social, and psychological obstacles in the path of the working-class child. In the process of research the whole notion of "innate ability" was attacked and the pyramidal and highly selective nature of English education was put in question. This wave of empirical research was accompanied by socio-historical analysis of the origins and development of the system. These studies disputed the educational inevitability of the current structure and emphasized the role of classes and interest groups in producing the peculiar system of English education. These researches provided much of the factual material on which educational reform groups, political leaders, and Government commissions relied in the campaigns which have led to a substantial expansion of higher education, a movement to replace selective grammar schools by comprehensive secondary schools, and a renewed interest in the education of the underprivileged (culturally deprived) child.

In the newly emerging structure and facing a new set of problems, research in the sociology of education has multiplied until it now includes all the spheres outlined here as essential for an adequate treatment of the whole field. As in other fields of sociology there is an increasing convergence of theoretical interest and methodological techniques in work done in Great Britain and in the United States. Although in no sense deploying the resources in either research funds or personnel of American sociology, the British sociologist concerned with the educational structure and process has certain advantages. The main one is the respectability of the field of investigation. Young sociologists do not feel "contaminated" by their contact with a discipline associated with teacher training. Some of the most respected of British sociologists have specialized for most or part of their careers in educational research. A second and associated advantage is the eagerness with which books and research reports on the sociology of education are taken up by the informed lay public and by policy makers. Professional and public reputations can be made as rapidly in the sociology of education as in any other sphere of sociological specialization. The mood of self-criticism and doubt that has swept British society in the last ten years has been directed to the educational system as much as to any other institution. The system is seen to be inefficient and inequitable, and to preserve antiquated values incompatible with a modern Britain. The older educational institutions—Oxford and Cambridge, the public Boarding Schools, the selective Grammar School, the "streamed" primary school, the teacher training college, the apprenticeship system for training skilled manual workers—have been exposed to increasing external criticism and wracked by internal self-doubts. In these circumstances the conditions for empirical research and sociological analysis are favorable. The main dangers are sloppy standards of empirical research and the premature use of value judgments (what has come to be known in Britain as "pop sociology") rather than excessive methodological sophistication and value neutrality.

ENGLISH AND AMERICAN EDUCATION COMPARED

It is impossible to provide a simple checklist of the similarities and differences in the English and North American educational settings. In *The First New Nation* Seymour Lipset has attempted to present a thumbnail sketch of the different value systems and forms of social integration of the United States, Great Britain, Canada, Australia, France, and Germany. To him "Britain has come to accept the values of achievement in its economic and educational system, and to some extent in its political system, but retains a substantial degree of elitism (the assumption that those who hold high position be given generalized deference) and ascription (that those born to high place should retain it)" (S. M. Lipset, *The First New Nation*, 1963, p. 215). The way in which the differing themes of achievement, ascription, and elitism have been combined or have been in conflict in the English educational system at different stages of its development has been perhaps the major theme of both documentary-historical and empirical investigation by British sociologists. The differences an observer from the United States will notice in, for example, the role of the teacher in the classroom and in society, the "realistic" level of aspiration of the average English child and young adult compared to his North American equivalent, the nature of parent-teacher, pupil-teacher, teacher-teacher relationships, the low rate of dropout and failure from English universities compared to the high rates from North American universities are all in the last analysis rooted in the power, class, and value structures of the two societies as they have developed and been modified over time.

In England the schools and the teachers have been insulated from popular pressure by the total institutional structure of which they are a part. The greater authority of the teachers in the English educational structure and their insulation from external pressures is reflected right down to the classroom learning situation. Similarly, all educational institutions in England from the primary school to the university aim to seal themselves off from outside pressures and to become self-sufficient communities.

The basic questions raised in the book by Corwin, Gerstl, and McGee appear to me to be the right ones and similar to those which British sociologists are raising in their work on educational institutions and processes. At all levels of sociological teaching and research the comparison of the two systems can perform both an important heuristic and methodological function.

Asher Tropp has been appointed to the Chair of Sociology at the new University of Surrey. Previously he was a Reader in Sociology at the London School of Economics and Political Science, where he received his Ph.D. in Sociology. He has been a Visiting Professor at the University of Puerto Rico and has carried out research and taught in Latin America, India, and the United States. He has published *The School Teachers: The Growth of the Teaching Profession in England and Wales from 1800 to the Present Day* (Heinemann, 1957).

REFERENCES

Baron, George (1965), *A Bibliographical Guide to the English Educational System,* University of London, Athlone Press, Third Edition.

Current Sociology, Volume VII, No. 3, 1958, "The Sociology of Education. A Trend Report and Bibliography."

Halsey, A. H., Jean Floud, and C. Arnold Anderson (ed.) (1961), *Education, Economy and Society. A Reader in the Sociology of Education*, Free Press, New York. See in particular the articles by R. H. Turner, T. H. Marshall, D. V. Glass and by G. Baron and A. Tropp for sociological analyses of the British and American systems.

Sociology of Education Abstracts (Liverpool, England) (contains full references to British as well as North American and other research).

Young, M. (1965), *Innovation and Research in Education*, Routledge and Kegan Paul, London.

Author Index

Subject Index